FOR FRIENDS AT HOME

D1534729

Matilda C.H. Sept 22nd 1854

My Dear Sister

I have been a long time
in answering your last letter, but I hope
you will excuse me as I have been quite busy
through the summer. It was only last night
that I returned from a short trip up Country.
We staid a couple of days at Wm Scotts, They have
had a very sickly summer about Toronto. Mary Ann
and little Mary have both had the ague, and their
servant girl and some of their hired men were
shaking with the same disease when we were
there, the others are well and send their kind
respects to all friends in Scotland —. —

But Helen, I must explain a little, so that
you may know who my travelling companion was
that I speak of as visiting at Cousin Scotts, and in
doing so I must go a little round about —
I must tell you what a picnic party is — —
A Picnic is a meeting of neighbours and friends
assembled in some shady spot in the woods, for
the purpose of enjoying a days recreation or amusement, each individual or family furnish
some thing in the shape of provisions some

Extract from One of James Thomson's Letters

FOR FRIENDS AT HOME

A Scottish Emigrant's Letters
from Canada, California
and the Cariboo
1844–1864

EDITED BY RICHARD ARTHUR PRESTON

McGILL-QUEEN'S UNIVERSITY PRESS
MONTREAL AND LONDON

1974

© MCGILL–QUEEN'S UNIVERSITY PRESS 1974
INTERNATIONAL STANDARD BOOK NUMBER 0–7735–0147–9
LIBRARY OF CONGRESS CATALOG CARD NUMBER 73–79501
LEGAL DEPOSIT 3RD QUARTER 1974
DESIGN BY RONALD CAPLAN
PRINTED IN GREAT BRITAIN BY
R. & R. CLARK LTD EDINBURGH

For
David, Carol, and Peter,
Dedicated Canadians

Contents

Illustrations

PREFACE

Most of the papers printed here are letters of James Thomson (1823-95). The remainder were written to him or about him and were found in the same collection. These were included when they helped to round out the story. There are also excerpts from a diary which he kept in the Cariboo.

Thomson's wife, the former Mary Armstrong, always spelled the name with a *p*, 'Thompson'. That form was also used by his sons and daughters. James used it himself for a time when on the Cariboo trip, but the monument erected to his memory in Cardinal cemetery gives the spelling 'Thomson' for him and for his father and his sister. 'Thompson' is used for his wife and children. In this book the spelling in the original is followed in each case except that, to give consistency, 'Thomson' is used in headings for James himself.

To make the letters easier to read, paragraphing has been introduced and all sentences made to begin with a capital letter and end with a suitable punctuation mark. In a few cases, where necessary for clarification, commas have also been added within sentences. Obvious slips of the pen have been silently corrected. Otherwise, Thomson's original capitalization, punctuation, spelling, and abbreviations have been preserved. Some passages that were repetitive or inconsequential have been omitted and this is indicated by the use of ellipses.

The original papers were in many cases difficult to read. In some instances the letters were written both across the paper and also up and down. My personal thanks are therefore due to Mrs. Azzie Mae Griffin, who patiently made the preliminary transcription.

I am also indebted to the reference staffs at the Perkins Library at Duke University, at the Massey Library, Royal Military College, and at the Douglas Library, Queen's University, for much help; as also to the staffs of the Manuscript and Documents Departments at Duke and of the Archives and Special Collections at Queen's.

I should like to thank Mrs. Agnes Green of Peterborough, Ontario for providing the daguerreotypes of her grandparents in early married life, and also Art Downs of Surrey, British Columbia for permission to reproduce two maps of the Cariboo from his *Wagon Road North*, in which they appear as the frontispiece and on pages 40–41.

Miss Penelope Maunsell helped with the preparation of the manuscript for publication and H. Pearson Gundy of Queen's University gave advice and great help with editing.

Finally, thanks are due most of all to Mr. and Mrs. George B. McClean, who brought the letters to my attention, and to them and the rest of their family for depositing the letters at Queen's, permitting Duke manuscript department to make and retain copies, and agreeing to publication in this form.

INTRODUCTION

James Thomson, Emigrant

In 1844 James Thomson, a baker's apprentice about twenty-two years old, emigrated from his native Scotland to Canada. Thomson had no specific destination in mind, only a vague intention to go to the Toronto area where a cousin was farming. As he had a letter of reference to a Scottish minister in Montreal, he called there and secured employment in his trade, staying through the winter. In the spring he decided to 'go West' and a chance encounter took him to Edwardsburgh on the St. Lawrence River, once again to work as a baker. Four years later, in 1849, he moved on to Chicago where he found employment in the office of a lumber firm. The next year he went overland to the California goldfields where he mixed mining with lumbering and baking. Within three years he made enough money to enable him to visit his old home in Scotland and to buy a farm in Edwardsburgh. James Thomson then married and raised a family. He died in 1895 at the age of seventy two, a highly respected member of the community, now called Cardinal, which he had served as reeve for several years.

Until 1856 Thomson wrote at irregular intervals to his father and a sister in Scotland. When the father and sister fell on hard times, he assisted them, and a nephew and two nieces, to come to Edwardsburgh. Presumably they brought his letters at that time. Six years later Thomson once again tried his hand at prospecting for gold, this time in the Cariboo. On that trip he wrote letters to his wife and also kept a diary, in which there suddenly occurs the moving passage that provides the title of this book: 'I feel thankful that I have such a wife & family. Oh that we may meet soon and live happy. I feel lonely enough but I feel more for friends at home than for myself.'

In 1962 Thomson's letters were found by a granddaughter, Mrs. George B. McClean, among the effects of his last surviving son, Edwin Scott Thompson, as the family now spelled the name. Realizing that these letters tell the story of an immigrant's adaptation to Canada in a uniquely complete way, Mrs. McClean permitted them to be prepared for publication and deposited them in the Douglas Library at Queen's University.

There are many first-hand accounts of Canada in the mid-nineteenth century, but mainly by visitors of the upper and middle classes. There are also reminiscences by men who made good and told their story late in life. But few immigrants of the lower order were literate. Complete collections of their letters have rarely survived. No collection of this kind has been published to provide a primary account of an immigrant's acclimatization and progress in his new home. In Thomson's case it was the emigration of the recipients (who brought his letters to Canada) and the subsequent preservation of these papers by his wife and descendants that has made publication possible. Together with a few other letters and documents in the collection and with excerpts from the Cariboo diary, Thomson's letters give a remarkably graphic and complete narrative of his life during the years when they were written.

James Thomson had the knack of taking up his story where the last letter had left off. He was also observant, not merely of conditions in his new home, but also of important contemporary happenings. Although, in the early days particularly, he spelled badly and ignored punctuation, he had a natural flair for writing and his serially-told tale grips the attention of the reader. Relatively few passages are repetitive or without general interest. It is a story of success through hard work and common sense, the making of a typical Canadian; it is also a self-portrait which succeeds in conveying the humour, curiosity, deep feeling, and the prejudice in matters of race and religion that were a part of the writer's nature and of his time. Thomson's early life is vividly evoked in the letters and his story needs little further elaboration, except to place it in its background of migration, settlement, and development on the St. Lawrence, and the two gold rushes. Places, people, and events have been further identified in footnotes.

The Great Migration of the Nineteenth Century

The great movement of people from Europe to North America, which had produced the astonishing growth of the Thirteen Colonies, had slowed during the wars that ushered in the nineteenth century; but when peace came in 1815, removal of wartime restrictions on emigration quickly led to a renewed flow that was greater than anything seen before. This vast migration was not merely the result of unsettled postwar conditions; its chief cause was the Industrial Revolution.

3

Men and women uprooted from a relatively secure, if meagre, existence in rural Europe, and sucked into new industrial towns, found themselves at the mercy of the vagaries of a capricious world-wide market economy. Their brothers and sisters who had stayed on the farm were little better placed. For vast numbers a move to new homes overseas seemed the only hope for a more prosperous and stable life.

The majority of the emigrants went to the United States. In the 1840s the Republic received more than twice as many as Canada and Australasia combined. Despite the efforts of imperially-minded colonial promoters to divert the flow from the United Kingdom to the newer colonies in the southern ocean, these received only half the number who went to the British colonies in North America. Many chose Canada because it was closer and less expensive to reach, and because it seemed to offer prospects similar to those in the United States but under their own flag. Countless others treated it as a stepping stone to the Republic.[1] A publicist for the British colony claimed that between 1829 and 1836 a quarter of a million persons had come to Upper Canada as immigrants.[2]

This great migration was seen as a solution for otherwise insoluble problems of poverty and over-population; and so it was supported by contemporary economic thought and public policy. Like all Western Europe, the British Isles were experiencing a phenomenal population explosion and the surplus could not be absorbed by the new factories. The unemployed, and sometimes also the unemployable, were actively assisted by charitable organizations and philanthropic individuals (including landlords who had other use

4

for their lands) to seek new homes in distant countries. The conditions under which these people moved were often shocking, almost as bad as those of slaves transported from Africa. As both the British and Colonial governments publicized this emigration, they were compelled to step in to supervise its operation and mitigate its evils. Thus a British act in 1835 required that ships with more than a hundred passengers should carry a surgeon and provide food from the time that passengers came aboard even though the vessel did not sail immediately.[3] But many emigrant ships were smaller than this, and the law was difficult to enforce. In 1838 Canada appointed an immigration agent at Quebec, Alexander Buchanan, who was authorized to inspect incoming ships and to see that the law had been obeyed. Conditions slowly improved.

Emigration from Scotland

James Thomson's boyhood home was in Aboyne, Aberdeenshire, where his father was a blacksmith. Aboyne is said to be derived from the Gaelic and to mean 'a stream of rippling waters'.[4] It lies upstream from Aberdeen at an important crossing of the Dee and at an entrance to the Highlands. Known since 1867 as a meeting place for the Highland games,[5] Aboyne is closely associated with that romantic part of Scotland. In the eighteenth century there had been tragic and notorious clearances of the Highlands by unscrupulous landlords; and whole clans had also been forced to migrate for political reasons. But overpopulation had since become worse, as a result of the clan system with its built-in protection for its members, the reduction in the death-rate due to improved medicine, including inoculation against smallpox, and the introduction of potato culture that made possible excessive subdivision of holdings. When rising prices forced absentee landlords to seek new sources of income from their Highland estates, they turned to sheep-farming because wool was in great demand for the new power mills. Their factors then evicted more crofters to make room for sheep. In 1836-37, when the Highlands were hit by famine, eviction reached the level of a new 'clearance of the Highlands'. After 1841 decennial censuses showed a declining population.[6]

Few Highlanders had enough money to pay their way to North America. Many therefore drifted to the coastal areas which became congested with workers dependent on the seasonal harvesting of kelp, a form of seaweed valued for its iodine content. Others moved into the new industrial cities and towns of Scotland where they met a greater wave of Irish fleeing their homes in search of work.

Aberdeenshire was not 'crofting country'. In fact its eastern half was not even considered to be in the Highlands.[7] It was a relatively prosperous county as a result of agricultural reforms and industrialization. It therefore received a net increase of population at this time by the inflow of Irish and Highlanders.[8] Although James Thomson, as a baker, had a trade that must have been in reasonable demand in an area where poor people were numerous, he may have found difficulty in getting employment as a journeyman after he had served his time as an apprentice. Many young men who suffered the same fate moved to the growing industrial towns of the British Isles. A smaller number crossed the Atlantic. After the American Revolution it became customary for emigrating Highlanders to go to Canada, allegedly because of their clannish instinct and desire to be with their own kind. James's financial circumstances, or those of his family, apparently enabled him to follow this path.

Thomson was thus an emigrant of a somewhat different type from those paupers who were shipped out of Scotland during the Highland clearances of 1837–38 and from Ireland during the potato famine of 1845. He paid his own way and went to Canada not because he was driven by poverty and sheer necessity, but because he was attracted by the hope of improving his lot. Men of this type were in a better position to make a success of their new homes and were good material for building a new country.

The later migration of James's father and sister, with two nieces and a nephew, was quite another matter. After the young man left home, his family fell on evil times. His father had to give up the smithy and he was installed by the laird, the Marquis of Huntly, as a bridgekeeper. This gave him a free house and a small wage. But the laird himself was soon in financial trouble. As a young man he had been a handsome soldier with a gallant bearing and the sprightly manners characteristic of his family who were known as 'the gay Gordons'. He had been a great ladies' man, so much so that at the French court before the Revolution he had quite captivated Queen Marie Antoinette, who liked to dance Scottish reels, and there had been scandalous rumours. In 1792 Colonel Gordon married into an English landowning family, and left the army. In 1836 when a distant kinsman, the Marquis of Huntly and Earl of Aboyne, died without heirs, the young gallant (turned English landowner, now styled Baron Meldrum of Morven) became head of his house and the premier marquis of Scotland. But these were empty honours which brought him no additional income. The family estates had been alienated, and Huntly's efforts to buy them back, perhaps injudicious in themselves, ended in disaster when an Edinburgh lawyer, a trusted agent, absconded with over £80,000. The marquis was bankrupt.[9] His factor stopped paying Alexander Thomson his small wage and also threatened to deprive him of his house. James Thomson therefore brought him, his daughter Helen, and a nephew and two nieces who had lost their mother and had been deserted by their father, to Edwardsburgh. James and Mary Thomson cheerfully accepted this additional responsibility along with that of raising their own growing family.

Settlement in Canada

In 1842 prospects for new immigrants had seemed good. Only four or five years earlier, the two British provinces of Upper and Lower Canada, continually racked by political disputes and obstructed by political stalemate, had been shaken by rebellion and invaded by self-styled 'patriots' from across the American border. Business was at a standstill, provincial treasuries were empty, and the public works needed to develop the country, especially canal construction, had been brought to a halt. Lord Durham, sent to report, ascribed much of the blame to racial tension between English- and French-speaking Canadians and the people's lack of an adequate voice in government. The remedies that he prescribed were the union of the provinces and responsible government.

The British government acted almost immediately to introduce union. It was achieved by 10 February 1841, and followed by a remarkable revival of confidence. So when James Thomson arrived in Canada the country was experiencing the euphoria of a very recent marriage. The new province was vast in extent. It stretched from the Gaspé peninsula to the head of Lake Superior and included the whole basin of the 'commercial empire of the St. Lawrence'. It had over a million inhabitants, more than half of them in Canada East where the vast majority, about half a million, was French in origin. There was thus a rough racial balance. The prospect seemed fair.[10]

Montreal

Montreal, James Thomson's first stopping place, had 40,000 inhabitants and was now larger than Quebec which had 35,000. While Quebec was two-thirds French, Montreal was half English-speaking. A large Irish Catholic element that spoke English complicated the racial and religious balance in the city.[11] This mixture of races and religions was at once a symbol of, and incentive to, active business life. Montreal was the acknowledged commercial hub of the new province, though not yet its political capital, which it became in 1844. It seemed to signify hope for a prosperous bicultural future. Charles Dickens, who visited

9

the city about this time, found it delightful by comparison with cruder midwestern American cities from which he had come. He admired Montreal's fine shops, its great cathedral, and its superior Government House. He even wrote favourably of the impoverished immigrants he saw passing through.[12] He glossed over the city's failings, narrow streets in the old French city where pestilence lurked, and low-lying new suburbs that hugged the river too closely and were subject to flooding. Montreal had a vigorous cultural and intellectual life, stimulated by the new McGill University out in the country below the Mountain, and enjoyed a lively social life led by the officers of the garrison. It clearly was destined to become one of the great cities of North America. It was an attractive place for a newcomer to Canada. But James Thomson had from the first planned to 'go West'.

The Development of the St. Lawrence

Above Montreal, between Lachine and the Thousand Islands, navigation on the St. Lawrence was interrupted by the series of great rapids of which the Long Sault was the largest and best known. The first Loyalist settlers in the region had taken up farms with a river frontage. Travellers going upstream half a century later noted that these farms were now a solid row all along the riverbank and that there was an air of prosperity. Thomas Rolph, a resident of Ancaster, who went from the Long Sault to Kingston, compared Canadian settlement favourably with that across the river. He said, 'The rich settlements on the Canadian side . . . large and well cultivated farms skirting the river from the township of Williamsburg to the beautiful village of Brockville . . . not only surpass in fertility of soil and excellence of cultivation the United States side, but may fairly challenge comparison with any of the most favoured parts of the States.'[13] The latter statement was gross exaggeration. Rolph was stressing the advantages of settlement in Canada over Australia. Other less partial travellers, however, also commented on the well-kept farms on the Canadian bank. Sir Richard Bonnycastle spoke of the north side from Cornwall to Prescott as a country 'full of apple orchards and flourishing farms'.[14]

English settlement on the Upper St. Lawrence was nearly as much a ribbon development as that in New France; the back country was not all developed. But although settlement along the river was continuous, almost a single street, subdivision had not gone as far as in Canada East. Better land further west attracted younger sons of Upper Canada families. Those who stayed along the St. Lawrence could make a living by farming but not much more. They appeared prosperous largely because their location on the main artery of Canada benefited them directly or indirectly.

The river was the chief highway of the province but because of the obstacle imposed by some of the most formidable rapids in the world its navigation was difficult. About 1780 British Royal Engineers had built small canals fit for bateaux with a thirty-inch draft but only for a short distance above Montreal. In 1800 these had been deepened to permit the passage of Durham boats. In 1841, although the Rideau waterway, also a barge canal, connected Montreal with

Lake Ontario by way of the Ottawa, on the St. Lawrence itself thirty miles of fast water had to be traversed
upriver by poling or by towing by horses or oxen.
Downstream bateaux and Durham boats shot the
rapids steered by skilled *Canadien* boatmen—a dangerous practice though accidents were surprisingly
few. As the distance was much shorter than by the
Rideau and Ottawa, the St. Lawrence continued to be
used.[15]

A road ran the entire length of the north shore of
the river but it was impeded by many streams and
swamps. Used by 'lumbering leathern conveniences',
this road, says Bonnycastle, would 'enter not into the
dreams of Britons'. Only the lower part, past the
Cascades, was planked and smooth. The remainder
was ankle- or knee-deep in mud in winter when it
was not frozen, and covered with dust in summer. It
clung to the river's edge and so gave the traveller
magnificent views of the rapids. For nervous passengers this was often distressing. Travellers preferred
to go by water wherever possible and they alternated
from coach or foot to boat and back again. Before the
canals permitted through navigation from end to end,
boat travel was precarious and uncomfortable. Bonnycastle tells that in 1841 small 'roasting' steamers were
crowded like cattle pens. The alternatives were the
canoe and the bateau, which he described as a sort of
coal barge. There were also small schooners 'where the
cabin could never permit you to display either your
length, your breadth, or your thickness, thus reducing
you to a point in creation, according to Euclid and
his commentators'.[16]

Plans to canalize the St. Lawrence had been

authorized by statute in 1833 and the work had begun in 1834. But the unsettled state of the province and lack of money brought the work to a halt. Union of the provinces got it started again in 1842 and by 1848 six canals had been constructed between Lachine and Lake Ontario. The first, the Cornwall canal, was completed in 1843. It was of a standard depth of nine feet in the sills. Thomson probably passed through this canal on his way to Edwardsburgh. The Beauharnois canal to deepen the ditch built by the Royal Engineers half a century earlier was completed in the same year. Four Williamsburg canals were begun in 1843 to by-pass bad water between Prescott and Dickenson's Landing. These were the Galoppes (or Galops), Point Iroquois, Rapide Flat, and Farrer's Point canals.[17] It was to supply bread to Irish labourers working on the Galops canal that Thomson went to work for the contractor at Edwardsburgh.

Edwardsburgh

Every community along the river dreamed of becoming a great metropolis. Cornwall township, at the foot of the main stretch of rapids, and Edwardsburgh, at its head, seemed to have special advantages. Above Edwardsburgh there was calm water all the way to Lake Ontario. In 1817 Edwardsburgh township had one thousand inhabitants including Loyalists and 'late Loyalists'. It had been settled by officers and other ranks of the 84th Regiment, the King's Royal Regiment of New York, Jessup's Loyal Rangers, and Butler's Rangers. (One of the first settlers was a Thomas Armstrong, a forebear of Mary, James Thomson's wife. He was listed as having 'served with General Burgoyne'.) By the early 1840s Edwardsburgh township had a population of 2,837. The land on the river was claimed to be 'generally good', the soil being sandy loam mixed with clay, but in the back of the township land was poor and produced barely enough to feed those who worked it. There were three grist and six sawmills in the township, one of which was worked by Henry Armstrong on his land at the very top of the Galops rapids. Bateaux and Durham boats going up the Galops rapids had to hire oxen to haul them round Point Cardinal, so that Henry Lewis's 'Hauling Point' there did a profitable business. Nearby was Hugh Munro's grist mill, later used also for carding. A village had grown up in the vicinity of the Hauling Point and the grist and carding mill. Within a mile radius there were also Lawrence Byrne's timber business, Duncan Clark's general store, and Henry Armstrong's sawmill.[18]

The contractor for a canal to by-pass the Galops rapids, a Lowland Scot named Andrew Elliott, cut it across the point from the head of the rapid to below Point Cardinal. About a mile and a half in length and nine feet deep, the dig was made with pick, shovel, and wheelbarrow by an army of Irish labourers. The work was completed by 1846. A secondary canal to connect the Galops canal with that down river at Iroquois was built in 1849–51.[19]

The coming of the canal-builders wrought great changes in Edwardsburgh. Some businesses were rendered unnecessary, for instance, Lewis's hauling trade. But the labourers on the canal had greatly increased the population in the area for a few years, and some of the Irish stayed on, changing the make-up of the township by the introduction of a considerable Catholic element.[20]

The growth expected from the new canals did not, however, benefit Canada as much as had been hoped. In earlier years Canada had profited because American goods, especially wheat, could pass through the colony and receive the preference in Britain as 'Canadian' wheat. The construction of the Erie canal in New York had checked this practice for a while, especially since it gave access to an ice-free port. The Canadian St. Lawrence canals had been designed to answer that New York challenge. They were expected to carry much heavier cargoes more cheaply. They did in fact reduce the cost of transportation from Kingston to Montreal by one half. However in 1845 and 1846 the Americans passed the Drawback Acts to give advantage to Canadian products and Canadian imports going through the United States; and about the same time Britain repealed the Corn Laws which gave preference to colonial wheat. To make matters worse there was soon worldwide depression. Canada had assumed a great public debt to pay for the canals, but the canals were half empty and business lagged. In June 1849 repeal of the British Navigation Acts, which brought foreign ships into Canadian ports, while regarded as natural compensation for the destruction of the old colonial system within which the Canadian economy had been fashioned, did not help Canada very much. It was accompanied by the belated concession of responsible government, by means of which Canada was given control of its own affairs. But those affairs were now in bad shape.[21]

Progress of the communities along the St. Lawrence, among them Edwardsburgh, was no doubt affected by this general malaise. Travellers now went mainly by ship, so that inns were not required as much as formerly. However, there were still seven in Edwardsburgh in 1850. Furthermore the population in the township had grown to 3,746; there were now four grist mills and twelve sawmills. The township also had eighteen public schools.[22] Edwardsburgh had thus continued to flourish after the canal was built despite the general depression. An important factor may have been the construction of the junction canal to link the Galops Canal with that at Iroquois, undertaken between 1849 and 1851. Meanwhile hard times had led Tories in Montreal to talk of annexation to the United States; and a Tory mob had destroyed the Parliament buildings. No doubt it was the general decline of trade in Canada at this time, rather than adversity in Edwardsburgh, that caused James Thomson to leave for the United States and then to head for the goldfields of California.

Chicago

Thomson's former employer and friend, Andrew Elliott, suggested that he should try Chicago because he thought it the city in the West with the greatest promise. When incorporated only twelve years before, in 1837, Chicago had been a hamlet with 350 inhabitants. In 1849 it was approaching 30,000. The secret of Chicago's success was its convenient location on Lake Michigan at the jumping-off point for the northern plains which were then rapidly being filled up. Communication with the East was by steamer across Lake Michigan. Railway connection was not established in that direction until 1852 (after Thomson had left). It is typical of Chicago's outlook that the first rails to enter the town in 1848 led off toward the West.

Everyone realized that Chicago had enormous potentiality as the gateway through which the great American plains would be developed. Yet it still had the appearance of a pioneer frontier town. Its buildings were almost all made of wood. It had no paved roads and in bad weather its streets were deep in mud. There were no services and the town was subject to periodic flooding.[23] When Thomson arrived Chicago was suffering from the depression that had struck everywhere else. He was therefore unable to get work at his trade. But with the city's need for buildings, the lumber business was still active and he soon secured employment as a clerk for a timber merchant. Chicago already showed signs of intellectual and cultural aspirations. Thomson took the opportunity to better himself by attending religious meetings and lectures.

Overland to the Gold Fields

A gold strike at Salter's Mill in 1848 had sparked the great gold rush that opened up California, recently acquired from Mexico as a result of the Mexican War. During the winter of 1848–49, two hundred thousand men and hundreds of wagons had congregated at Independence, Fort Leavenworth, St. Joseph, and Council Bluffs, all headed for California.

In 1849 many thousands also went to California by

way of Panama, but the cost was prohibitive. Most gold seekers therefore tried the cheaper overland route. The first wagon crossing had been made in 1843. From the Middle West it was obviously much the more convenient way to California; but there were serious dangers. There were no roads and few visible trails. Wide rivers had to be crossed, and in the mountains there were hazardous precipices. Most frightening of all, there were hostile Indians. In 1849 reliable guidebooks to show the way across the continent were lacking. The first based on actual experience were published only in 1851. Joseph Ware's *The Emigrant's Guide to California*,[24] which appeared in 1849, was not written from first-hand knowledge of the country. However, many thousands did make the crossing successfully in 1849 and thus the American nation burst across the continent to reach the Pacific in one bound.

The usual practice, which Thomson followed, was for a small group of men to form a 'company' which purchased a covered wagon, a tent, equipment, and supplies. More than one route was used but that which Thomson followed was one of the most popular. He struck out by way of Rock Island, Council Bluffs, Fort Laramie, the South Pass through the Rockies, and Salt Lake City. From there he crossed the Humboldt Sink in the desert, climbed the Sierra Nevada, passed through Placerville (popularly called Hangtown), and then went direct to diggings near Nevada City.

In 1850, when Thomson made the crossing, the worst hardships of the previous year had been eliminated. The cavalry had taken over Fort Laramie on

28 June 1849, and the Plains Indians were cowed by numbers and authority. Ferries had been installed at dangerous river crossings, and commercial stores for supplies were becoming available. But wagons still travelled in huge convoys for mutual protection and quarrels among the travellers were frequent. Few companies reached the Pacific slopes intact; by the time they had reached South Pass most of them had disintegrated. The way through the desert was strewn with surplus effects the overlanders had abandoned. From South Pass, the Indian menace being now behind them, wagons raced independently to the goldfields. But many had not succeeded in getting so far. Accidents, illness, especially Asiatic cholera, and death by violence were frequent.[25] Thomson and his partners were fortunate.

Mining in California

On 24 January 1848, ten days before the Treaty of Guadalupe, Hidalgo arranged for the cession of California and other territories to the United States, and three months before the treaty was ratified, James W. Marshall, an eccentric millwright and carpenter, had found pieces of gold in Colonel Sutter's millrace in Coloma. The news leaked out quickly and, after initial scepticism, flashed around the world. By November 1849 more than eighty thousand, the 'forty-niners' as they were termed, had reached California.

Gold worked in California during the gold rush was found in the valleys of the many tributaries of the

Sacramento and San Joaquin rivers that flowed from the Sierra into the Grand Valley. Miners were busy all along these Western slopes, from the Feather River in the north to the Tuolumne in the south, a distance of about 150 miles. This area is in the middle of the state directly behind San Francisco Bay. The early goldfields were thus fairly accessible. Actually gold deposits were much more widely spread but the primitive methods and tools of the miners could not exploit it all and they tackled what was easiest.

Gold found in river valleys could be separated from the dross by 'panning'. The 'forty-eighters' had favoured a rocker and cradle to do this on a large scale. But they had also had to resort to the pick and shovel. The 'forty-niners' had to dig deeper. They sank holes to the bedrock where gold had accumulated and then drove tunnels laterally in several directions. This process, known as 'coyoting', was laborious. As the miners in their haste often worked without timbering walls, it was also very dangerous. When retrieved, the pay dirt had to be carried some distance to be washed. Ditches had to be dug to bring water to dry diggings and mining was dependent on an ample flow of water which in California was seasonal. During the winter of 1849–50 the Long Tom was introduced. This was an improvement on the rocker. It was a rocker enlarged and immobilized by lengthening the hopper into a trough in which a heavy sheet iron sieve allowed the heavier gold to fall through. Because some gold escaped, the sieve emptied into one or more long troughs fitted with riffle bars where the process was repeated. But the Long Tom was much more dependent on water than the rocker and cradle and therefore needed more extensive ditching. In dry weather when streams dried up miners were unable to work and became restless.[26]

The vast horde of newcomers to California created problems for a territory that had become a state only in 1850. Provision for law enforcement was still sketchy and the miners took the law into their own hands. Men caught red-handed and suspected criminals were tried by 'miners' courts'. These trials were not merely arbitrary convictions. Juries of varying sizes decided on the question of guilt. Accused persons were given an opportunity to defend themselves and evidence was heard in regard to the facts, but the courts were impatient with argument. Punishment was swift. An oft-told story tells of the delegate sent from a miners' court to inform a new widow that her husband had been hanged for murder. 'But, madam, the joke's on us. He didn't do it.'[27]

In addition to law and government, other needs of the miners had to be improvised. Men suffering badly from gold fever concentrated on mining but others provided them with services. The wives of miners who took in laundry often made more money than their husbands. The need for lumber and for bread gave Thomson the opportunity to combine mining with those two occupations in which he already had experience; and these provided him with a steadier income than gold mining. Many men who thus opened up such businesses for the miners stayed on to become permanent settlers in California. Thomson was different in that almost from the time he arrived he was thinking of returning to settle permanently in Canada.

The Cariboo

James Thomson's second prospecting venture in the Cariboo, ten years later, provides interesting contrasts with that in California. There had been finds of gold in British Columbia since 1849, the year of the big California gold rush, but it was not until 1860 that rumours of big discoveries there began to spread. Once again the finds were in territory not yet organized. It was still part of the domain of the Hudson's Bay Company. Vancouver Island had recently been made a Crown Colony, but it had not yet grown out of its Company leading strings. That colony had only a few hundred inhabitants, mostly Company employees.

Over the course of about six years Hudson's Bay Company factors in British Columbia had collected gold from Indians in quantities not significant enough to be of much commercial value. The last thing the company wanted was to provoke an invasion of prospectors in search of gold. Hudson's Bay officials feared these would disturb the Indians and the fur-bearing animals, on which their main business depended. So, for a while, the gold was kept in store. In February 1858, 800 ounces of it were sent by the Company to San Francisco to be minted. In California, gold was still on everybody's mind. When news of the gold shipment became known, some miners decided to try prospecting in the Fraser Valley. They found gold on Hill's Bar near Hope in such quantities that a new rush was triggered. By May 1858 a thousand men were on the Fraser and the days of the quiet fur trade were numbered.

22

James Douglas, governor of Vancouver Island, feared that, as most of the newcomers were Americans, the influx might lead to eventual annexation. He instituted a license system for prospectors and hurriedly arranged for the creation of a new Crown Colony of British Columbia, of which he became governor. He also obtained from England small parties of British soldiers, men of the Royal Engineers, to help him provide necessary works and buildings and keep the peace. Among these were blacksmiths, painters, carpenters, surveyors, miners, and architects. The Royal Engineers surveyed townsites, built roads and trails, and provided military protection. Most important of all, they planned and began to construct a road at the beginning of the route to the goldfields up the Fraser River.

The biggest single finds came late in 1860, far up in the mountains, at Antler Creek, Williams Creek, and Lightning Creek. In 1861 this new goldfield yielded between two and a half and five million dollars. By the beginning of 1862 there were six thousand miners in the Cariboo creeks area centred on the town of Barkersville in a remote area of the mountains.[28] Once again miners had poured in from all parts of the world, some coming by way of Victoria, others overland, and not a few going direct from American ports without stopping at Vancouver Island. The ocean route from New York by which Thomson travelled meant braving Confederate cruisers in the Atlantic, crossing Panama, and making a long journey up the Pacific.

Late in 1858 a trail had been slashed around the Fraser Canyon to Lillouet, and in 1860 it had been widened to a carriage road. But this was a roundabout route over high mountains. It was possible to get by ship as far up the Fraser as Yale. From that point miners went on foot. In 1861 Governor Campbell undertook to build a wagon road north for 400 miles through the Fraser Canyon to the goldfields. As the permanent population of the colony was a mere 7,000, this was a phenomenal concept. The first six miles of the road had to be literally blasted from the face of the canyon cliff. This part of the Cariboo trail was built by Royal Engineers. Other parts of the road were put out to contract. By September 1863 a road had been built for 300 miles up to Soda Creek. Beyond that it was possible to travel by sternwheeler to Quesnel. But in 1861 and 1862 thousands of miners had struggled north by shorter routes through a variety of passes to the west of the river and the future Cariboo Wagon Road. There were many different trails through the wilderness.

In addition to being in remote and difficult country, the gold in the Cariboo was freakish and erratic in its location. It was said that any amateur could guess where it was located as accurately as any geologist. Sometimes the best diggings were on what was called the mother lode at the head of a creek. In other places they were to be found fifty feet deep under clay at the foot of a creek whose waters swirled down into a river. A fortune might come out of one claim. A hundred feet away its neighbour might produce nothing. A few miners struck it rich. The majority were disappointed.[29] However, contractors were working on the wagon road and Thomson and his friends from Port Elgin (an older name for Edwards-

burgh) were among the less fortunate who took this
kind of work. After several tries they had found only
a few specks of gold. Thomson had to work in a
lumber yard to earn enough money to buy his ticket
home. An anonymous historian writing in the Prescott
Journal in 1898 said that the Cardinal men came back
'with heavier purses'.[30] This was not true for James
Thomson.

Edwardsburgh Again

Thomson's decision, made long before this, to farm
in Edwardsburgh, had been taken despite an aware-
ness that this would lead only to a modest livelihood.
The money he had made on his first gold-seeking
expedition to California had been enough to set him
up as a farmer but he had deliberately chosen to
buy cheaper land in Edwardsburgh because he
knew the place and had friends there. Better land
further west would have meant starting all over again,
but might have been more profitable. In 1854, at the
age of thirty-one, James Thomson's marriage to
nineteen-year-old Mary Armstrong, the attractive,
high-spirited daughter of a United Empire Loyalist
family, completed the immigrant's assimilation into
the conservative society of the St. Lawrence valley.
As their letters reveal, it was to prove an exceptionally
happy and stable marriage.

James's choice of Edwardsburgh as a permanent
home was typical of his caution, but soon after he
bought the farm, fortune smiled upon him. The new
Grand Trunk railway was built across his land and
he obtained contracts to prepare part of the permanent
way in the vicinity. For a while conditions throughout

the provinces had been improving. Reciprocity in 1855 had helped the economy. The railway from Toronto to Montreal, which passed through Edwardsburgh, was opened in 1856. Once again Canada did not benefit as much as had been hoped. Earlier lines running down into the United States drained away some of the trade, and those coming down from the north to points in the river were hampered because the hinterland in the Laurentian Shield was infertile. Nevertheless the communities along the mainline of the Grand Trunk gained from the accelerated movement. Passengers could now get from Edwardsburgh to Montreal and back in one day, a great improvement upon the time when Thomson had first come to the township by coach, steamer, and on foot.

But the biggest contribution to the prosperity of Edwardsburgh was the introduction of industry. It was made possible because the new railway provided the transportation facilities to serve a new business that could use the water power of the river. In 1858 William Thomas Benson, an English manufacturer of chemicals, sold his business in Manchester and emigrated to Canada. He met a man in Montreal named Thomas Aspden who told him that, as there was no starch company in Canada, this was the opportunity he was seeking. The manufacture of starch from corn was then a new development. It was in great demand not only for food and laundry work but also for use in the manufacture of cloth, an industry which was opening up in the province. The fast flow of water in the Galops rapids could provide power, the railway and canals a means of bringing corn from the farms and sending starch to the market.

Benson and Aspden selected Point Cardinal, not far from where Lewis had had his hauling point, as the best site for their factory which began to grind 200 pounds of corn a day. The village of Edwardsburgh had thus found an industry to set it on its feet. Growth was rapid. In 1865 the firm was incorporated as the Edwardsburgh Starch Company, one of the constituent parts of what is now the Canada Starch Company.[31]

Starch benefited Thomson as well as Edwardsburgh. Probably after his return from his second, and fruitless, trip to seek a fortune in gold, he took up a position with the starch works, thereby abandoning the early dream of being his own master. When he went on his overland journey in 1850, and later when he was in business in California, and mining and lumbering in British Columbia, James Thomson had kept the books and had thereby earned the respect of his partners. He now put this talent and experience to good use. He became an assistant book-keeper in the starch works. This provided him with a steady income to supplement the meagre return from his land. An anonymous historian of Cardinal wrote in 1898, 'He handled money for the factory every day for twenty-two years and I never heard a complaint against him.'[32]

James remained a member of the Free Church of Scotland (later reunited with the Presbyterian Church), but in the censuses of 1861 and 1871, his wife Mary was listed as a Wesleyan Methodist, the denomination of her parents. The children all belonged to the Scottish church in which Thomson became an elder in 1876.[33] In 1878 when it was decided to incorporate the village, Edwardsburgh changed its name to Cardinal after the point on which it stood. James Thomson was elected a member of the town council which sat for the first time in January 1880. The following year he was elected reeve, an office he held for six years, longer than any other reeve in Cardinal's history.

James's father, Alexander, the former Aboyne blacksmith, had been installed in a small house on Thomson's farm and worked there until his death in 1864. His daughter Helen also lived in that house for a quarter of a century after she and her father came to Canada in 1856. The children they brought with them were put to trades. Ellen Smith lived with her aunt, and in the census of 1871 is described as a tailoress. She was then twenty-five. Mary Smith, four years younger, was a dressmaker living elsewhere in the village with Louisa Armstrong, aged twenty-two, probably a sister of James's wife. John Smith, the nephew, who had also come out from Scotland with Alexander, was listed in the census of 1861 when he was thirteen. Ten years later he had either left the village or died.[34]

James and Mary Thomson had seven children of their own. The first born died in infancy, and a girl, Lora, also died young. Three sons, James, Colin, and Edwin (or Edward) remained unmarried. Edwin, the youngest, went to business college in Kingston in 1886.[35] All three were partners in a large general store in Prescott which continued in business until Edwin died in 1962. James himself had died in 1895. His wife Mary Thomson (who always spelled the name in the Irish way with a 'p') lived until 1916. She died at the age of eighty. A daughter, Mary (Ella) married Stuart Alexander Lytell and died in 1930.Her sister Agnes

(Mrs. Logan), who died in 1968, was the last surviving child of that young Scottish baker's apprentice who had come to make his home in Canada a hundred and twenty-four years earlier.

Other letters in the Thomson collection not included in this volume reveal that in 1886 James and Mary visited his relatives in Scotland. Correspondence with a niece, perhaps on his mother's side of the family, suggests that the Scottish relatives had, in the end, fared almost as well at home as Thomson had in Canada. The niece, who struck up a friendship with Mary Thompson, was a clerk in a telegraph office in Aberdeen. In her letters there is a reference to 'my uncle the blacksmith', which may indicate that James's elder brother Sandy had found work in his old trade after the rest of his family left Scotland and had at last prospered.

The Thomson letters give an intimate view of a Canadian in the making. James Thomson showed many of the characteristics which seem typical of his adopted country—diligence, caution, sobriety, devoutness, willing acceptance of responsibilities, love of family and of his new home, and respect and affection for the country of his origin. His ambitions were modest. By emigrating he had bettered his lot, but not much more than he might have done if he had stayed at home. This surely is the story of pioneer Canada: not a tale of great and sudden prosperity and power, but a popular migration in which men, by virtue of hard work, sacrifice, and probity, built a new nation in a country where people could live a little more comfortably than if they had stayed in the British Isles.

NOTES

1. See William A. Carrothers, *Emigration from the British Isles with Special Reference to the Development of the Overseas Dominions* (London: P. S. King & Sons, 1929), *passim*; Stanley C. Johnson, *A History of Emigration from the United Kingdom to North America, 1763–1912* (London: G. Routledge & Sons, 1913); and Brinley Thomas, *Migration and Economic Growth: a Study of Great Britain and the Atlantic Economy* (Cambridge: University Press, 1959), pp. 57, 59.

2. Thomas Rolph, *Canada and Australia: Their Relative Merits Considered in an Answer to a Pamphlet by Thornton Leigh Hunt, Esq.*, entitled '*Canada and Australia*' (London: Smith, Elder, 1939), p. 28.

3. Johnson, *Emigration from the United Kingdom*, p. 105.

4. Charles, XI Marquis of Huntly, *The Records of Aboyne, MCXXX–MDCLXXXI* (Aberdeen: New Spalding Club, 1894), p. viii. But see James Macdonald, ed., *Place Names of West Aberdeenshire* (Aberdeen: New Spalding Club, 1899), p. 3, where the derivation of Aboyne is said to be possibly a personal name.

5. Moray McLaren, *The Shell Guide to Scotland* (London: Ebury Press, 1965), p. 69.

6. Sir Adam Collier, *The Crofting Problem* (Cambridge: University Press, 1953), pp. 1–8, 21–22, 44–47; Carrothers, *Emigration from the British Isles*, pp. 1–2, 171–84.

7. Collier, *Crofting Problem*, p. 13.

8. D. F. Macdonald, *Scotland's Shifting Population, 1770–1850* (Glasgow: Jackson, 1937), pp. 23–26.

9. James Taylor, *The Great Historic Families of Scotland*, 2 vols. (London: J. S. Virtue, [n.d.]), II, 344–45; *Gentleman's Magazine*, XL n.s., III, (1853), 198–99.

10. Gerald M. Craig, *Upper Canada: The Formative Years, 1784–1841* (London: McClelland & Stewart, 1963), pp. 274–75; J. M. S. Careless, *The Union of the Canadas: the Growth of Canadian Institutions, 1841–1857* (Toronto: McClelland & Stewart, 1967), pp. 20–27.

11. Careless, *Union of the Canadas*, p. 2.

12. Stephen Leacock, *Montreal: Seaport and City* (Garden City, N.Y.: Doubleday, Doran, 1942), pp. 162–63; Kathleen Jenkins, *Montreal: Island City of the St. Lawrence* (New York: Doubleday, 1968), pp. 317–18.

13. Rolph, *Canada and Australia*, p. 9.

14. Sir Richard H. Bonnycastle, *The Canadas in* 1841, 2 vols. (London: Henry Colburn, 1841), I, 89–90, 98.

15. Craig, *Upper Canada: The Formative Years*, p. 150.

16. Sir Richard H. Bonnycastle, *Canada and the Canadians in* 1846 (London: Henry Colburn, 1846), I, 92.

17. Gilbert Norman Tucker, *The Canadian Commercial Revolution, 1845–1851* (New Haven: Yale University Press, 1936), p. 43; Craig, pp. 150–60.

18. Fred Byers, et al., *A History of Cardinal* ([Cardinal, Ontario]: Privately Printed, 1967), *passim*; Wm. H. Smith, *Smith's Canadian Gazetteer . . .* (Toronto: H. & W. Rowell, 1846), p. 52.

19. Byers, *History of Cardinal*, p. 32.

20. Ruther McKenzie, *Leeds and Grenville: Their First Two Hundred Years* (Toronto and Montreal: McClelland & Stewart, 1967), pp. 218–19.

21. Careless, *Union of the Canadas*, pp. 108, 110, 117.

22. W. H. Smith, *Canada: Past, Present and Future*, 2 vols. (Toronto: Thomas Maclear, 1852), II, 310.

23. Bessie Louise Pierce, *A History of Chicago*, 4 vols. (New York: Knopf, 1940), II, 3.

24. Published in St. Louis, Mo. by J. Halsall; reprinted with introduction and notes by John Caughey (Princeton: Princeton University Press, 1932).

25. Andrew Child, *Overland Route to California . . .* (Los Angeles: N. A. Kovak, 1946), pp. i–iii; Jay (James) Monaghan, *The Overland Trail* (Indianapolis: Bobbs-Merril, 1947), pp. 343–49; John Walton Caughey, *Gold is the Cornerstone* (Berkeley: University of California Press, 1948), pp. 97–98.

26. Caughey, *Gold is the Cornerstone*, pp. 161–64; Rodman W. Paul, *California Gold . . .* (Cambridge: Harvard University Press, 1947), pp. 61–62.

27. Caughey, *Gold is the Cornerstone*, p. 236.

28. Agnes Laut, *The Cariboo Trail: Chronicles of Canada, No. 23* (Toronto: Glasgow Brook, 1935), *passim*; Rev. A. G. Morice, *The History of the Northern Territory of British Columbia* (London: John Lane, 1906), pp. 298, 304; Art Downs, *The Story of the Cariboo Gold Rush in Photos* (Quesnel: Northwest Digest, 1960), *passim*.

29. Laut, *Cariboo Trail*, p. 47 *passim*; Downs, *Cariboo Gold Rush*, p. 2.

30. Byers, *History of Cardinal*, pp. 103, 105.

31. McKenzie, *Leeds and Grenville*, pp. 185–86; Byers, *History of Cardinal*, pp. 57–61.

32. Byers, *History of Cardinal*, p. 106.

33. P.A.C., Canada West Census, 1861 (Reel C 1025) Grenville County, Edwardsburgh, p. 8; ibid., Ontario Census 1871 (Reel C 647) South Grenville, Edwardsburgh, pp. 5, 17–18.

34. P.A.C., Canada West Census, Edwardsburgh, p. 8; ibid., Ontario, Edwardsburgh, pp. 5, 17–18.

35. Richard A. Preston, 'A Business College Student's Letters, 1886–87', *Historic Kingston*, no. 19 (February 1971) 81–86.

EMIGRATION TO
MONTREAL

To Alexander Thomson 6 June 1844
Addressed: Alexander Thomson, Blacksmith,
Aboyne, Aberdeenshire, Scotland [via] Halifax.
Postmarked: Quebec, June 6, 1844.

From the Quarantine Station
thirty miles below Quebec.[1]

Dear Father,

As we are now drawing near [our destination] I take
the opportunity of our lying at [anchor to send a
few] words, as you will perhaps be looking for [news
as soon as a letter] can reach you. Our seventh week
is now [begun. Unless] the wind change we need
not [expect to be aboard more] than another day. I
hope this letter will find you all as well as I am while
writing it. I am as well as ever I was for which and
for conducting me in safety across a stormy ocean
I would thank Almighty God and at the same time
ask his blessing protection for the future. I will not
at present enter into any account of our voyage. It
has been rather longer than most of us expected
however we are all quite well and aparently in good
spirits and when we compare our passage with
other ships that we have spoken we have cause to be
thankful. The quarantine doctor has just left our
ship after examining the passengers with the appearance of whom he was well pleased. One ship is at

1. The quarantine station was on Grosse Isle.

present riding quarantine in consequence of sickness on board. Very few of our passengers are to stop at Quebec and as there are so many going up the river we are expecting to get a steam boat to come alongside the ship which would save a deal of trouble.

With many thanks and good wishes to all kind friends in Scotland I remain your affectionate son.

James Thomson

June 6 2 p.m.   we are now moored about half a mile from the [wharf at Quebec] and all well. I intend to go ashore tonight [to see the place] and post this letter and deliver Andrew [Begg's letters if I can] find the owners. More news soon.

J T

To Alexander Thomson 14 June 1844

Montreal June 14, 1844

Wednesday June 5th   Rose at five am to assist at
weighing anchor. The wind was still a head but the
tide here runs ten miles an hour so we go on pretty
well. About nine oclock we came in sight of the
quarantine & the Brilliant hoisting her sails to leave
it. In the course of the morning our beds were all
emptied of chaff and the place well cleaned. At ten
we cast anchor at the quarantine station and soon
after the doctor came on board. We were all ordered
upon deck and the doctor went below. After he came
up we were all put to one end of the ship and a rope
put across and we passed the doctor one by one as
fast as we could walk, we had no customers for him.
One of the passengers of the [Brilliant] was detained
being sick. There is an hospital here the doctors
house and a few more houses also a Roman Catholic
and an Episcopal chapel. The latter has a congregation of thirteen. Some of our cabin passengers went
ashore in the doctors boat. They were not allowed
to go far inland as we had not yet passed the Customhouse. A boat from the shore came along side with
some goods for sale. They had tea at three pence an
ounce sugar at five pence a pound strong beer at
sixpence a quart. At five pm we were under weigh.
At ten dropped anchor.

Thursday June 6th   After a very hard lie all night
rose about five. A boat came along side with fresh
fish. They are nearly as large as a salmon and taste

35

very like a trout or fresh herring. They were sold for sixpence each. We got one that served us to breakfast and dinner. About nine am we were opposite a church the bell of which was ringing and the congregation assembling. We are supposing them to be Roman Catholics and this some holiday. I never saw so many gigs comming to a church before. More than one half are driving. The church is situated upon the large Island of Orleans along the side of which we have been sailing for some time. It is as thickly inhabited as the other side and has most beautiful scenery. This island bears a place in the history of British America. When the British fleet under General Wolfe were going to attack Quebec they sailed up one side of the island while the French fleet who were on the lookout for them sailed down the other side. This gave the British a great advantage.[1] The weather is now foggy and sometimes heavy rain but quite mild and agreable. Ten. We are begining to see the spires of Quebec through the mist.

Eleven am. We were moored about half a mile from the wharf at Quebec. The weather is now dry and clear and we have a fine view of the city with its fortress frowning upon the river, its houses rising row above row the whole surmounted by its stately steeples and splendid domes. Imagine all these with their tinplated roofs glittering in the noonday sun, and then you will not wonder if it looked like enchantment to eyes which for weeks had only beheld a dreary waste of waters. In the evening I got a

1. This is an inaccurate version of the story of Wolfe's approach to Quebec.

36

James Thomson in Early Married Life

Mary Thomson in Early Married Life

James Thomson in Later Life

Mary Thompson in Later Life

chance of a boat and got ashore a short time and got
a look of part of the upper town. I had no time to go
to the lower which I do not regret much as I got a
good and I believe a true description of it at any
rate it was a short one. I was told there is nothing in
it but Irishmen and pigs. In the upper town there
are some good houses and shops the streets like
those of most old fortified cities being narrow and
crooked. We went to our old quarters all night.

Friday.   When ashore yesterday the captain engaged
a steamboat to come alongside. The one that was
going up the river with us could not come but a
spare one came for us and three hundred Irish that
were moored a little off. We had thus to shift all our
luggage twice which with passing the customhouse
officer made a good days work till five pm when we
left for Montreal. Some of the steamers on the river
are very large and splendidly finished. The one we
went with is larger than the city of Aberdeen and
has a deck supported on pillars above the usual one.
The upper deck forms a very agreable walk it is
covered overhead with canvass in warm weather.
Not withstanding her large size she was well filled
on this occasion. There was three hundred Irish
nearly the whole of the passengers by the St Lawrence & Brilliant. A great many Canadian lumberers
or raftsmen making in all about seven hundred. The
Aberdonians kept pretty close together and kept
brother Pat on the other side. After starting we had a
fine view of the fort and the monument erected to
the memory of Generals Wolfe and Montcalm. After
passing the fort a little we were showed the place

where Wolfe went up and where he fell victorious.

We had not gone far up the river when we saw some more wonders. You will think it was no great wonder after all when I tell you it was only a float of wood comming down the water but it was none of your Water of Dee floats with Sandy Rae on one end and John Michie on the other. It was an immense field of floating timber the logs squared and built one upon another I dont know how deep. There were a dozen masts upon it with a sail on each a great many men with wooden houses and fires and the whole pulled along by a steamer. The first one was scarcely passed when we saw another. The wind was right ahead and by evening very cold so that the upper deck was nearly deserted. There was a sleeping place below but the greater part kept beside their luggage.

Saturday. At two am the Queen (vessels name) stopped at a place called Three Rivers. I was comfortable below and did not come to see it. The next place we stoped at was Port St Francis on the other side of the river. Here some passengers left and some came on. Among the former were a family from Morayshire who were near neighbours to us in the St Lawrence. We felt as sorry at parting as if we had been acquainted all our days. It was like the first breach in the family now that we were among strange faces and strange tongues. We looked upon a St Lawrence person as a near relative.

The other place we touched at was a village named William Henery.[1] Here some goods and passengers

1. Sorel.

were taken on board and a lot of wives and children selling gingerbread and sweetmeats came on as long as the ship lay (about ten minutes). They had also roasted fish similar to those we bought below Quebec and hard boiled eggs.

At eleven am we were at Montreal. The boats starting at five from Quebec are generally at Montreal by eight next morning but the Queen on this occasion had a strong head wind and a strong tide to encounter. She was also loaded until she was eighteen inches deeper than usual. Still you see she went about mail coach rate. The distance is a hundred and eighty miles, and the fare a dollar no charge for luggage. There are a great many small islands in the river all the way up and a good many small lighthouses along the banks. They need no compass but steer by the sight of the banks. For this purpose the wheel that turns the helm is placed far forward and a good piece raised above the deck. There are always two men at the wheel. There are two engines of two hundred horse power each. There are a good many steamers here a little less than the Queen and there are others a good deal less on the canal leading to the upper province.

Henderson got a situation in Quebec he did not intend to stop long but only to get up to the ways of this country. Watson has got a place a few miles from Montreal with an acquaintance that he happened to meet. Let Andrew Begg[1] know that I did not see Mr Chambers. Enquired and got direction

1. Thomson carried a letter to Andrew Begg's son who lodged with a Mr. Chambers in Quebec.

where to find him but my time was limited and the boat would not wait. I gave the letters to Henderson who will deliver them. I will I hope get word from him before I write you again.

My compliments to all my friends and may this through God's blessing find you all well as it leaves me. Mr James Smith is quite well.[1] I have not had much time of him yet. I had a long news with Mr Esson.[2] More soon.

Your loving son

James Thomson.

I have now dear reader brought you as far as Montreal and I have got no further myself. I shall not at present say anything about this city as it will need a page for itself. In the meantime I will only add that I am highly pleased with its appearance.

1. James Smith worked at the Bank of British North America. Thomson carried a letter of introduction addressed to him.

2. The Reverend Henry Essen, M.A., a distinguished Scottish Presbyterian minister, a gifted scholar, and a brilliant talker. He was born at Deeside, Aberdeenshire in 1793 and was invited to St. Gabriel Street Church in 1817 by Montreal merchants who had come from his part of Scotland. In 1844 he was 'carried on top of the wave' of Free Church sentiment, a movement originating in Scotland over the issue of the freedom of the congregation to choose its own minister. As ministers in Canada were usually 'called' by a congregation, the Scottish dispute really had little relevance across the Atlantic. Nevertheless it split the Presbyterian Church in Canada. Essen was one of the leaders of the 'non-inclusion' party which became the Free Church. In November 1844, after Thomson met him, he resigned from St. Gabriel Street to become a professor at Knox College, Toronto, set up by Free Church adherents in competition with Queen's College, the Presbyterian Church's seminary. See Rev. Robert Campbell, *History of St. Gabriel Street Church* (Montreal: Drysdale, 1887), pp. 276–96.

44

Through the kindness of Mr. Esson I have got a
situation the duties of which I enter on this afternoon. Since my arival in the city I have been living
in a lodging house kept by Mr McHardy who twelve
years ago was a coach guard on the Deeside road.
We have always beef steak and potatoes to breakfast
and also to tea and roast beef and potatoes to dinner
besides a number of other dishes. The whole con-
cludes with a glass of cold water there being no
beer unless called for.

To Helen Thomson 18 July 1844

Montreal July 18th 1844.

Dear Sister[1]

After a somewhat long and rather stormy voyage, by
the good providence of Almighty God I arrived safe
and well in this city, just seven weeks after parting
with so many kind, dear friends at Aberdeen. I will
not here enter into any particular description of my
passage as I sent a long account of it to Father on
my arrival here.[2] I may mention however that I was
not sick above two days altogether, although I did
not feel inclined to take much food the first fortnight. After that I got a nice appetite and could have
eaten four or five times a day. Almost the only food
that I could take was water brose.[3] Tea and coffee
was not relished at all. During our first week at sea
the fire was but little used and those who wanted to
cook first in the morning had to light it for themselves. When stomachs began to get a little larger
that plan was found not to work well, so every grown
up passenger subscribed twopense and with this
sum (about fourteen or fifteen shilling) we engaged
two men to light the fire every morning at six oclock.
This did first rate as a good fire soon set the brose
kettles and the porrage pans a-boiling. Breakfast was
generally over by eight oclock. By nine the fire was

1. James's unmarried sister who lived with his father. Her name is
variously spelled Helen, Hellen and Ellen.
2. This letter, elsewhere described as a 'journal', was circulated
among Thomson's friends and relatives at home. It is not among the
present collection of his papers.
3. Oatmeal porridge.

filled with the first round of dinner pots. Notwithstanding which the last dinner parties (if the weather
was at all moderate) generally had to keep fashion-
able hours.

The almost universal supper was brachin[1] and
treacle the cooking of which commenced about five
oclock and lasted a couple of hours, as cooking and
eating was nearly all we had either for work or
amusement you need not be surprised when I say
that we had some new fashioned dishes at times.
We made several puddings out of broken ship biscuits and got them baked in the cooks oven, and we
more than once had pancakes or sauty bannocks.[2]
Some tried to make sowens[3] without sids[4] and some
who had seen farther before them had brought sowens
in a dry state like a cheese or lump of chalk. As the
cook had sometimes a pie to cover and other little
jobs in the baking line the bakers were great favour-
ites of Peters and also no losers as we had sometimes
a turnip or stock of green kail to put in our broth
after we were a month at sea.

We made out pretty well with the cooking but we
had always the best dinner when we made it along
with the Barrons. They afforded the materials the
one day and us the other and here I must mention
that of all the kind neighbours we had aboard the
St. Lawrence, Ann Barron (the stout girl that left
Simpson the minister) was the kindest and the best.

1. A water-gruel with butter.
2. Oatmeal pancakes or griddle cakes.
3. A dish made by steeping and fermenting the husks, seeds, or
sifting of oats in water and boiling.
4. The husks of oats for making sowens.

47

She was our doctor and nurse when we were sick and our cook when we were well. Our bed was as regularly made and our share of the floor kept as clean as any on board and when the weather was fine she washed our towels and pocket handkerchifs. Her and her sister were not the least sick. Her brother was a few days and her mother fully a month. Poor old body, I felt sorry for her she could not smoke her pipe nor drink tea. The only thing she could take was oranges of which they had none. I had thus an opportunity in a small measure of returning their kindness, as I stood in little want of those I had. The ships water was sometimes not very good but with a little crem of tartar or even oatmeal I could always drink it. There were several passengers who had been at America before, who said the worst of it was good compared with what they got on other ships. We had a good deal more provisions than we used but were very lucky in getting the greater part sold. There were some things that we would have been the better of that we had not. But as long as they were aboard the ship we never wanted. We bartered biscuits for oatmeal and butter and sugar for treacle.

The bannocks you made me were as good three weeks after as when baked. I have no doubt they would have kept the whole of the voyage as many others did who were made the same way. They were better than those baked in an oven. The eggs I had kept good five or six week. We did not give any of them a longer trial. They were better than the others, as they had some taste of the straw that they were packed among. But they were all very good.

We sold a great deal of our beef about the half of

48

our sugar and a good many biscuits besides bartering a great many more. After the meal I brought was
done my red box was filled and emptyed more than
once. The only commodity that remained unsold
by the time we got to the river was one pound of tea
of which we did not use above an ounce and also the
greater part of the coffee. These things were relished
by no body on board not even the old wives. We left
a few pounds of biscuits too, which when we were
at Quebec we divided among some families who
were going to the far west, and who had then a
fortnights more sailing before them. After thus buying and selling and bartering and when the partner
ship was about to be broken up we counted the contents of our till and found about thirty shillings,
which brought down the cost of our provisions for
the voyage to about one pound fifteen each certainly
not very extragavant for seven weeks board and good
board too.

The first land we saw was calculated to give us a
very poor idea of America but the farther we went it
got the better until we were near Quebec where it
was truly beautiful. Our farming passengers would
wish no better, and we stood mostly by farmers and
farm labourers. There were four or five blacksmiths
three bakers half a dozen wrights and joiners and a
tailor who might almost be said to have crossed the
atlantic on his goose and needle as he sewed all the
time unless when the rolling of the ship turned him
off his chest lid. We had also two fiddlers and a
poet. Henderson is the only one of our number who
remained in Quebec and there are only about half a
dozen in Montreal.

I had only an hour or two in Quebec on the evening of our arrival. The upper town is build on a high rock the French and English Churches are also on very high ground and both very large. The houses are all covered tinplate (white iron) and when glittering in the sunshine they have a very dazeling appearance. The fort is on one side of the town having a full command of the town and the river. Here I saw hills of cannon and mountains of balls. Near the battery there is a monument erected to the memory of Generals Wolfe and Montcalm. The one was the English soldier who fell at the moment of victory taking the city. The other was the Frenchman who was defending it. It is a long square tower very like the monument at the Aberdeen Lunatic Asylum. There is no inscription on it but the name Wolfe on one side and that of Montcalm on the other. . . .

There are no public clocks as the frost in winter would destroy them. To make up in some measure for this want a cannon is fired at certain hours every day. . . .

The Custom house officers were even less strict here than at home as we had not to open our trunks at all. They merely asked if we had got anything to sell.

From the confusion that was in the steerage when you were down you could have no idea of how comfortable and happy we were on the St. Lawrence. . . .

I must now bid adieu to the St. Lawrence and step on board the Queen a large and powerful steamer where everything is as bright and beautiful as carving gilding and painting can make it. Her decks

are all painted white and kept as clean as the floor
of a drawing room. In a few hours she was at Montreal which is a much finer city than Quebec. The
streets are long and straight and level the principal
ones paved with wood. The foot paths are allmost
entirely wood which is laid the same as the floor of
a house only the boards are thicker. It is very nice
to walk on. The streets here have generally their
names put up in French and English. Rue is the
French for street thus St. Jame's Street is on one
corner and Rue St Jacques on the other. About the
center of the town there is a large square called the
Place de Arme's. On one side of it stands the French
Church[1] the largest one I ever saw. It covers about
an acre of ground and holds a great many thousand
people. It is open everyday. I was in it two or three
times the days that I was idle. There are some wax
candles ten or twelve feet high and a great many
chandeliers all hung with glass. There are paintings
of the apostles in one of the windows and a fine
statue of the virgin Mary near the altar. On the front
of it there are two large steeples one of them contains the largest bell ever cast in Britain. It weighs
seven tons six hundredweight and cost twelve hundred pounds. It was cast in London about two years
ago and was consecrated with great pomp and
christened the Monster Bell, on its arrival here.[2]
As it is still considered a curiosity, there are people
in attendance to show it. The charge of admittance

1. Notre Dame Parish Church.

2. The first Gros Bourdon bell, cast in February 1843, weighed
16,352 pounds and was the largest bell on the continent. It broke in
May 1845 and was sent back to England to be recast. The second
Gros Bourdon bell, weighing 24,780 pounds, was installed in 1848.

is tran sou but they did not catch mine. It is only
rung on great festivals. In the other steeple are ten
music bells. The first sunday I was here was a great
day among the Roman Catholics. All the principal
streets were ornamented with evergreens and some
of the Churches and nuneries were decked with
flowers as pretty as the mail coaches are in Aberdeen
on a Queens birthday. They intended to have a
grand procession but the weather said no, as it rained
heavily the whole day. So I understand they went
through the ceremony in the church.

The principal street of Montreal is Notre dame St
or Rue Notre Dame which is longer than Union St
Aberdeen and goes through the Place de Armes the
same as Silver St does the Golden Square. Then
came Rue St Paul Rue McGill Rue Craig Rue Wellington all long streets. There are some streets have
a tremendious jaw breakers of names such as
Laguchetere the name of the street where Mr Esson
lives.

Among the first places that I called at was the
Bank of British North America where I found Mr
Smith. He came to my lodgings the same evening.
I also called on Mr. Esson who was very kind and
spoke to his baker about me with whom I engaged.
There are two of them in company both Scotsmen.
McDougal and Morrison. The latter is a native of
Huntly. They have both been a good while in this
country. McDougal works in the house and Morrison
goes out with the wagon and bread. They employ
three men. When I came they had two Canadians
and an Irishman. The former speak French and are
poor hands at English. I have got a promise of work

for the winter if I choose to remain. The baking is
harder work here than in Aberdeen but they are
better paid and also better fed.

Sunday July 21st.—Mr Esson preached his second
sermon since the disruption.[1] The first sunday I
was in his church Mr Lewis of Dundee preached.
He is one of the deputation to America from the
Free Church. Mr Esson was at the synod of Canada
about a fortnight where upon the motion of whether
they would remain in connexion with the Established Church of Scotland the synod split and each
party held meetings by itself. Mr Esson is a staunch
Non.[2] At the time I called on him he told me that
he was preparing for the press. That was before the
meeting and he told Morrison the other night that
he must again address the public through the press.
His Church[3] is a neat comfortable one I should
think would hold a thousand hearers. The congregation appear to be highly respectable. He thinks a
few will perhaps leave in consequense of recent
events. There are two or three Moderate ministers
in town. It is expected that as many will leave them
as will form another congregation. There is a large
church here called the American Presbyterians. They
are favourable to the Free Church as are also the
other evangelical christians. The methodists are
very strong here they are at present building a splendid new church. There are several Independent
congregations and a jewish synagogue.

1. The schism in the Presbyterian church.
2. A member of the Non-inclusion party, or Free Church.
3. St. Gabriel Street Church.

July 25. Dear Sister want of time compels me to bring this letter to a close the mail leaves Halifax on the Third of August and the box closes at Montreal a week previous to the time of sailing. Be so good as call on Mr. Shanks[1] and let him Know what kind of a passage I had and where I am. I again thank them all for their kindness. As the baking is different here from what it is at home I was advised to stay some time in this place before going up the country. Mr Shanks will know that we do not go much idle here if you tell him that three of us and one of the masters bake between sixty and seventy barrels of flour a week. Our oven holds three barrels at a batch and we have her filled three and sometimes four times a day. The common wages for journeymen bakers here is from ten or sixteen dollars a month five shillings being a dollar. They are always boarded with their employers same as at home. There are some splendid confectionary stores here but I have seen no gingerbread loaves like what I got from Mr Shanks part of which I still have. The Canadians were surprised that it should be so good after being so long at sea.

When you write to Auchinblae[2] send my compliment to all our kind friends there. . . . Among other friends in Aberdeen be sure to give my best respects and thanks to Mrs Gray. I will never forget her kindness. I had part of her present till we were on the banks of Newfoundland at which place it is usual

1. The baker with whom James Thomson had served his apprenticeship.

2. A market village in south central Kincardine, five and a half miles from Aboyne across the mountains. The Scott relatives there were probably James Thomson's mother's family.

to give the sailors a glass of some thing or other.
When I was at Quebec I had no time to call on James
Begg. I gave the letters to Henderson and wrote
him last week to see if he had found owner. He had
found Mr Chambers house. James Begg is still there
but did not see him. The person that spoke to Henderson
said that but for Mr Chambers James Begg
would not have been well off before this time. Perhaps
that would account for his long silence. Be so
good as let me know the first time you write if his
friends have got any letter from him yet. I will
expect a letter from some of you soon. The mails go
every fortnight so you could be in little mistake
what time you wrote. I do not know when they leave
Liverpool, they leave Halifax on the third and eighteenth
of each month.

I am pretty well supplied with Aberdeen papers as
Mr. Morrison gets the Review regular only if you
had an opportunity you might send me a Banner
once in six months or so as I have very little time
to read them. . . .

I must allow that the heat of a Canadian July sun
is no joke but not worse than I expected. I have got
a broad brimmed straw hat.

I remain dear sister your loving brother

James Thomson

PS. my address is care of Mr. McDougall Baker,
Wellington Street, Montreal, North America. The
address I sent to Father would also find me. Anderson
was the former tennent and his sign is still up
but Mr McDougall is now well known.

55

PS. I will be depending on Hellon for a good deal
of Aboyne news soon. I will expect a letter from
home before I write again, and if any body be asking
about the letters they gave me one answer will do
for all. I put them in the post office.

Montreal August 8 1844

Dear Sister I was too long in going to the post office
with my letter: the Halifax bag was closed before I
went. This will leave Montreal about the tenth or
eleventh inst. Halifax on the eighteenth and reach
Aberdeen I hope if not in this month, at least before
September be many days old, when I hope it will
find you quite well. I have enquired at several persons about David Currie but can get no certain
account of him. Mr McDougall wrought with him
in the same bake house some years ago, and says
he was the most terrible man for drink that he ever
saw. He nearly killed himself with drink when here.
McHardy at whose house I lodged a few days says
that he lay sick in his house three months, went up
the country and he hears is doing pretty well and
keeping steady. Curry was an accquaintence of Mr.
Shanks when they were journey men. You may also
tell Mr. Shanks that I have seen and spoken several
times to Mr. John Scott, Candlemaker. He has given
up his own business and now carries on a brewery
where he makes soda water ginger beer and lemonade. He has a spring cart that he drives his teetotal
drink through the town in.

I am beginning to understand a little French. The
Foreman gives me french for as much english as I

can remember. Last week Mr. Morrison bought several tons of bran that had been damaged by water. On saturday I was sent to sell it at what it would bring. It was mostly French Canadians and Irish who came to buy for their horses and pigs. They generally had a little english, and with my few words of french we mostly got on pretty well. Only once I had to ask a passerby to act as interpreter. The english here call a half penny, a copper, the french call it an sou. A shilling sterling is here fifteen pence or tran sou. Five shillings currency or four shillings sterling is a dollar or un paistre.

I have seen the way that Mr Morrisons newspapers are addressed. You might address my letters Care of Messrs McDougall & Morrison, Wellington Street, Griffinton, Montreal. Griffinton[1] is the name of a district of the city same as Footdee is in Aberdeen.

No more time at present your loving brother

James Thomson

1. Griffintown, named after a merchant Robert Griffin, was a low-lying riverside district which, until 1888, was subject to annual spring floods.

To Alexander Thomson 6 October 1844

Montreal October 6 1844

Dear Father

September fifth put me in possession of your kind
letter of eight of August. I was beggining to weary
before its arrival although I did not expect it much
sooner as I knew from the sailing of the mails that
you could not have my address before the middle of
July and then I did not know exactly when the mail
left England. However the welcome intelegence
that the letter contains of your welfare made up for
the delay.

I am glad also to see that you had a hopeful communion Sabbath and so good a minister. We have
had no communion in St. Gabriel Street church
since my arrival. Mr. Essen explained the reason a
few sundays ago. He said he had thought proper to
put back the celebration of the Lords supper for
some time as owing to the disruption there was a
great deal of excitement among the people and as
there were several eminent ministers on their way
from Scotland he thought it would be better to wait
till they should arrive and till some settlement was
made when they could sit down to the holy ordi-
nance with calm and untroubled minds. I may here
mention that the moderates[1] here were quite as
furious as they were at home. Mr. Essens congregation were almost unanimous in their aproval of his
conduct yet the few who left tried to get him put
out of the church. There are forty managers to whom

1. The established Presbyterian Church of Scotland.

the church belongs. A meeting of them was held
when only four were in favour of remaining in connexion with the Established church of Scotland and
these four are to carry the case before the civil courts.
Some of them were so wild as to lock up the door
of their pew when they left the church but those
who remained served the locks much the same way
as the Nons at home used to do the interdicts. Ever
since the meeting of synod the church has been quite
crowded. We have had some fine ministers from
Scotland the last few sundays. Mr. Burns[1] has been
preaching every evening since he came in the Place
de Armes a large square in front of the French
Church but the Roman Catholics would not hear
him. Great crowds collected and were like to illuse
him but he still persevered with wonderful patience
untill he was stopped by order of the magistrates.
This week he is to preach every evening in Mr.
Essons church. The new synod meets at Toronto on
wednesday.

You mention that several of my acquaintances
have read the journal that I kept at sea. I am sorry it
was not better worth their perusal but whether to
blame the cold weather the rough sea or my own
carelesness most, I shall not take upon me to say.
Perhaps all were art and part.

Although the weather was very cold all the voyage
I believe that to that under the blessing of God may
in a great measure be ascribed the general good
health that we enjoyed. I know the only inconven-

1. William C. Burns, a Free Church minister from Scotland, who
preached in the streets in French (Campbell, *St. Gabriel Street*,
pp. 516-17).

ience that I felt was cold feet. They were seldom
warm but when in bed as I had plenty of blankets
and bed fellows we held the cold at defiance pretty
well. Perhaps we have the same cause to thank for
our freedom from vermins. We were as clean in that
respect when we left as when we entered the St.
Lawrence. I believe there were a few families on
board who by the end of the voyage could have
supplied the Scots Grays with a few recruits but I
can't say that I ever saw them parading the decks as
a neighbour of yours did. Only I saw as much as
to make me believe his statement to be perfectly
correct.

On our arrival at Montreal I saw none of those
daring characters which some have met with. The
only persons who minded us were a few poor Irish
who asked if we had any paraties[1] for sale or any
old chests. The different steam boat companies on
the canal have agents who wait the arrival of the
Quebec steamers and try to get the passengers to
come to their respective boats the one telling we
have a boat ready to sail, the other that we will take
you cheapest and so on. Besides these no one minded
us and all went on as well as it would have done at
any British port.

The baking here is very different from what it was
at home and one newly arrived does not get so much
pay as one that has been awhile in the country. As
it is I have got ten shillings a week with bed board
and washing in the house. They count a good deal
on washing here. We are well wrought and well fed.

1. Potatoes.

The baking is not a desirable job it being all night
work commencing about ten pm.

My employers are both very steady quiet men and
kind to me. McDougalls mother is our house keeper.
She has three other sons one a school master one a
confectioner and one who is boarding with us is
learning to be a moulder. They are Baptists and
Morrison and I are Essonists as some of the Moderates call us. We have had several changes among
our workmen they being mostly Canadiens. All
those who are descended from french parents and
who speak that language are called Canadiens. They
are all Roman Catholics. Joe our foreman will eat
no meat on fridays goes to Church at five oclock on
sunday morning and to the bush with his gun same
afternoon.

When I wrote my last letter I dont think that I gave
you any account of Montreal. I have some times
thought of describing it by comparing it with Aberdeen but I am afraid I have not head for that only
I may mention a few points in which the two resemble
each other and also some in which they differ. Montreal then lies in nearly the position to the St. Lawrence as Aberdeen to the Dee only the river the
harbour and the wharf here lie nearly south and
north as do also some of the principal streets including the one I live in. The other street runs in
the opposite direction they being nearly all straight.
The harbour here is quite as good and large as at
Aberdeen and there is a great deal of more shipping
in summer and mostly large ships from Liverpool
London and Glasgow. If the Aberdonians had a wing
of the St Lawrence as we have it would save them

the trouble of making wet docks. There is also a
great deal of traffic on the canal mostly with steam
boats. They go up the canal and come down the
river on their way to and from Canada West. It is
called the Lachine (pronounced Lasheen) canal and
runs in a south westerly course and joins the river
nine miles up. It is to enable them to pass the rapids
of Lachine which they cannot go up although they
venture down. By these steamers the emigrants go
to the upper province. They go to Kingston in about
three days. There is a quicker mode of conveyance
for those who have heavy purses and light luggage
by steamers who keep the river all the way the passengers going past the rapids from one boat to
another by stage coaches. By this conveyance the
trip to Kingston is made in twenty six hours. What
is called Durham boats are large open boats towed
by horses and only used for fire wood or other bulky
goods that will not afford them steam boat fare.

There is a large steamer goes three times a day to
Lapprairie a town nine miles off on the opposite side
of the river and on the line of road from this to New
York. By the aid of steam and current the Prince
Albert as she is called comes down from Lapprairie
in forty five minutes bringing at each time a great
many country people with their farm produce.
Another small steam ferry boat crosses the river
opposite the town. Fare twopence. The river here
runs as fast as Dee does where the burn of craigen-
dommie comes into her, so you must not grudge
Prince Albert two hours to go up what he came down
in three quarters.

One thing that a stranger notices especially one

just came from a large manufacturing town is the
want of tall chimneys there being no factories here.
Instead of manufacturers we have importers. I do
not know whether there be any cloth at all made in
Montreal but in all my drives about town I never
heard a single shuttle going and I have not seen
weavers going about with thrums[1] or tows[2] upon
their bonnets as one would soon do about the
Minenilchbrae or the Gallowgate.[3] If we be behind
Aberdeen at manufacturing wool and cotton we
would tip them at the wood. We have wooden
wharfs, streets, houses, churches, and steeples all of
which answer their purposes admirably. Perhaps
you granate church backers would laugh at reading
in the newspapers of a church steeple being blown
into the river during a hurricane and taken out little
damaged twenty or thirty miles below the place
where it formerly settled.

There are three or four machines here moved by
steam for plaining wood. The deal is fixed on a
frame the same way as in a circular drilling mill and
pushed forward in the same way and what was a
rough deal at one end is at the other well plained on
both sides and ploughed on one edge and (I dont
know what you call it)[4] on the other ready for being
joined together. Wood is the only fuel used in
private houses. The principal supply comes up the
river. It varies in price according to the quality and

1. Threads needed for the yarn when commencing weaving.
2. Flax or hemp in a prepared state for use in weaving.
3. Gallowgate, a street in Aberdeen. Minenilchbrae has not been
identified.
4. Tongue and groove.

kind of wood from nine to eighteen shillings a cord.
It is cut in lengths of three and a half or four feet and
a pile of these eight feet long and four high makes a
cord.

I was a good deal bothered at first with so many
different kinds of money. Our copper money is the
same as at home only there is a great many bad half
pennies. Silver money we have a States piece worth
sixpence. We have the English sixpence worth seven
pence half penny, a broad thin ugly tenpence piece
when or where made they have lost the power of
telling, the shilling sterling or quarter dollar worth
one and three pence, and a Spanish piece same value
the English half crown worth three shilling and a
halfpenny, a bank token three shilling and a American dollar value five shillings and a penny, the half-
sovereign twelve and threepence, sovereigns etc.
Then we have dollar bills one two five ten and so
on.
I am near the end of my paper and must conclude
for the present. I am sorry I have so little time to
write. . . .

James Thomson

To Helen Thomson 3 November 1844

Montreal November 3rd 1844

Dear Sister Helen

On the eight of October I received a letter twenty
five days old from Mary Ann[1] containing the pleasing inteligence that you were all well. I see by the
letter too that there had been unfavourable reports
circulated about the St. Lawrence which by the
blessing of God were not correct. We are still the
spared monuments of his long suffering mercy and
as the God of Providence have still to thank the
Almighty for bringing us in safety accross a stormy
ocean. . . .

Today I heard sermon by Mr McNaughton of
Paisly. He preached to us about a month ago. Since
that time he has been at the upper province with
Mr. Esson. There was a meeting of synod. Mr Burn
officiated for Mr Esson and for a fortnight had public worship every evening and prayer meetings in
the mornings two or three times a week. The Roman
Catholics are too bigoted to give him a fair hearing.
They are by far the majority in this city there being
so many French and Irish. The French or as they are
called Canadiens are generally quiet decent citizens.
They are clean and neat in their houses and clothes.
As servants they are not much trusted by old country
people. The Irish are just Irish, what would improve
them I cannot say but certainly transplanting does
not. . . .

1. Mary Ann Smith, née Thomson, an elder sister who had raised
James after his mother died. She had married and now lived in
Aberdeen.

I had a letter from Henderson last week. In it he says 'there is a great fuss here that the end of the world is to take place next week. I do not exactly believe it but let us be preparing for it and live every day as if it were our last and then we need not fear the day of judgement but rather wish for it'. . . .

There are still numbers going to the west. It will be a cold America to them the first six months they are in it. I have good opportunities of seeing the emigrants as I am aboard some of the steam boats almost every day. . . .

On the twenty eighth of october snow began to fall and next day there was about a foot of snow on the ground. The last two days have been soft and the storm is nearly gone. I have ordered a great coat of thick canadian gray, and a pair of long boots to go above my trousers. With these and plenty of underclothes I think I will hold out pretty well if it is not all the more severe.

As I had such a long trip this spring you could not expect that I would travel much after my arrival here. My farthest travel has been once across the river in a steam boat to a place called Longueville[1] and once to a place called Cote des Neiges two miles off at the back of the mountain where there is a baker that wrought in Aberdeen.

Speaking about the mountain you must not imagine that it is a great hill towering to the clouds with its head covered with eternal snow like the Andies or the Alps. It will not stand comparison even with your Scottish mountains Ben Macdhui or Lochnagar nor Morven or Mortlack but the nearest resemblence

1. Longueuil.

that I remember to it is the Knockie.[1] Only the
mountain as it is always called is rather steepe on
one side and in summer it is so closely covered with
trees of different kinds that no one can see from a
distance what like its surface is. Autum however
has striped it of its green mantle and exposing its
rocky head to all the rigour of winter. At its foot on
the side next the town stands the English or as it is
generally called the McGill College in honour of its
founder. I go to it three times a week with bread. It
was a nice pleasant drive when summer days were
fine. The road to it is as thick with apple trees as
firs are at home which but a short time ago were
bending and groaning under their well stocked
branches.

I have as many customers as takes me about three
hours every day to go through them with a horse and
spring cart. It is a great improvement upon carrying
the baskets. The customers that I go to Mr. McDougall used to serve himself. Since I came he does not
go out. Morrison is not a baker to trade. He drives
bread the whole day. Mrs McDougall keeps the
shop and we have a servant girl from Glasgow.
Servants here are all engaged by the month, wages
about four dollars. The girls dress almost as fine as
their mistresses. In summer white dresses black
veils and silk parasols are quite common among
them. In that respect they are only like other people
here as all classes are better dressed than at home at

1. Knock is the name of numerous hills in Scotland, either alone
or in combination with a particular name. This 'Knockie' is probably
Knock Hill, 717 feet, near Auchinblae, where Thomson's relatives
lived.

least if not better they are more fopishly attired and I have seen fewer ragged people than in Aberdeen. The country people are all clad in stout gray home-made like clothes. They are all most as uniform in their dress as a regiment of soldiers. In that respect when you see one you see them all. There are a few indians about town. The squaws (women) go about selling ladies bags and slippers finely sewed and ornamented with beads. The men like very well to go idle. They have a wigwam or village a little bit up the river side.

November 10. As to morrow or next day is mail time I must finish my letter tonight. I have little time to write but in other respects I like the place well. I intend to remain all winter and go up the country early in spring. Until that time I would not take upon me to give anyone advice about comming to America although what I have seen confirms me in the opinion that any steady person who is willing to work would do better than at home. My complements to all kind enquiring friends. . . .

Mary asks about paying postage. I believe either way would do but I think it is time enough to pay when we receive then if any be lost the loss will be the less. . . .

Your loving brother

James Thomson

To Alexander Thomson 22 December 1844

Montreal December 22, 1844

Dear Father
I am now experiencing the severity of a Canadian
winter. The frost has been very hard for some weeks
but little snow has fallen. The river is not yet closed
but does not want much. It takes very severe frost
to close her unless snow falls. As far as I have seen
of the winter I think I will stand it out pretty well.
The air to be sure is very cold but it is clear and
healthy and seldom any wind. People say it will be
colder after the new year. It was after new years day
before the river closed last winter and it is generally
thought will be so this. All the ice that is now at
each side will shoot, as they call it and a new ice
close the river. The shooting of the ice is sometimes
dangerous, such large pieces are turned up one year
it knocked down a house on the wharf and damaged
others. From being blocked up with the ice the
water rises six or eight feet some times. The cellars
in Griffintown are yearly filled with water and sometimes as much in the streets as float a canoe. These
things last only a few days and we are daily expecting a visit of the water and many people are wishing
the river would close, as that event is the signal for
lowering the markets as there is then an abundant
supply of everything from the States and from the
inland townships where there is no water carriage
and roads not the best untill frost and snow make
them all good enough for sleighing. At present the
farmers of our tight little island are making a fine

69

job. They find that the half frosen state of the river
is a better protection for agriculture than Sir Charles
Metcalfs[1] or Sir Robert Peels corn laws. There is no
coast guard required to prevent smuggling.

The farmers around Montreal depend greatly on
their potato crop which has this year proved a failure.
Potatoes sell at one and ninepence a bushel. The
oats that they bring to market are very bad. They
would not turn out much meal. They are used only
for horses. There is only one mill in Montreal where
oat meal is made. The Scotch people all seem to
turn English when they come here and to live on
roast beef and white bread.

Since I last wrote you Mr Esson Has left Montreal.
You have likely seen some account of his departure
in the news papers. He preached his farewell sermon
on the seventeenth November. He has been nearly
thirty years minister of that church so it need not be
wondered that his parting with his flock was an
affecting scene, rendered more so perhaps from the
new position in which they have been so lately
placed. They are the only congregation and he the
only minister in this city who have maintained in all
their purity the great principles of Presbyterianism.
Mr Esson in praying for all his flock did not forget
those, few though they be, who have opposed him
and the great majority of the congregation. He said
of them, what I believe might be said with equal
truth of many at home, that he was sure they could
not pray to God for success on their opposition and
he prayed earnestly that they might not go to a death-
bed with such conduct unrepented of.

1. Governor General of British North America, 1843–45.

On the nineteenth ultimo Mr Esson was invited to
a farewell soiree. It was attended by several hundreds of the respectable inhabitants of Montreal.
There were six or seven ministers of different denominations. All of whom who spoke did so in very
high terms of Mr Essons character as a scholar a
minister and a christian friend. In particular they
honoured him for the noble testimony he had been
enabled to make in support of a doctrine of our holy
religen and that too after being deserted by the other
two ministers of the same church Dr's Mathieson
and Black. Mr Esson is to be succeeded by a Mr
Miller not your kind neighbour but one from Dundee who has been labouring sometime in Nova
Scotia. He was expected here before this time. At
present Mr. Burns occupies the pulpit. I sent a newspaper to Mr Esson Balnacraig[1] with a short account
of the soiree in it. If he has got it he has had better
luck than me. I have got no papers yet. Mr Morrison
told me today that there was a letter from Mr Esson.
He has got seventeen students already.[2] If he stays
in Toronto I may see him again as I intend to see
the capital of Canada West before six months.

There is a small monthly paper the Ecclesiastical
and Missionary Record of the Presbyterian Church
in Canada printed in Hamilton to which I am a sub-
scriber. I am told it will go with the post as any other
newspaper. You may expect a copy soon.

This I believe is the shortest day. We certainly have
the advantage of you Britainers in that respect if day

1. Mr. Essen of Balnacraig, Argyll, probably a relative of the
Reverend Henry Essen.
2. At Knox College, Toronto.

light be an advantage. It is pretty light here at half
past seven am and the sun does not go down behind
the mountain till four pm. This circumstance and
the greater severity of the winter look rather strange.
The one says as plainly as can be that we are nearer
the equator than you, while ones nose in a cold day
almost says alone we are in the artic circle. Those
who have long head and pretend to know about these
things say that it is owing to our distance from the
sea and the great frozen continent to the north of us.
If so be thankful of having John O'Groats for your
northern boundary, you must not think that we
Canadians are a poor shivering blue nosed race
without any comfort during winter. The buffaloes
and beavers of the west and the finely fured animals
of the cold north have supplied us with means of
warmth when out of doors and a good stove with
plenty of meanee[1] and pine keeps the houses very
comfortable.

There are various shapes of stoves. Some are about
the size and shape of a chest of Drawers and have
generally an oven in them. Others where there is
much cooking are lower and have places in them
where five or six pots and pans may be boiled and
places below for keeping dishes warm holding the
tea pot etc. etc. Where there is plenty of room they
are placed in the middle of the floor. The smoke and
heat is carried to the vent by sheet iron pipes about
six inches diameter. There is no heat lost and the
same quality of fuel will keep the house much
warmer than an open fire place would.

1. He may mean spruce.

We will soon have Christmas. It will be a great day here among the Roman Catholics. I do not expect to get any sowens this year but I have a piece of Mr Shanks gingerbread loaf and I guess as a yankee would say I'll finish it on tuesday night. It is as good yet as it was in April. I dont think I'll get any whiskey either as this is a temperate house. I have been almost a practical teetotlar since I came to America, there has not been a drop of beer in the house since I came but after dinner we get a cup of coffee which I like quite as well. The mails now only go monthly. . . .

To Helen and Alexander Thomson
14 February 1845

Montreal February 14, 1845

Dear Hellen

I received your letter of twentysixth December on
third of February, . . . and Mary Anns letter on the
26. That will give you some idea of posting in Canada
at this season. I see by the papers that a better plan
is now to take place. The British government have
made arrangements with the States government to
have the Canadian mails carried through that part
of their teritory which lies between Boston and this
province so the Mail Steamer will not touch at Halifax but go to Boston from which place we will send
or get letters in $2\frac{1}{2}$ days instead of two or three weeks
as was sometimes the case in winter between this
and Halifax.

You mention that Mrs. Reid is intending to come to
Canada this spring and you were going to send a
parcel with her. If she is coming and not away when
this reaches you, if she is coming no farther than
Montreal, I will be away before her arrival so that
she would have to give the parcel to some of the
forwarding companies who have steam boats going
to the upper province. They only go to Kingston so
it would have to change hands there again, as it is
rare to find a steamer from Montreal to Toronto
direct. If you do try the experiment let it be with
some thing of little value, till we see whether it
arrive or not. I do not know where I may be by that
time but I believe I might take the liberty of adopt-

ing the following address, that of Henderson's friend,
as I think from his being in the town he would have
a better chance of receiving any thing than William
Scott[1] would have and whether I stop in Toronto or
not I hope Henderson and I will still correspond. I
believe I stated in some former letter that I would
leave Montreal early in spring, from that you will
perhaps be thinking that I am already off to the west.
But no, you must remember that early spring in
Scotland and early spring in Canada are two very
different things. In the one case I suppose you understand about the beginning of March but in the other
case for March you must read May. It is generally
the latter end of April before the river breaks and
commerce is stopped a few days longer by the floating ice, so I am fixed until the first of may. You ask
me some questions about my washing and my bed.
To those questions I can scarcely answer, yes. I do
not pretend to be a judge of fine washing but I know
what pleases my self and I shall only say that if this
washing be worth a dollar a month I would give
you seven and sixpence. As to our bedroom I think
it would do first rate with the Duke of Beccleugh.[2]
I see by the newspapers you sent me that his grace
is a great advocate for ventalation to the dwellings
of the working classes. It we had him in our garrat
we would give him as much pure air as he gives his
Free Church tennantry on the braes of Yarrow on a
sunday. Although it is not quite so comfortable as

1. A cousin on his mother's side, from Auchinblae.
2. William Francis Scott, 5th Duke of Buccleuch and 7th Duke of
Queensbury (1806–84). At this time he was Lord Privy Seal. He was
also President of the Highland Agricultural Society.

75

could be wished I have felt no bad effects from it. I
have not had a cold this whole winter. . . . Yesterday
March 5 it snowed all day about three inches deep.
We were just in want as the streets were getting bare
and sleighing bad. I was afraid I would have to
mount the old cart again. . . .

We have got another minister to our church
Mr Bonar of Lar Beert.[1] He is to stop some time.
Mr Burns is away on a missionary tour among the
Canadiens. . . .

I remain your loving and affectionate brother

James Thomson

Montreal February 14, 184

Dear Father
. . . I mentioned before we had a snow storm in the
end of October which went all away in a few days.
From that up to the middle of January I may almost
say we had open weather, as up to that time we had
not more than three inches snow which fell at different times. About the middle of January we had a
stormy day which added about four or five inches to
our stock of snow and the fourth and fifth of this
month were very stormy. A good deal of snow fell
and drifted into wreaths which blocked up some of
the roads a day or two. If there is no more stormy
days ahead we have seen nothing here yet so bad as
the twenty fourth of February last year in Scotland.
Your opinion of the snow has been rather too extragavant but the frost is so severe that you can

1. Larbert, Stirlingshire.

hardly think too severely of it. Nothing like it at home.

The river closed about the beginning of the year. We have now a splendid bridge some three miles across and as far up and down as the eye can reach. The ice is not smooth as on still water. It is the snow and loose ice floating down that gets jamed together. This raises the water untill the ice that was about the sides is shoved away and then so much of it floating down soon closes and forms a bridge. The different roads are all marked by small trees or poles, as people might lose their way in snow storms and in some places there are air holes in the ice. The river before she closed rose to about ten feet above her summer level. We had two feet water in our cellar. You would wonder to see the blocks of ice that are cast on our wharf, which has now a very desolate appearance. No more sign of navigation than on the top of Morven.

Not a ship or steam boat to be seen but we are not without visitors. At this cold season hundreds of sleighs come to town every day loaded with wood, hay, oats, flour, fowls, mutton, beef, pork, and many other things. Beef and mutton are very cheap. Two pence a lb is quite common or if you buy a leg or a side from a country fellow you may have it for three coppers. The Canadians and Irish are great admirers of Sandy Campbells flesh so that pork always keeps the top of the market. Very little fish is used unless cod fish and herrings and some Lake Huron white fish. I have never seen a yellow haddock. If some Findon Nannie would come here with her creel, I guess she would soon get it empty.

77

I see by your last letter that you do not think very
highly of our Republican neighbours, and I must
allow that my opinion of them is not much better.
We may perhaps be mistaken, as those who take upon
them to enlighten the British public on that subject
are generally no friends to the Republican form of
government. If I do pay Brother Jonathan a visit I
shall try to keep my eyes about me, and, send you
so far as my humble abilities will allow, an account
of things as they appear to me whether it be to con-
firm you in your present opinion or to make you
think a little more favourably of the yankee character.

In the meantime however I intend to keep the
Canadian side of the line at least till I have seen the
capital of C.W. This is perhaps the last time that I
will adress you from Montreal.

I can give you little information about the political
affairs of the place. If you have got all the newspapers that I have sent you will know as much about
it as I do. During summer I seldom read a paper and
my shopmates are very ignorant. The Parliament
house is not a new building. It was used some years
as a market and altered last summer to answer its
present purpose. I see party spirit runs very high in
the house, sometimes even to a disgraceful height.
At the late elections there was great rioting. But for
the strong military force, the loyal party could not
live here, the Irish are such a blackguard set. The
Canadians although equally displeased with the
government do not resort to physical force. On the
day of election there were soldiers at every polling
place infantry with their muskets and cavalry with
drawn swords, and in some streets a party of artilery

with a great Mons Meg looking gun which would
have sent the canadiens to their long homes by the
dozen. Notwithstanding all that there were several
persons assalted and church windows broken.

Newspapers are very cheap. The Transcript costs
a penny and the Gazette three coppers. In summer
there are three or four daily papers and others tri
and semi weekly.

Montreal contains a population of forty four thous-
and. Of these 30,000 belong to the Church of Rome
6700 to Church of England the rest are composed of
5000 Presbyterians, and other denominations number nearly 3000. There are 19 Protestant Churches
and Chapels, there are colleges academies and con-
vents 23, Elementary Schools 68, Scholars 3700.
There are 3000 Scotch and 10,000 Irish.

We have got no steady minister in our church yet.
Mr Burns generally officiates. . . .

I remain Dear Father your affectionate son

James Thomson

BAKING FOR
THE IRISH CANALLERS

To Helen Thomson and Mary Ann Smith
25 June 1845

Edwardsburgh June 25 1845

Dear Sister

I am only here yet. By the last letter that I sent to
Scotland you will be thinking that I am at least two
hundred miles farther from home than I really am.
When I wrote Aunts letter it was my full intention to
have left Montreal for Toronto at the first of May.
When that day arrived I actually left my place. My
employers were unwilling to let me go away and by
fair words and good promises, they got me advised
to stay a few days longer till they could get one in
my place to suit them. Time went on. Days became
weeks and the end of May found me still toiling
away in Griffintown. But the warm weather made
the long fatiguing hours so very disagreeable that I
was determined to put up with it no longer, although
I was getting good wages. I had 17/6 currency a week
and board. I gave due notice that with the end of
May my engagement would expire. I stayed with
them till monday the 2nd of June. On that morning
when settling with my masters, a gentleman came
into the shop wanting a baker to go up the country
to a village near Prescott on the river. He wanted
one to start immediately and being all ready I suited
him in that respect and it being so far on my way to

the west I engaged to make a trial of it for a month.

By the time I got directions and a letter of introduction it was getting late for the stage coaches. I got a caleche (a sort of gig with a seat for the driver on the front) and with my small chest alongside of me, by half past ten I was driving through the beautiful island of Montreal. I left my other chest. The gentleman with whom I engaged was to forward it with some goods that he was purchasing.

An hours drive brought me to Lachine nine miles from Montreal. I got aboard the mail steamer Cheftain and at noon we started. The sun in her meredian strength made us feel rather too comfortable. Opposite Lachine there is a large village called by the indians Cockneywaggon.[1] A little below is the rapids of Lachine on account of which the canal from Montreal is necessary. From this place the river gradually widens. One would think they were going out to sea, only when I came up there was no waves. The paddles of the Cheftain alone riffled the mirror like surface of the water. Soon after we started we passed the mouth of the Ottawa on the north side and the Chateaugay on the opposite bank. The latter is a large rapid stream not navigable. It belongs to Canada fifty or sixty miles up. It then belongs to the States. The scenery on either side was delightful and the many islands in the river covered with bush to the waters edge makes the trip a very pleasant one. We met several rafts barges and steamboats downward bound.

At four oclock we arrived at Cascades, where we left the boat and got into stage coaches. They are

1. Caughnawaga.

82

very large and easy to ride in. Hold nine passengers
and a immense quantity of luggage on the top. We
had a fine drive on a plank road sixteen miles long.
This took us past three rapids of the St Lawrence
namely Cascades, Cedars, and Coteau du Lac. We
saw them all. Some of my fellow passengers were
raftsmen, who knew what it was to go down the
rapids. Two of them were very chatty and told us
the names of places as we went along frequently
remarking to each other when we were opposite the
worst places 'rough weather there I guess.' Rafts are
many times wrecked going down these places and
some of the men sometimes get drowned.

A little above the latter rapid there is a village of the
same name, where another boat the Canada waited
our arrival and as soon as all were aboard she started.
The boats here are not so large as the Montreal and
Quebec ones but I think rather larger than the Aberdeen and Leith steamers. It was 6 oclock when we
left La Coteau as it is generally called. We had a fine
cool breeze ahead and a rapid current in some places.
About seven I went below and had supper. The
steward in the steerage was a smart little highland
man. None of the crew of the boat were french canadians and only two or three on the Cheftain were
French. About sunset the boat called at Lancaster.
After dark we got into the long Sault canal and called
at Cornwall. About four am the sun rose in the
eastern sky large and red. We were then steering
right away from him. Soon after we stopped Williamsburgh or Mariastown as the village is called and at
7 am June 3 I was landed at Matilda fifteen miles
below Prescott.

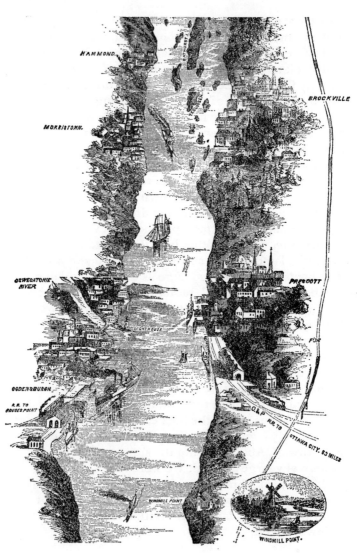

HAMMOND.

MORRISTOWN.

OSWEGATCHIE RIVER

OGDENSBURGH.

R.R. TO ROUSES POINT

LIGHTHOUSE

BROCKVILLE

PRESCOTT

FOR

O&P R.R. TO

OTTAWA CITY. 53 MILES

WINDMILL POINT

WINDMILL POINT.

Panorama of the

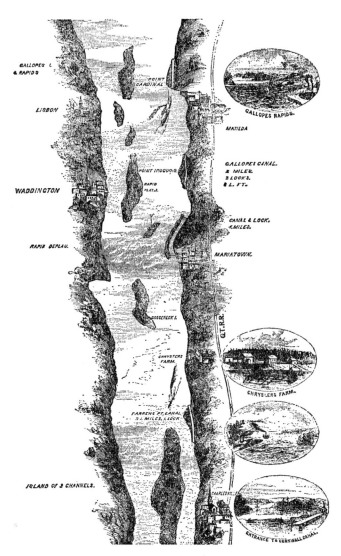

St. Lawrence Settlements

From this place I had to walk six miles to Edwardsburgh. I met with an Irishman at the wharf
who gave me directions how I would know Edwardsburgh when I should reach it. I put my trunk into
a store and with a small bundle under my arm set
out to tramp the wilds of Canada. Matilda is a poor
looking place scarcely anything to be seen but shanties or log houses in which the canalers live. This
was a poor beginning, but I went on.

The country which had looked so well from the
river looked no worse from the road. All the way
was well settled and cleared. Some good farm houses
that would do credit to any road side in Scotland
and every one with a large orchard. The road side
all along was full of apple and cherry trees as well
loaded with blossom and young fruit as if they had
been in Carse o' Gowrie.[1] The weather was delightfully fine, and in due time I came to the big house
past the two taverns, as the old Greek (as they call
the Irish in Montreal) told me. I had then to go a
little farther to the store to the keeper of which (Mr.
McPherson) my letter was addressed. He came and
showed me the bakehouse and I began to prepare
to give them bread the following day.

My employer Mr Elliott[2] is an extensive contractor on the canal now forming along the banks of the
St Lawrence. He has three sections one down at
Beauharnois on the south side of the river, below
Cascades, one at Williamsburgh, and here he has a
section of the canal, a farm, a store, a bake house,
a wife and three children. He is seldom at home

1. A fertile valley south of Aboyne.
2. Andrew Elliott, Mayor of Cornwall, 1852–54.

being generally at some of the other jobs.

There are about a hundred men at this job. There is a master or as they call them in Canada a Boss to every twenty or thirty men. There is a head Boss over them, and a government Boss who sometimes comes round and looks over them all.

I board in Mr Elliots house, and I would not wish a better. One of the masters on the canal, Mr. McPherson, and two of the teamsters (farm servants) also board in the house. I have not quite so good wages as when I left Montreal but in all other respects decidedly better.

No night work here. I can do all my work any day in eight or nine hours. Our principal customers are the canalers, who are nearly all Irish with of course plenty of young Greeks. A waggon is brought to the bakehouse door every day and takes the bread away to the store, and brings me flour when I want it. There is generally one day in the week that I do not work.

I have been at Matilda since I came and at Prescott. One of the teamsters are at some of these places every week. Their waggons have no springs but they put two long sticks from end to end with the seat in the middle which gives enough of spring. That and a buffalo hide two or three times doubled makes a very good seat. A pair of splendid horses goes a long the road eight or nine miles an hour. The road to Prescott is along the river side. There is plenty of good farm houses with well cleared farms and large orchards along the wayside. When near Prescott the road goes past the remains of an old wind mill and a number of roofless stone houses, the

monuments of war. At this place, what is known as
the windmill fight took place in 1837 or 38, between
the rebels and royalists. The village was burnt by
some of them. A little farther on just at the entrance
to the town there is a barracks surounded by a forti-
fication[1] and battery the big guns of which looks
anything but smiles to the yankees over the water.
The town of Prescott is a stirring little place. I think
about as large as Stonehaven.[2] About the same size
and directly opposite is the town of Ogdensburgh,
State of New York.

As my driver had some business to do on the other
side I went over with him to see the yankee city and
when landed I was for the first time in my life out of
Victoria's dominions, but I did not stay long under
President Polk. I saw nothing very remarkable in
the town. The streets are not so well paved as Union
Place.[3] If a person did not look to his feet he would
run a fair chance of getting his ankles knocked out of
joint and where the pavement is wood he would be
all the better that his legs did not possess the faculty
of breaking. A steam ferry boat crosses the river, fare
for each passenger a york shilling, seven pence halfpenny canadian currency, sixpence Aberdeen currency.[4] It was from a company in Ogdensburgh that
we got our superfine flour in Montreal. I get some of
it here too. It is equal to the finest town made Lon-

1. Fort Wellington.

2. Stonehaven, Kincardineshire, had a population of 3,240 in 1851.
Prescott's population in the same year was 2,156.

3. Union Street is the main street of Aberdeen.

4. A York shilling was Upper Canadian currency; seven pence
halfpenny. 'Canadian' probably means Lower Canadian currency;
and Aberdeen currency means British sterling.

don flour. It allways brings half a dollar a barrell more than the best Canada flour.

The village of Edwardsburg consists of a few good large houses two taverns, several grocery and dry-goods stores and a presbyterian church. The canalers live in shanties generally their own property, value nine or ten dollars. They are in no regular order but scattered about every where, you might as well look for a street in Drumleithie as among them. A good many of them speak the Irish language. I am as bad at it as I was at French last year.

The only French that I hear now is a few indians who sometimes come round selling fish. They have a little English but they are better at French.

The river here is narrow and rapid. The other side belongs to the State of N Y. We are about two hundred yards back from the river on rising ground. From my bakehouse window I can see all the steamboats barges and rafts that pass on the river and a mile or two of the yankee side. The place opposite to us they call New Lisbon.[1] There are three mail steamers on the line between Kingston and Coteau du Lac. One goes up every morning and one down every afternoon. All the steamers between Montreal and Kingston who go up the grand river and Rideau canal, go down the St. Lawrence. They will come this way next summer when the canals past the rapids are finished. The steamers have enough to do geting past this place. A person might walk along side as fast. Once they are a mile above this they have no more rapids. They go sweeping down here

1. There is no New Lisbon on the map. Lisbon is a short distance away from the river.

at the rate of twenty miles an hour.

Father will see by his map where about this place is. The names of several places near this are on the american side but he will see that the places are on the Canada side. Edwardsburgh should have been marked near the red strip a little above Matilda. The road which goes back into and divides the concessions passes between our house and store. Twenty three miles back is the Rideau canal and river.

There are few new settlers in this district. Several that I have spoken to have been from ten to nearly thirty years.

I have met with only one Aberdeenshire man. His name is Charles Hunter. He was nine years a game keeper to Lumsden of Clover. Came here nine years ago. Is a day labourer a fiddler and precentor in the village church. When I asked him if he had a farm he said I have no land, no wife, no nothing but myself. He says there is a Tarland tailor a few miles back who came out about the same time as him. He has been often at Aboyne but did not know that his Lordship[1] was a Marquis and a Bankrupt.

Mr Elliott is from the Scottish borders, Mrs Elliot from the English borders. Mr McPherson is from the north of Scotland. Mr MacDougald the gentlemen who engaged me in Montreal to come here is a partner in some of the sections of the canal and has a store at Cornwall. . . .

My fellow passengers who came with the St Lawrence who stopped in Montreal were all well when I left. . . .

Board in Montreal is two dollars a week, with

1. George Gordon, 9th Marquis of Huntly.

washing eleven shillings. House rent and firewood
is high. Everything else is cheaper than at home.
Clothes are not much dearer when the difference
between currency and sterling are deducted. Shoes
are cheaper.

A few weeks before I left we were turned out of
St Gabriel Street Church (Mr Essen's). A temporary
wooden Church was erected and opened on sunday
May 18th by the Rev Mr Bonar. Four deacons were
previously chosen and four additional elders. One
of the new elders was to give a thousand pounds to
the erection of a new church. Others of the congregation came forward with hundreds. They were to
commence right off. They have also given handsome
sums for the minister stipend.

The Church here is at present vacant. The Presbytery of (I think) Kingston are about to place a minister. At present there is only a missionary who does
not come every sunday. There is an Episcopal
Church about a mile below, public worship every
second sunday. And two miles farther there is a
Methodist Church with a minister regular. He sometimes comes up this way on sunday evenings. The
canalers have a temporary Chapel and a priest near
Matilda.

I wrote to William Scott since I came here. I could
not tell him when I would be up the country. I may
take a summer in this place. For anything I know it
is expected that this part of the canal will be finished
about the end of this year. . . .

This is a very healthy place and I believe it might
be called a beautiful place too. The farmers seem to
be thriving. They have one advantage over the many

places. They can always get ready money for their
productions. We met with a farmer the other day
when we were going to Prescott. He had traveled
eight hundred miles in the western states within the
last two weeks to see if he thought he would be
better there than here. He met with some people
with which he was acquainted before and they told
him that they could get plenty to eat and drink but
very little money. He saw that want of good money
was the prevailing evil of these places. He guesses
he will stop in Canada. I should like very well to go
to the west a little bit, but I think it is better to hold
by a good place when I have it.

You have heard about Quebec.[1] The dreadful
news was comming day after day to Montreal.

I remain Dear Sister your loving and affectionate
brother

James Thomson

June 26

Dear Mary

I thought when I left Scotland that by this time I
would have been able to give an opinion as to whether
it would be advisable for a person to emigrate, but
I have seen too little of this country and I feel that I
have far too little experience to say anything decided
on important a matter where so much depends on
the individuals own disposition and exertions. A
person who intends to emigrate should be fully
resolved in his own mind that he can leave home

1. A disastrous fire, which started in a brewery in Quebec City,
destroyed some 1,500 to 2,000 homes.

92

and friends, and at least for some time put up with
fatigue and disapointment but on no account get
disheartned, always hope the best. There is no doubt
cases of poverty and suffering in this country, but I
can safely say that so far as I have seen the great
mass of the people are much better off than in Scotland. Tradesmen in Montreal are much better paid
than same classes in Aberdeen and farm servants in
the country are better too. As to settlers with small
capital I have not seen any of them yet but I believe
that with industry and economy they can in a few
years better their condition vastly more so than in
Scotland. At least those who have families have a
much better prospect of seeing their children provided for in a decent way. When you write you might
mention whether Sandy[1] says anything about coming to this country. If he were resolved to come I
should be most happy to do all in my power to give
him advice and assistance. There is not a better paid
trade in Canada than a blacksmith.

James Thomson

1. Alexander Thomson, junior, an older brother, apparently
trained as a blacksmith by his father.

To Helen Thomson 24 January 1846

Edwardsburgh January 24th 1846

My Dear Sister[1]

When I remember the length of time that has elapsed,
since I wrote home before, particularly as from the
contents of that letter you could scarcely expected to
have seen Edwardsburgh at the head of another
from me, I surely ought to commence this one by
making some apology for my neglect of duty. . . .

Although it is now a considerable time since the
canaling was closed for the season, still it is only a
few weeks since I made up my mind to remain here
all winter. . . . When the work did close I intended to
go to Toronto, but Mr Elliot wished me to stay and
he would find something for me to do during the
winter. The school was at that time without a teacher.
He wanted me to accept of that office. As he has a
good deal of influence in the neighborhood he could
have got me into it but I did not think that I was
properly qualified for such a situation, and therefore
declined it.

About the end of last month Mr McPherson the
clerk bought the store and bakehouse from Mr Eliot.
I then engaged with him to assist in the store and
bake occasionally if required, untill the work would
begin in spring. The store stood a little off the road,
and being an old uncomfortable building Mr. McPher-

1. This letter, which mentions the proposal that Thomson should
become a school teacher, is written in a better hand, a conscious
attempt at self-improvement which is evident throughout Thomson's letters.

son rented a log house which stood on the old road
now broken up by the canal.[1] We got thirty or forty
men one day, raised the entire building, fixed two
logs below it for runners put twelve or fourteen
horses to it, turned it right round and brought the
whole concern along the old road to where it joins
the new. It is now boarded out side and inside and
fitted up as well as any village shop in Scotland.
There is upwards of £300 worth of goods in it now,
and McPherson has been in Montreal all this week
purchasing more, and I am store keeper. . . .

Mary Ann mentioned that my old shopmate
D McKay intends comming to America next spring,
and asks if it would be advisable to send any thing
by him. I think not, as he is going to the States and
I am not much in want of anything. I have lots of
stockings and shirts yet and as many mitts as do me
this winter. I can get clothes here almost as cheap as
at home. Those for summer wear cheaper. I am now
pretty well acquainted in this neighbourhood.

There are few of the farmers very wealthy but they
are generally in easy circumstances, some have extensive orchards. The farm that Mr Elliot rents has
six hundred apple trees in one field and others around
are larger. They make a good deal of cider. The
apples that they want for winter use they preserve
by paring, taking out the seed, stringing upon thread
and letting them dry. In the end of autumn after
gathering in their fruit, they invite all the young
people around who assemble in the evening and
after paring and stringing apples for two or three

1. The Galops canal completed in 1846 was used for passage
upstream only.

hours, get a fiddler and dance and drink cider as long as they have a mind to.

There is now about two feet of snow on the ground. There has been very little severe frost. The river closed at Prescott on saturday last and they were crossing to and from Ogdensburgh in light sleighs on Monday. The river is too rapid down here for the ice to close.

Since the navigation closed in there has been a great deal of traffic along the roads. The mail Sleighs between Montreal and Kingston one up and one down passes our door daily. We are about 200 yards from the Post Office. I had a fine drive on New Years day back to Spencerville, a village on the Nation river twelve miles from this which is the farthest of my travels in the bush.

A few weeks ago the Rev Mr Gaggys was inducted into the pastoral charge of the congregations of Edwardsburgh and Spencerville by the Presbytery of Kingston. On the second of this month a travelling missionary connected with the Canada Sunday School Society gave an address in our church with the view of establishing a sunday school and library. His plan is where the people can raise fourteen dollars he gives a library of 100 volumes and value 28 dollars. For every dollar we give for tracts the society gives 2 dls worth. The money was soon got. . . .

James Thomson

To Alexander and Helen Thomson
24 April 1846

Edwardsburgh April 24th 1846

Dear Father

.... The new corn bill of Sir Robert Peel is looked upon by different parties with different feelings in this country as well as at home. Some say (Isaac Buchanan[1] of Toronto for instance) that it will either ruin Canada or break her connection with the mother country. Some say it will do neither.

The long talked of subject of war had been nearly hushed untill a short time ago when news arrived of Mr I K Polks special message to Congress recommending an increase in their army and navy,[2] and Englands order to the cannon makers at Woolwich to have some hundred large guns ready for our river and lakes. These orders made some to fear and some to hope that there would be war. There are some old veterans in this neighbourhood who fought against the Americans in 1812 & 13 to whom nothing would give greater pleasure than a declaration of war.

I was not aware till I received your letter that my shipmate Henderson had gone to Scotland last fall. I should be most happy to see him on his return to Canada.

There is to be a line of steamers between Montreal and Oswego this summer in opposition to the mail line. There is a wharf built at this place but it is not yet decided whether the boats will call.

1. Isaac Buchanan of Toronto, merchant and politician, sometimes described as the 'father' of Macdonald's National Policy.
2. The message which precipitated the Oregon crisis.

97

The mail steamer Gildersleeve has been running
from Kingston to the head of the Cornwall canal for
the last ten days. She is the first that has disturbed
the St Lawrence for four months. The snow has now
completely disapeared, gloomy winter now ended.
In some respects winter is not a gloomy season here
although the ice bound river prevents navigation and
the whole ground covered with snow hides it from
the view. Yet the almost incessant jingling of sleigh
bells shows winter to be more than any other period
of the year the season of business and pleasure while
the pure cold air renders it healthy and invigorating.
But the picture has a gloomy side too. On the approach of winter almost every living thing forsakes
us, birds wing their way to milder climates, insects
reptiles and the smaller animals sleep away the
dreary months in a torpid state from which they can
be aroused only by the voice of spring. The first of
our voluntary exiles who paid their anual visit was
the crows. They arrived about the end of March and
soon after there was birds singing in every tree and
frogs croaking in every pond.

In answer to a request in your letter I will now
give you some account of my primary circumstances
since my arrival in Canada. When I arrived in Montreal, through your kindness and that of other Dear
relatives I had upwards of twelve sovereign which
I have still by me. Out of my years wages in Montreal I saved about fifteen pounds currency part of
which I deposited in the Montreal Provident and
Savings Bank at four per cent interest which I see
by an advertisement has since been increased to five
per cent. Since I came to Edwardsburgh I had from

June to December 17 Dollars or £4.5/- a month. For
three month in winter as there was little doing my
wages was 12 Dollars a month and from first of April
they are up to £4.10/- a month with perhaps another
rise by June. Out of that I pay for board 7 Dollars
£1.15/- a month. I have a first rate boarding house,
no two tables in Elliots. My washing I get done in
another house for 3/- per dozen articles, handker-
chiefs not included. Through the blessing of God I
write this in good health and I hope it will find you
all enjoying the same great blessing. I must leave a
page for Hellen.

I remain your affectionate son

James Thomson

My Dear Sister
. . . This is the season of making maple sugar in this
part of the country. Some of the farmers tap or bore
several hundred maple trees. They place a trough or
bucket at each tree. The whole sap is collected at
night to a hut in the bush and boiled down to the
thickness of Molasses, strained and cooled. It is then
boiled to the proper thickness and poured into
moulds or dishes. When brought for sale it is in hard
cakes and a good deal darker than common sugar.
Some families make several hundred pounds weight
of it. It is worth from 5^d to 8^d per lb. . . .

James Thomson

To Alexander and Helen Thomson
8 June 1846

Edwardsburgh June 8th 1846

Dear Father

.... There are great numbers of emigrants going up
the river every day. The fares are considerably re-
duced on the river and Lakes this season. The deck
passage from Quebec to Montreal is for steerage 1/3
by 1/ sterling. From Montreal to Kingston $3 or 15/.
But the opposition boats will commence in a few
days and probably bring the fare to $1\frac{1}{2}$ dollars 7/6.
From Kingston to Toronto they go for $7\frac{1}{2}$d a york
shilling. Last year it was ten shilling Halifax Currency. From Toronto to Hamilton forty miles for
what you please. About a fortnight ago two of the
steamers on the river ran foul of each other. The
Gildersleve knocked off one of the Canadas paddles
which laid her up a few days. Her place was supplied by an old boat named the Shannon who could
not go up the Galloos[1] (the rapids at this place) without assistance. When she got to the place she had to
lie in a bay by the canal bank untill the Highlander
a powerful boat on her way down would turn round
and pull her to the top of the rapids. In consequence
of the Shannon lying here several times I had an
opportunity of seeing a great many emigrants. It
brought fresh to my memory the spring of '44', when
I too was a homeless wanderer in a strange land....

I see you had some trouble with the letter that I
prepaid. I remember paying it and am not much

1. Galoos was an earlier form of Galops.

surprised at a mistake from this quarter, our Post Master is a well meaning, blundering, half blind sort of a yankee. However that is a mistake that I can prevent him making in future. . . .

The old country mail arrived here on saturday the 6th bringing the important intelligence that the new Corn Law was allmost become law.

We are not so far advanced in military affairs as you imagine there is no militia raised in this part of the province. On the other side of the river they are raising volunteers for the Mexican war, I believe with little success in the northern States. In the American papers Matamoras[1] and the Rio Grande have taken the place of Oregon and the Columbia, but the public prints will give you a better account of public affairs then I can do.

Last sunday we had no serman in consequence of our minister being at the meeting of the Synod of the Presbyterian Church of Canada (Free Church) at Hamilton. . . .

James Thomson

June 10th

Dear Hellen

It is just mail time and I have hardly time to thank you for your kindness in sending me so handsome a present. It is comming from Montreal along with McPhersons goods. . . .

Your ever loving brother

J Thomson

1. Matamoras is a Mexican town on the Rio Grande river. It was occupied by Zachary Taylor in 1846.

To Alexander and Helen Thomson
October 1846

Edwardsburgh Canada West
October 1846

My Dear Father

As the British Mail will be closed here tomorrow
and there being no serman in our Church today, I
intend to spend an hour or two in doing what should
have been done long ere now writing you a letter. . . .
I now thank you for the present you sent me this
summer. The parcel did not reach me so soon as I
expected but when it did come the articles were all
right. I hope some time or other to be able to send
to Hellen something more appropriate than mere
thanks, for her trouble and kindness and for your
nice selection of pamphlets. You will see from this
that I am still in my old quarters. I expect to remain
for the winter.

Mr Elliot finished his section of the canal here
about a month ago.

I have not baked any since and dont know
whether I will any more this winter. The day that
Mr E. finished here he got another job amounting to
about £5000 at which he has now a hundred men
working. It was a large section commenced about
three years ago but the contractor (Mr. Hillday) in
consequence of too low an estimate or by mis-
management or I believe both the causes united
failed to perform his contract. New tenders were
taken for the completion of the section and Mr.
Elliott although not lowest was accepted. He has

finished all his former contracts to the satisfaction of
the Board of Public Works and their Engineers.
There will be winter work for a hundred men on the
new job. There is 12000 square yards of rock to blast
and take out. 16000 sq yds of clay excavation and
9000 yds of embankment.

[Mr McPherson] is still to clerk for Elliot. He is
to open store tomorrow at the new place. We are to
keep this store too. I will be at one of the places I
expect for the most part here. The other place is five
miles below this in the township of Matilda. Mr
Elliots family will not remove this winter. I would
rather remain here as go below. I am best accquainted in this neighbourhood. I like very well to
stay here although I believe I have not seen a single
person since I came here that I ever recolect to have
seen before. . . .

This place is no exception from the almost universal ravages of the potatoe disease. Some farmers
here have not gone to the trouble of digging their
potatoes at all and others who have done so have
found it to be labour in vain. But there is some ex-
ceptions. We have plenty of good potatoes in our
house while our neighbours with only a fence between the fields have scarcly a sound one at all.
Since the arrival of the September English Mail the
price of flour has risen tremendously. Little more
than a month ago we could get Superfine flour delivered at our door for four dollars per Barrel or at
the rate of about £1.2.6 sterling per sack and a few
days afterwards when the mail arrived we could
scarcly get the same article under six dollars per
bbl [barrel]. So much for bad potatoes in Europe.

I have mentioned that our new place of business is in a Township of Matilda. You must remember that we have no parochial divisions here as in Scotland. Our divisions are Districts, Countys, Townships and Concessions. My place of residence is 1st Concession, Township of Edwardsburgh Grenville County, Johnstown District Canada West. This Township has a front to the St Lawrence of about five miles and extends back 24 miles to the Rideau River. It has 16 Concessions of $1\frac{1}{2}$ miles broad and the whole length of the front. There is a road (not a turnpike) between each concession and a road back between each township. The concessions are divided into farms or lots. A lot in the 1st Con- has a front to the river of a quarter of a mile and goes back $1\frac{1}{2}$ miles to the 2nd Con road. The 2nd Con- lots extend to the 3rd Con road and so on farther than ever I was. . . .

James Thomson

Dear Hellen
This day fortnight the weather was so warm that the girls could not come to church without their parasols. Since then we have had two or three days of snow and frost and lastly rain which has taken away the snow and left the weather fine and the roads bad. But a few weeks will give us roads hard as Aberdeen granate and smooth as polished chimney pieces. . . .

James Thomson

To Alexander Thomson
24 March 1847

Edwardsburgh CW. March 24th 1847

Dear Father
The sleighing has been beautiful all winter and still
continues good. I had twenty miles of a sleigh ride
yesterday evening. We had one cold day in February. I dont know how far the thermometer was
below the freezing point but I thought my nose and
ears was not far above it when going to breakfast.

We are to have a telegraph along this road to connect Montreal and Toronto with Buffalo and the
principal towns in the US. The wire is to be supported on posts 20 feet high 30 to a mile. One of the
poles is close by our door. The people here, the great
majority of whom read but little and consequently
are not over stocked with scientific knowledge have
curious ideas of the telegraph. It would make any
one smile to hear two or three of them discussing the
matter among themselves. Some think that a letter
will be put in the wire & pulled along with a string.
Others think that the invention consists in applying
some unknown power to the letter which makes it
go without a string. Others who object to this theory
will ask them how it will get past the top of the
poles without being torn and how will it do in a
heavy shower. Although they can thus silence others
they allow that they themselves know no more about
it than a cow does about fiddling. One old woman a
neighbour of ours who has seen over fourscore win-
ters believes that railways, steamboats and tele-

graphs are the invention of the emissaries of his Satanic Majesty and are the means [of] bringing down famine on her native land. If they set up a pole at her door she is determined to set fire to it.

We are at present doing something for the relief of the distressed Irish & Scotch. A meeting of this Township was held at Spencerville a few days ago when a commitee was appointed to receive contributions in Money or grain the whole to be converted into Flour or Meal and sent home. Mr McPherson is a member of commitee for the neighbourhood and Mr Elliot below. We opened our list at noon yesterday and before night we had about £10. from twenty subscribers which from a small neighborhood and comparitively poor people is very liberal. McPherson headed the list with £1.10/ the writer of this followed with £1.5/ most of the others gave from £1. to 5/ I think by the end of the week we will have about £20 including grain. Mr Elliot was boasting that he would beat us. We shall be glad if he does. He is to give five pounds himself. In our list we opened two columns one for the Irish and one for the Scotch so that contributors could give to either or to each nation as they pleased. I see the majority have given a half to each. Only two or three that were called on refused to give something. It certainly is the duty of everyone to do all in their power in such a case. Our fields are extensive and have hitherto been fertile but we know not how soon the labour of the husbandman may fail and the fields give no meat.

There is a report here today that Santa Anna with a large Mexican force has got between the American

armies under Scott & Taylor[1] that he has whipt the
latter and that the Yankees are retreating. As it comes
from Ogdensburgh there is likely some truth in
it. . . .

James Thomson

1. Taylor had defeated Santa Anna at the Battle of Buena Vista,
22–23 February 1847 but had failed to follow up his success. By this
time Scott had been sent to capture Vera Cruz by sea.

To Alexander and Helen Thomson
26 August 1847

Port Edwardburgh August 26 1847

Dear Father

I had always some notion of leaving this place during the summer and put off writing from one mail day to another until now that the September mail is almost being made up and me only commencing my letter. I believe that I mentioned in some of my previous letters that I intended to leave early in the season but I have talked so long about it and done nothing else that I have given up fixing any date for that event as I know as much about when I would leave three months ago as I do today. However I dont care much as long as I can earn fifty pounds a year with a straight back and some leisure hours you will easily believe that I am not very anxious to go digging in a dough trough sixteen hours a day.

During the month of May Mr McPherson had a severe attack of rheumatism fever which confined him to bed nearly a fortnight and disabled him from writing for several weeks during which time I was kept pretty busy. I went to the store at Matilda four or five times a week to take in the mens time from the foremen, make up the amount of their pay every fortnight and on pay nights clerk for Elliot and collect the amount of one hundred and fifty canalers store accounts. I got along with them better than I expected although some of them do not understand a word of English and I know as little Irish.

This has been the warmest summer in this part of
the country for more than a dozen years. During
July the thermometer some times stood as high as
95 degrees in the shade. There has been a good deal
of sickness and deaths but the mortality has been far
greatest among the emigrants from Ireland. It is
almost sickning to see the miserable condition in
regard to health and poverty of the immense crowd
that almost daily pass up the river. Temporary hos-
pitals have been erected and filled at every town
from Quebec to I dont know where. This place is
likely soon to become a considerable village. You
will see by the top of this letter that it has got a small
prefix to the name in consequence of the customs
department having made it a port of entry and clear-
ence. A collector has been appointed to receive
duties and prevent smuggling from the yankee side.
Mr Lewis one of the proprietors has laid out part of
his property adjoining the canal in streets and building lots of $\frac{1}{4}$ of an acre 100 feet square all of which he
has sold and some of them are being built upon.
McPherson has bought 6 lots including the building
we now occupy as a store for 500 dollars. Mr Jessup,
clerk of Peace Johnstown District the other proprietor has just finished surveying part of his property
in Lots 50 feet front by 125 feet deep. Mr Jessup has
the privilege of a Mill site at the lower lock in the
canal. He is to erect mills next summer. The Board
of Public Works has already spent £500 making a
mill race as a remuneration for an old mill that stood
in the way of the canal. I have been thinking of purchasing a lot and if the place should come to anything I would build an oven and commence busi-

ness. In summer there is a great demand by boats
passing through the canal. . . .

I send a Cornwall Observer. The reason of my
sending so few papers of late is that I gave up the
Banner when I thought of leaving. We get some
New York papers but they will not go by this country mail.

James Thomson

Dear Hellen

. . . One request you make I am afraid I cannot accomplish in a letter, to describe the working of the
Telegraph. We have one passing within a few feet of
our door but all one can see is a wire about the thickness of a garden line stretched upon poles 20 feet
high like a long clothes line. The apparatus at the
stations is quite small and simple but I cannot describe it although I have seen one in operation in
Prescott. Montreal is now connected with New York
by way of Toronto and Buffalo. I intended to have
gone on a visit to Toronto this summer but I had
not good [sic] getting away and there is so many sick
and aging passengers on the boats that it is unpleasant traveling until the weather getting colder.
By Gods blessing I have hitherto enjoyed good
health and I hope this will find you all the same.

Your loving brother

James Thomson

To Alexander and Helen Thomson
15 December 1847

Edwardsburgh. December 15th 1847

My Dear Father
I received your letter of 30th Sept on 25th Octr the
same day that I returned from a very pleasant tour
round Lake Ontario. The canal at Matilda was
finished about the end of Sept which closed our
business there. The young man who attended store
below not being engaged at that time I got him in
my place and took a fortnights liberty.

One of Elliots foremen was going to Hamilton. I
waited a few days untill he was ready. On Sunday
morning Oct 11th we went to Prescott by waggon.
At 9 am as we expected the new iron steamer Pass-
port came along and we got aboard. The weather
being fine we took deck passage, called at the thriving village of Brockville, passed through the really
beautiful scenery of the Thousand Islands called at
Gananaque and got to Kingston at 3 pm 70 miles
from Prescott. Took dinner saw as much of the city
as we could in two hours, got aboard the Princess
Royal mail Steamer and in half an hour more were
under way for Toronto. As it was to be a night job
and some appearance of storm we took cabin passage. At 4 oclock am of 12th we called at Coburg
changed some passengers and mail bags. Could not
see the town. An hour and a half afterwards went
through the same ceremony at Port Hope and got to
Toronto at noon. Kingston to Coburg 94 miles. Co-
burgh to Toronto 70 miles. The afternoon was rainy.

We hired a cab and drove five miles out the Lake
shore road. When at Humber bridge we enquired for
Scotts[1] residence and were told that he and Mrs. had
just gone into town. We returned to Toronto and
called at several places where we were told he
generally puts up but could not find him.

We staid all night in the Rob Roy Hotel Young
Street and started next morning for Hamilton which
we reached at noon 45 miles from Toronto. Spent a
fine afternoon in this rapidly growing city and neighborhood. Sir Allan N McNab MPP has a fine seat
a little from town at the head of the lake. The finest
house I have seen in Canada.[2] Oct 14th 9 am bade
adieu to my traveling companion and Hamilton
City and got to Toronto per Steamer Magnet at noon.
Walked out to Mimico 6 miles. Found all well. Got
a hearty welcome from my friends. I of course had
to introduce myself. William Scott rents a fine farm
upwards of a thousand acres. Has a good house on a
pleasant spot near the Lake Shore with a fine view
of Toronto harbour. Mrs Scott is a very sensible
woman and very kind. They have four fine children
the oldest boy Stephen is a smart little chap. Will
soon be able to assist his father. Friday 15th being
the day fixed for the public entrance of the Governor
General into Toronto, Mrs Scott and I drove into
town to see the ceremony. Through the kindness of
some of her friends we got a place at a window from
which we had a good view of Lord and Lady Elgin,
and a very gaudy procession of citizens. I have not

1. Thomson's relatives from Auchinblae.
2. Dundern Castle.

seen such a display of plaids and tartans since I left
Scotland.

On Sunday we again went to town, Mrs S and I in
the gig William on horseback. We went to hear Dr
Burns. The Free congregation is large and respectable. Their Church was latly burnt down. They meet
at present in Temperance Hall. A fine new Church
is in course of erection. When comming out of Church
I met Thos Duncan from Turriff an old shipmate.
Mon 18th Bade adieu to kind friends at Mimico,
spent the rest of the day in Toronto, called on an old
acquaintance Alex Findlay, Baker.

Slept at the Rob Roy. The house was almost full
of Highlanders. From the name of the house the
looks and language (gaelic) of the inmates one
might almost fancy himself transported accross the
Atlantic to the Clachan of Aberfoil and backward in
the course of time to the days of the Bold Outlaw
whose motto was 'let him take who hath the power
let him keep who can'. Only Bailie Nicol Jarvie
might spend a night here without having to use a
hot poker in self defence.[1]

Tuesday 19 left Toronto per steamer Admiral for
Niagara & Queenston. The former place is at the
mouth of the river. There is a fort on each side the
one Canadian the other United States with rows of
cannon facing each other. Queenston is 7 miles
farther up the river and 7 miles below the falls. The
boat stopped at Queenston I went to the Falls by
railroad cars drawn by horses.

1. A reference to Walter Scott's *Rob Roy*. A clachan is a small
village in the Highlands in which there is usually the parish
church, or, as in this case, an inn.

On this part of my journey I was fortunate in having for travelling companions two Queenston Ladies mother & daughter. They pointed out to me all the interesting scenes in this very interesting part of country including some of the grandest scenery I ever saw. Gave me a history of the war the battle of Queenston Heights Brocks monument battle of Lundys Lane, best places for seeing the falls etc. Near the Falls there is several good Hotels a fine Museum pleasure grounds walks & Summer houses.

I need not try to describe the great cataract as you have seen a description by abler pens than mine. On turning to my note book which I wrote as I went along I find the following on one of its pages (I write this in a beautiful Pagoda in full view of Niagara Falls on a beautiful autumn afternoon amidst the eternal thunder of the descending waters and surrounded by the never ceasing but ever ascending spray of this wonderous work of an Almighty Creator. The rays of the afternoon sun and the mist of the falls is forming a beautiful rainbow like a fairy bridge across the foaming abyss of troubled waters. Whoever stands in this place may well say what is man ?)

After tea I went and saw the falls by the light of the pale moon and spent the following forenoon in that romantic neighbourhood and I may well say it is truly awful and grand.

At one oclock pm of 20th I left the falls went to Chipawa two miles up the river which Place I left an hour afterwards on board steamer Emerald for Buffalo, passing on our way Schlosser famous for the

burning of the Caroline[1] from which place she went
down the river and over the falls. Navy Island cele-
brated during the late rebellion. When entering
Lake Erie we met a stiff gale and heavy sea. We got
our decks washed a little before getting into Buffalo
harbour. On board this boat I happened to hear
some emigrant passengers talking Aberdeenshire
English. On getting into conversation with them I
found they were the families from Braemar going
to the Londen District. I forgot their name. One of
them was a blacksmith. They were all well. I saw
them again after they were aboard a Lake Erie
steamer bound for Chatham C.W.

Buffalo, State of New York is a large commercial
city at the foot of Lake Erie and head of the Erie
Canal, great place for shipping. The harbour is large
and quite full of steamboats mostly of a large class
that go to all ports in Erie and Michigan and other
places far west. Here I staid one night and the following morning left per rail way (locomotive engine)
with a train of four or five cars each containing about
sixty passengers. By this conveyance I came to
Niagara Falls a distance of 22 miles.

Here we left the greater part of our fellow travelers,
exchanged our large splendid cars for others of
smaller size, and our never tireing iron sinewed fire
and boiling water horse, for 3 or 4 of flesh and blood.
The track here runs along within a few feet of the
edge of the river which for some miles below the
falls is about 200 feet high of steep rocky banks on
each side and quite narrow. It is enough to make
weak nerves tremble to look from the carriage win-

1. The *Caroline* was boarded at the American Fort Schlosser.

dows down such a giddy depth to the now smooth
waters gliding along their narrow channel. 8 miles
of this track brought us to Lewiston a small town
opposite Queenston to which place I crossed over
for my traveling bag which I left on my way up. The
ferry boat here goes by horses in place of steamer.

Crossed again to Lewiston. Got on board the U.S.
Mail Steamer Lady of the Lake which left at 4 pm
for Ogdensburgh, calling during the night at
Rochester and at 9 am of Friday at Oswego. The
Lake was very rough. After getting out of bed I felt
a little seasick. Soon got better. Took very little
breakfast but made up for it at dinner. Afternoon
called at Sackets Harbour NY. Went over to Kingston CW about dusk and down the river to Ogdensburgh some time during the night. I kept my bed
till daylight. Saturday morning went over to Prescott. Saw no chance of a conveyance home. Took the
afternoon steamer. Came to Matilda. Staid at Mr
Elliots till monday morning. McPherson got word
I was there and sent his horse for me so I got safe
home after my fortnights agreable ramble. . . .

James Thomson

[Letterhead Sketch of the Falls of Niagara]

Ellen,
When at Niagara Falls I got a small piece of Table
Rock with a motto carved on it. I have enclosed it in
a newspaper and sent it to you. If it goes safe you
will then have a piece of the rock that overhangs the
dreadful abyss of foaming waters. It should come
along with this in a Prescott Telegraph.

To Helen Thomson 21 June 1848

Edwardsburgh June 21st 1848

My Dear Sister

... The past winter was remarkably open and mild.
We had not over two feet snow at any time and only
3 or 4 weeks good sleighing. The spring came in
early fully a month sooner than last year but it has
been dry during May and up to this time in June
and very changeable. The last few days of May was
very warm. On the morning of the first of June there
was ice as thick as a shilling which hurt a good
many crops. It continued cold several days and is
to this date very dry, but some days almost warm
enough to roast a negro. There is a good many emigrants gone up the river but nothing besides what
went last summer. They are generally healthy and
not so very poor as formerly. . . .

I have received a good many Aberdeen Journals
lately. One as I expected with my last letter. The
Journal has got to be such a respectable size now,
that our postmaster has great thumbing at it thinking there is two papers in the parcel. I enclosed you
an american paper inside a Canadian one some time
ago I dont know if it went.

I see the Queen intends visiting Ireland & Aberdeenshire this summer. However she may be received
in the Green Isle, I have no doubt she will receive a
hearty Highland welcome to the heather clad mountains around Balmoral[1]. . . .

I am my Dear Sister your ever loving & affectionate Brother

James Thomson

1. Prince Albert acquired Balmoral Castle in 1847 and the royal
family arrived there on 1 September 1848.

To Helen Thomson 15 January 1849

Edwardsburgh January 15 1849

My Dear Sister

. . . When you wrote your last letter the Queen was
visiting Deeside. It is a truth that the longer one
lives the more they see. If anyone had said at the
time I left Aboyne that in four years from then the
Queen of Great Britain would be dining in the
Huntly Arms Inn, he would have almost been considered a fit inmate of a Bedlam. . . . It seems they
have pretty hard times in Abdn. The Aberdonians
are not alone in that respect for we feel it even in the
back woods of Canada. . . .

I will expect a letter from Father pretty soon. I
think Sandy and him might go in Co[mpany] and
give the Cunard Steamers a little freight[1]...I intend
to leave Edwardsburgh next spring. I have not yet
decided on what course I will steer. I will write again
before going.

James Thomson

I hope you have received the Brother Jonathon news
paper I sent last month

JT

PS. I wish you would send me a few sprigs of bonny
blooming heather, in a letter or paper next spring
as it is quite a rarity in this country.

1. That is, that his father and brother should come to Canada.

To Alexander Thomson 20 April 1849

Edwardsburgh April 20th 1849

My Dear Father

Another revolution of this fair world . . . has brought
us back again to the twentieth of April, which being
a memorable day in my journal (the fifth anniversary
of my leaving Scotland) I have thought proper to
devote a small portion of it to the pleasing duty of
writing this letter. The annual return of such a day,
will very naturally bring to the recolection of an
exile the scenes and events of former years, even if
those years had been passed in a less beloved land
than Scotland, and among less beloved relatives than
I had the privilege of passing the years of my infancy and childhood. Never then can I forget the
land of my birth, or the friends of my childhood. I
am ever proud to own Scotland as the land of my
nativity, and however humble I may be, I can claim
kindred with the descendants of those brave men
who set limits to the grasping power of ambitious
Rome and who told the haughty Edward of England
at the ever memorable battle of Bannockburn,
hitherto thou mayest come but no farther, and here
shall thy proud conquests be stayed. And also of
those brave and devoted Covenanters, the fathers of
our church, who taught the bigoted Charles, the
folly of attempting to thrust upon a religious people
a detested form of religion. While we thus justifiably
feel proud of our noble countrymen let us also endeavour to improve the inestimable privileges, trans-
mitted by them to us, remembering that righteous-
ness alone exalteth a nation.

I think I mentioned in a previous letter that I intended to leave Edwardsburgh this spring. I now wait the full opening of the navigation to put that intention in execution. I intend to go west. Dont know exactly how far. Perhaps up to Chicago, Illinois, twelve or fifteen hundred miles southwest of this place. On the map you will find Chicago at the southend of Lake Michigan.

Before going west however I intend to go down to Montreal. When I was staying there I put a little money into the Savings Bank, which has since gone to pot. They are now paying depositors with a dividend, I want to go and get what I can.

I suppose you will think from the glowing descriptions of California, as given in the newspapers that I will be off to the 'diggins' gathering gold by the bushel, but I have not started yet. The gold fever has not exactly reached the moving point with me. A few individuals went from Prescott and Brockville and at one time you would have thought that half the Township would go, to hear them talk. Some chaps had it all nicely planned out. How they would go, how long they would stay there, and also the style in which they would come back, driving a coach and six with the boxes of gold strapped in behind. That however looks too much like counting the chickens before the eggs are laid for an Aberdonian to be catched in such a speculation.

Perhaps you dont know that we are all become teetotlars about Edbg, but I can tell you that such is the case almost to a man. About Christmas last the Rev Mr Wadsworth of Montreal delivered a temperance lecture in the Presbyterian Church, a number

signed the total abstinance pledge, and formed a
society. Among other regulations, one was that there
should be a monthly public meeting for the purpose
of advocating the cause of temperance. We got a
medical gentleman, who lives in the neighbourhood
to deliver the first lecture which took place in February. At the close of the meeting I was appointed
to address the next meeting which took place on the
5th of March. I stated the evils of intemperance to
the meeting as well as I could. All seemed pleased
and a good many signed the pledge. The April
meeting was addressed by a Scotchman who keeps
a store, a little below this place and the next meeting
is to take place on the first monday of May when the
Rev Robert Boyd of Brockville will lecture. Boyd is
a Scotchman too so you see Caledonia's sons stand
high in the estimation of the Canadians about these
parts. The society now numbers upwards of a hundred members, within a circuit of less than two
miles.

You will very likely be a little puzzeld to find out
when I qualified myself for becoming a public
speaker, and occupying a platform where Revd &
Medical Gentlemen had been my predecessors and
were to be my successors. The only clue I can give
you to assist you in unriddling the mystery, is that
I have read a good deal, and endeavoured to understand and remember what I did read. With all that
however I dont know that I could have stood up and
addressed a large meeting, as I had to do, had it not
been for a little training I went through last winter,
a course of training by the by which is within the
reach of all, if a few will only lay their heads to-

gether. In the month of November last a few of us
in this place, including two schoolmasters, and some
leading members of the Methodist and Episcopal
churches, got up a debating club. We met in the
school house every Friday evening, and discussed
what ever subject had been agreed on at our previous meeting. We elected a chairman who was to
hear both sides impartially and decide not on the
merits of the question, but on which side the greatest weight of argument had been brought forward.
One rule of the society was that no allusion should
be made to sectarian or religious principles. As a
specimen of the questions discussed I may mention
the following. Is Nature or Art most pleasing to the
eye? Is a Monarchy or Republic the best form of
government? Has Politics or Religion caused the
most blood shed?[1]

May 21st.   You will see that a month has elapsed
since I wrote the foregoing part of this letter. The
reason is that I did not want to send it off untill I
would be ready to leave this place, which I think I
will do about the 23rd inst. I was at Montreal beginning of this month. The day I left Montreal two
Glasgow vessels came in the first from sea this
season. For the money I had in the Bank I got fourteen shillings to the £. You will see by the newspapers that we have had stirring times in Canada
lately. The Tories were turned out of office at last

1. Thomson made his debut as a successful debater on the subject,
'Which affords the greatest pleasure, married life or single life?'
Prescott Journal, April 1898, quoted in F. Byers, et al., *A History
of Cardinal* (Cardinal, Ontario; Privately Printed, 1967), p. 105.

election, which they took sadly to heart as they had
long enjoyed the sweets of office. They are making a
great fuss about a Bill for paying the Rebellion
losses in Lower Canada. On the 25th of April they
burnt the Parliament House and assaulted Lord
Elgin in the streets of Montreal. If attempting to
take the life of Her Majestys Representative be
loyalty then the tories are most loyal. If burning and
destroying public and private property be support-
ing law order and the constitution then the tories
are good citizens. Petitions are now getting up by
one party, the tories, to have Lord Elgin recalled,
and by the reformers to have him stay here. . . .

I think it would be well for some of your ministers
to be as moderate at the bottle as they are in church
politics. . . .

James Thomson

A LUMBER YARD
IN CHICAGO

To Alexander Thomson   16 July 1849

care of D. Clark & Co.
Lumber Merchants
Chicago Illinois,
United States

Chicago, Illinois   July 16th 1849

My Dear Father

... On account of the dullness of business in Edwardsburgh and in Canada generally I last winter
made up my mind to seek out a new and more
active locality. I applied for advice to my friend Mr
Elliot whom I knew to be well acquainted with the
country and on whose judgement and advice I
could rely with confidence. He at once recomended
me to try Chicago as in his travels in the west he
had seen no place where I would be more likely to
succeed and he gave me a letter of introduction and
a very high recomendation to a gentleman in this
place with whom he is accquainted.

I left Edwardsburgh on Monday May 28th. Several
kind friends volunteered to drive me to Prescott
which place I reached in time for the morning mail
boat. I got to Kingston about 2 pm. Some business I
had to transact for Mr McPherson detained me in
Kingston till the following afternoon when I left per
Steamer Magnet for Toronto. The boat was crowded
with travellers, upwards of a hundred cabin pas-

sengers and decks well filled. In consequence of
opposition among the boats the fare is at present
very low, cabin two dollars, deck seven and a half
pence. I arrived in Toronto at 10 a.m. of the 30th,
rode out to Mimico and staid till the following day.
Cousin and family are pretty well. . . .

Thursday afternoon Wm drove me into town. He
was anxious that I should see the inside of Knoxs
Church.[1] We hunted a long time for the doorkeeper
but could not find him. The Free Church people
may be justly proud of such a building. It is one of
the finest in Canada. Foiled in our endeavour to get
into the church, we went to the Horticultural So-
cietys exhibition, the first for the season being held
that day in the fine pleasure grounds around the
Government House.[2] To look at the beautiful flowers
and large and mature vegetables one would think
that in comming in at the gate they had stepped
from May to July or August.

Wm was to write to Scot shortly after I was there
so you have probably heard that I was so far on my
way to the west.

I staid all night at the Edinburgh Castle Hotel,
and on the morning of the first of June left Toronto
and Canada, for Lewiston. It being only a four hours
sail I took deck passage paid my 7½d and got to
yankeetown about 11 am. Got in the railroad cars for
Buffalo, passing rapidly over and in full view of the
classic ground and sublime scenery between the

1. Old Knox's Church built in 1848 to replace one destroyed by
fire the year before.
2. Government House on King Street was the residence of the
Lieutenant-Governors of Upper Canada and Ontario for almost a
century until 1912.

Lakes Ontario and Erie including Queenson Heights, Genl Brocks Monument, Suspension Bridge, Niagara Falls, Lundys Lane, Navy Island, and other places of natural beauty and historical interest. Reached Buffalo same evening. Staid overnight in a very large temperance Hotel, and left the following day at 10 oclock for Detroit, on board the finest steamboat that I ever saw called the 'MayFlower'. I have heard of a floating pallace before but never saw one till then. She made the trip through to Detroit in seventeen hours.

It being sunday morning when we arrived I put up at a Hotel. Went to the Presbyterian Church in the forenoon. Little difference from a church in Scotland only they have an organ.

At 4 oclock pm of the 3rd left Detroit per Railroad for New Buffalo the western terminus of the RR on Lake Michigan at which place a steamer waited our arrival and took us into Chicago about 9 am. of the fourth of June exactly a week from the time I left Edsbg. By deducting the time I stopped at the different places you will see that the actual running time occupied in comming here does not exceed three days. The route I took by the Michigan Railroad is more than four hundred miles shorter than by the Lakes. By taking that near cut the distance from Edwardsburgh to this place will be about 1000 miles. The americans are so accustomed to travelling that they think no more of that distance than you would think of a trip to Edinburgh.

When I came to Chicago business was very dull. One week from the time of my arrival however I got a place in a dry goods retail store, one of the clerks being absent on visiting trip to the south. There I continued a fortnight until his return. One day after leaving that place I got into my present situation, clerk in a Lumber Merchants office, which I like very well. My employers D. Clark & Co have a steam sawmill in Green Bay, State of Wisconsin. The Lumber business in Chicago is very extensive, all imported from Michigan & Wisconsin as there is no timber in Illinois. The first three weeks I was here I staid in the Chicago Temperance House. I now board with a private family near the office. Deaths by Cholera in Chicago average five or six daily. . . .

James Thomson

To Alexander and Helen Thomson
18 March 1850

Chicago Ill. March 18th 1850

My Dear Father

... Since I came to Chicago I have had a very comfortable place, my employers are very kind they
have treated me more like a son or brother
than as a stranger. I have had many opportunities
during the winter of attending lectures by able
speakers on different subjects, in all calculated to
improve the mind. In regard to opportunities for
religious instruction Chicago is ahead of most towns
of the same size in Scotland. The gospel is preached
by many able clergymen on sundays and also week-
day evenings with a devotedness and zeal worthy
of their high calling.

Notwithstanding all these advantages I have made
up my mind to leave this the Garden City of the
Prairie State, in fact before you read these lines I
expect to be many miles on my journey towards the
setting sun. In your last letter you expressed a hope
that you will again see me on the banks of the Dee.
I trust that hope will be realised and that too at no
very distant date. You will no doubt think when you
read this letter that I am about to take a very strange
road to get to Scotland.

That rich territory that 'Uncle Sam' accquired by
whiping the Mexicans, has excited a great deal of
interest in this and other countries during the last
two or three years. This year thousands will go to
that Eldorado of the West. I have made up my mind

to have a trial of gold digging too. I don't know what your opinion is on this subject, but I have thought the matter over pretty well and believe that the best thing a young man with two or three hundred dollars can do is to go to California. No doubt hundreds who go there will be disappointed, still there is better chance of success in going there than by embarking in any sort of business with the same amount of capital. Some of our ablest business men are going, and many are leaving wives and families and good situations, and setting out for the Far West. Should I be successful and accquire even a small amt. my greatest happiness would consist in paying you a visit at as early a date as possible, and should I be fortunate enough to accquire wealth, I would value it not for its own sake, but only as a means by which I might improve my own mind and benefit my fellowmen.

A good many have left Chicago this winter for San Francisco by way of New York, Chagres,[1] and Panama but those who have travelled both ways recomend the overland route, especially from places so far west as this. The distance from Chicago to the 'diggings' across the Plains is estimated at about two thousand five hundred miles, rather a long journey to go in a waggon I admit, but my love of seeing the world feelings were always pretty strong, and I can't feel satisfied until I have seen the 'Far West' (if there be such a place) and gazed upon the broad bosom of the mighty Pacific Ocean which stretches from the golden hills of California to the shores of the Celestial Empire. I go in company

1. Chagres is on the Caribbean shore of the Canal Zone.

130

with three others all older than myself, two of them leaving wives and families. Their names are Horace Clark,—McAulay, and I don't mind the other fellows name. Our wagon (like all California wagons) is covered with canvas, drawn by four horses. We also take a canvass tent about ten feet square, which we can pitch in five minutes, a sheet iron cooking stove and four months provisions & cc. Our intended route is westward through the State of Illinois, crossing the Mississippi about Rock Island, thence through the State of Iowa to St Joseph's or Council Bluffs on the Missouri river, west along the banks of Platte river, a tributary of the Missouri, crossing the Rocky Mountains at the South Pass in the same degree of latitude (42°) as Chicago, thence via the Morman City at Salt Lake, and over the Sierra Nevada mountains on the western slope of which is the gold diggings.

It may not probably be in power to write to you for some time but I will embrace the earliest opportunity of doing so. The hope of being able to visit my native country will cheer me on the long journey now before me.

James Thomson

Ellen,

When I get back from California, I will come right straight home and see all my friends and see if I can't get a wife out among your acquaintences. I suppose if I had my pockets full of gold dust I could, but I don't believe in buying a wife, nor marrying a pile of dollars bills with a young girl into the bargain.

James Thomson

To Alexander Thomson 20 September 1850
From G. B. Baldwin, Lumber Merchant, Ottawa

Ottawa Sept 20th 1850

Mr Thompson
Dear Sir
Having resided in Chicago sometime I then became
acquainted with your son James who left this place
[Chicago] about the 1st April for California. When
about leaving he requested me to write you a few
lines if ever I heard anything about his Company. I
recd a letter from him dated Fort Laramie[1] June 13th
which must have been detained some time I having
recd it but two days ago. Fort Larami is about 1000
miles from Chicago. The Company were well fitted
out with good horses and every convenience for the
journey. They joined in with another Company at
Council Bluffs and Elected offices when James was
chosen Treasurer. He seemed to be in Good health
and spirits. When in this place he enjoyed the
utmost confidence of his employers & was liked by
all whom knew him. He was my only companion &
I would as soon part with a brother (If any one
should prosper in California He will). Of sound
constitution enured to Labour of Good natural
abilites and education and above all of Temperate
habits (such a person will prosper in any part of the
United States).

Hoping your son every manner of success in his

1. Fort Laramie, Wyoming, a stockade built in 1834 and rebuilt
for use as protection for travellers on the Oregon Trail.

133

enterprise and wishing that father and Son may soon
meet to enjoy each others society once more.
I remain yours truly

G B Baldwin

Please if you rec^e this send a few lines or a News
paper. Directed to me Care of John Hossack, Lumber Merchant, Ottawa

THE CALIFORNIA GOLD FIELDS

To Alexander and Helen Thomson
6 October 1850

Nevada City California Oct 6th 1850

My Dear Father
Now that I have got to the end of my long and tedious journey over the mountains and deserts of America and arrived safely in this the golden El Dorado of the west I embrace the earliest opportunity of making you acquainted with my welfare since I last wrote to you. When I was at Fort Laramie five hundred miles up the river Platte I wrote to a young man in Chicago a friend of mine and requested him to write to you stating that I was so far in my journey all well. I hope he [has] done so. I hear so many complaints about the Post Office arrangements of this country that I consider it extremely doubtful if these lines [will] ever reach you but I shall continue to write occasionally and expect an answer as soon as possible.

I kept a journal of my journey over the Plains but to give you an account of the every day occurrences of such a length of time would go beyond the limits of this sheet. Suffice it for the present to say that I left Chicago on the 6th of April crossed the Mississippi at Dubuque on the 14th crossed the Missouri at Council Bluffs May 20 passed Fort Laramie June

14th crossed the Rocky Mountains at the South Pass
June 28th reached the Sink of Humboldt or St
Marys on the 4th of august. On the 17th of August
took dinner on the tip top of the Sierra Nevada
Mountains upwards of nine thousand feet above the
level of the sea having travelled part of the forenoon
on the top of snow banks deeper than any that ever
graced the rocky caverns of Lochnagar, and arrived
safely at Placerville (generally called Hangtown)[1]
the first diggings on the 20th of August, having enjoyed excellent health and met with no accident
during the entire route.

We staid a few days in Hangtown but from the
large number of emigrants daily arriving found that
the best diggings were occupied. We got all the
information we could and concluded to try the
northern mines. Having sold our horses we put the
heaviest of our luggage in a store house and with a
change of clothing and a few cooking utensils on
our backs we started for Nevada City sixty miles
north. The weather being warm and some very
steep hills to ascend and descend we took our time
and arrived at this place on the 30th of Augt.

Here as elsewhere in California we found some
people making fortunes and others scarcely making
their board. The bottoms of rivers and streams are
pretty well dug out or occupied. Numbers are now
digging in the hillsides sinking shafts in regular
mining style from twenty to eighty feet deep until
they strike the granite rock immediately above
which the gold is deposited. Some get as high as

1. Placerville, sixty miles south of Nevada City, apparently the
site of lynchings.

50,000 dollars out of one hole and others get hardly enough to pay expenses.

Since I came to California I have been in company with a man from Canada who came through with me and one from the State of Iowa whom we got accquainted with in Hangtown. They are both respectable and agreeable companions. We have done little at mining only washed out a little dust with a tin pan or basin. We have not yet bought mining tools finding we could do better at other employment.

There being a great deal of building going on in the city we resolved on going into the lumber business, manufacturing boards. Although in a different style from that pursued in other countries, the boards made and used here are four feet long six or eight inches wide, $\frac{1}{4}$ inch thick and instead of being sawed are split. We commenced two weeks ago and have made a hundred and fifty dollars each clear in that time. We work in the woods half a mile from town having built ourselves a small cabin. We do our own cooking. Our board costs us about nine dollars a week each. By making a good article of lumber we can sell at the tree as many as we can make at sixty dollars per thousand. We three can easily get out 800 boards per day. The pine splits beautifully when we happen to get the right sort of tree which is some what difficult in the vicinity of the city. It would almost astonish even a Glen tanner man to see the trees that grow in this country many of them upwards of 300 feet high. The one we have been working is 260 feet long 8 feet diameter at the base 5 feet diameter at 60 feet from the ground and

2 feet do 200 feet from the ground. We are now
sawing where it is five feet through pretty hard
crosscutting you can believe me. One cut will make
a thousand boards and bring us $60. We will not be
able to work up all the tree unless we get a longer
saw.

This place is 75 miles from Sacramento City. The
carriage of goods cost 9 or 10 dollars per 100 lbs
from the place. Provisions of all sorts are sold in this
country by the lb. Flour 20 cents potatoes 25 Beef 30
Pork 40 Sugar 50, Butter, Cheese Onions & Cabbage
a dollar per lb each Tea $1.50 Hay 25 cents. Tea you
will see is the cheapest article being little more
than it is in Scotland. You will see it is no joke
keeping a horse in this place with Hay £100 per
ton and Barley 4/sterling per lb. I have not seen
many oats. In Hotels and boarding houses the
charge is one $20 per week. Clothing is not as dear
in proportion as provisions.

There is no paper money in circulation here but
gold dust goes as readily as coin at $16 per ounce.
A British sovereign passes for $5 the same as an
American half eagle. The Mexican Doubloon goes
for $16 and a British shilling for 25 cents. The
weather here is not so changable as in Scotland. It
rains four months in the year and during the remainder it does not rain at all. The rainy season
generally sets in about the middle of November. We
have some intention of moving our quarters before
the rain commences. One of my comrades wants to
go to Oregon. I do not know yet whether we will but
I hope you will write on receipt of this and address
my letter to Sacramento City. My kind respects to

all. Hoping that by Gods blessing this will find you
all in good health. I remain your affectionate son

James Thomson

Ellen
Enclosed is a small specimen of California gold. A
great deal of the gold found here is as fine as the
sand on your floor. These are about the largest pieces
that I can pick out of two hundred dollars worth of
dust. On some of the rivers however, the pieces are
much larger some of them weighing several ounces.
I have merely sent you this to let you see the pure
California metal. Remember me to Brother Sister
and all friends.

Your loving Brother

James Thomson

To Alexander Thomson [and family]
22 February 1851

Nevada City, California Feby 22nd 1851

My Dear Father, Brother & Sisters

Twelve months have now rolled away since I have
had any inteligence from home. Five months have
passed and gone and yet I have received no answer
to my first letter written in California. Under these
circumstances is it any wonder that my mind oft
times wanders back to the scenes of my childhood,
the home of dear relatives, and esteemed friends,
who it may be are now charging me with ingratitude
for not writing, as it is extremly doubtful whether
you have ever received my previous letters. I know
from the testimony of many persons that the Post
office department in this country has until lately
been miserably managed, or rather mismanaged. I
hope things are now different. Since 'Uncle Sam'
admitted us into the Union we have got a new P.M.
at Sacramento and also a Post office at Nevada City,
so I have resolved to try once more if I cannot send a
letter and receive an answer from the other side of
the Atlantic. If I could only receive intelligence of
your being all well I could rest satisfied and put up
with the inconvenience of this new country for some
time longer.

The winter months so far have been the most
delightful I ever saw. So far as weather is concerned,
California far outshines any other country I ever
lived in. Scotland, Canada, Illinois, neither dare
compare with El Dorado. I doubt whether Italy with

the boasted auzure skies could beat the weather that
we have had this winter. Instead of the rain and mud
and wind and storm which I expected during the
rainy season, we have had only a few wet days and
all the rest as fine as ever shone in May. One night
about the end of Nov. it did seem as if old Boreal
was about to assert his supremacy over the elements,
as he does in other countries at this season. That
night the rain fell fast the wind blew as t'would
blawn its last just as it did on that eventful night
when Tam O Shanter was making his way home via
Alloway Kirk.[1]

In my last I mentioned that I was engaged in the
Lumber business. Building in Nevada City did not
continue much longer and I went to mining. As yet
I cannot give a very favourable report of my success,
although the star of hope is still in the ascendent.
In the month of December I in company with two
partners purchased a claim for a thousand dollars, a
pretty large price for a piece of ground 30 by 90 feet,
when we might have had it for nothing if we had
only been there a few weeks sooner. It is in a dry
ravine two miles from town and the want of rain has
been a very serious hindrance to us. However we
have now got water independent of the rain. We in
Co with those who have diggings adjoining ours
numbering about fifty men, have just completed a
ditch from a mountain stream $4\frac{1}{2}$ miles distant over
as rough looking ground as water was ever brought
over being great part of the way through rocks and
fine roots, and accross deep ravines in troughs. In
fact such a work as Californians alone would try and

1. A reference to Robert Burns's poem.

nothing but gold would prompt even them to attempt
it. Now for the results. We have about 1/3 of our
claim worked out and the Cr side of Claim account
shows that we have washed out twelve hundred
dollars. Some parts of the claim are much richer
than others. One part pays about $6 to a pail full of
gravel. The greater part will not pay more than from
ten to fifteen cents, but even at that we can make
fair wages say an ounce (16 dollars) a day to each
man.

Washing with a cradle or rocker is a slow process
and not much used unless where water is scarce.
We wash with what is called a Long Tom, a spout
or trough, 16 feet long 16 inches wide and 6 inches
deep. At the lower end the bottom consists of a
screen or riddle of sheet iron punched with $\frac{1}{4}$ of an
inch holes, through which the water sand and gold
passes, keeping back the larger gravel. Under the
screen is a shallow box seven feet long and the same
width and depth as the tom, with bars accross the
bottom inside. Here the gold by its superior weight
settles and nearly every other substance is washed
away. Two men washing the gravel up and down the
Tom with shovels or spades keeps one busy shovel-
ing in. A stream of water, as large as would run
through a pipe 2 inches diameter is continually
running through the Tom. Our ditch supplies 20
Toms and we have a surplus which we sell to a few
who do not belong to the concern at ten dollars a
day per Tom. I was elected Secretary & Treasurer
to the ditch Coy.

I have still to thank a kind and merciful Providence for good health & many comforts, and I pray

the Almighty Ruler of the Universe may bless you all with every blessing and I hope the time will come when I may be enabled to leave the far west and once more visit the scenes I have left far away but not forgotten and I hope it is needless to remind you that a letter is anxiously looked for by the exile of Scotia. As this place is likely to be my place of residence for some time, please address my letter to Nevada City California. A number of letters have been brought here from Sacramento P.O bearing my name but not for me. In order to save me some trouble please put the letter B between my names. On Christmas day I wrote to Mr McPherson, Canada and requested him to write to you,

James B. Thomson

To Alexander Thomson 21 March 1851
From Kenneth McPherson, Merchant, Edwardsburgh

Edwardsburgh 21st March 1851

My Dear Sir

You will be astonished on receiving this letter from
me an entire stranger to you—but I do so by request
of your son James, who is now in *California*. I had
the pleasure of getting a letter from him four days
ago, in which he stated that he had written you a
letter in September last but in consequence of the
Post Office business being so badly managed in that
far distant country—he fears that said letter might
miss carry and consequently never arrive at its
destination—Therefore in case you have not recd his
letter and in complyence with his requests I hasten
to say that James has arrived in California on the
20th August last after an overland journey which
must have been an awful task.

Yet after enduring hardships in all its different
forms, he enjoyed good health and which blessing
has attended him up to the date of his letter to me—
He is in company with a few other young men who
started there along with him, one of them he says a
young Scotch Canadian. They are doing well each
earning per day (digging gold) from 10 to 16 dollars,
and their expences costs each one dollar per day—
So you will observe that by their present earnings
that can soon make a fortune if they continue in
good health—and I am proud to say that if any
person will do well your son shall as he is a young
man that is an honour to the family he belongs to—

an honest sober persevering, and industrous person, just the qualities required for making well in that or any other country—And I will further venture to say that in course of a couple of years or perhaps less— he may return with a *fortune*. I have known many that has done so in six months from the same place —I know of nothing that could give me and my family greater pleasure than receiving this letter from James, as we felt most anxious for his safety during his overland journey, and because we thought as much of him as if he was one of our own—he being so long (and *faithfully too*) in my employment —and might have been yet if desired to continue. However he is now in a country that he will soon do well. His employment is digging the preacious metal—he has sent me enclosed a sample of the stuff part of which you will find enclosed here as a specimen of your sons labour—which specimen shall have travelled over ten thousand miles ere it reaches you—James address is James Thompson, Nevada City, Via Sacramento, California, United States America.

I have nothing more of any consequence to communicate to you, and shall conclude with Best respects will I remain to be My dear Sir Yours very faithful, Kenneth McPherson, Merchant, Edwardsburgh, Canada West

To Alexander Thomson 11 April 1851

Nevada City, Cal. April 11th 1851

Dear Father

I received your long looked for and anxiously
expected letter of 30th Dec. on 23rd of March conveying to me the mournful intelligence of the loss of
a well beloved sister. I mourn, not for Mary Ann, but
for myself and those she has left in this vale of tears.
I sincerly sympathize with her bereaved husband
and those dear little ones now left motherless. . . .
Dear Helen if those children are entrusted to your
care train them up as their mother would have done,
had she been spared with them and you will reap a
rich reward.

I wrote about the latter part of Feby which letter I
hope has reached its destination. You will learn by
it that I gave up the board business and turned to the
great staple business of this country, mining. We
have had a very fine winter. The only winter we have
had was between the 20 March and 5 April. During
that fortnight we had rain or snow almost everyday.
The snow fell very fast but never got over a foot
deep. Farther north on Yuba and Feather rivers[1] the
snow is very deep. The winter here is again beautiful. This day has been almost warm enough for the
fourth of July. I intend to move farther north about
the first of June.

I will now endeavour to answer a few of the many
questions you ask, with this short preface that we
are not quite so bad off for the necessaries of life as

1. Tributaries of the Sacramento.

146

you seem to think. The boards that we used to make
certainly very thin are almost the only material used
for building in the mining district of California. The
miners cabins or shantys around Nevada are mostly
built of logs and roofed with boards. There is plenty
of good building stone around Nevada, real Aberdeen looking granate, but none of it used. Everything here in the shape of building is done in temporary style only calculated to last a few seasons.
Here we build a house in a week. A merchant in
this country will sometimes put up a house, sell his
stock of goods make his fortune and go home in
little more time than it takes any Aberdonian to plan
his building, advertise for estimates, and lay the
foundation stone.

If you send any of your sawyers here to cut up our
big logs tell them to bring twelve feet saws with
them and then we can stick them on to a log where
they will only have two feet stroke. There is now
three saw mills in this vicinity one water one steam
and one horse power. They sell their lumber at 175
dollars per thousand feet (board measure). Sawed
stuff is used for flooring and inside work, and making Toms for washing gold.

This is a well watered country considering the
long dry season. We have a good spring within a
few yards of our cabin. There is very little farming
up here in the mountains, only a few little flats are
being fenced and cleared for gardens where there is
a chance to irrigate them with water from some
mountain stream. But down in the valley of the
Sacramento there is some fine farming land and the
greatest cattle raising places in the world. Some old

settlers principally Mexicans own a great many thousands running almost as wild as Buffaloes. They catch them with the lasso and brand them as the Scotch farmers do their sheep only they use a hot iron instead of tar. Some of the old Californians are great at throwing the lasso. They will ride up to the wildest bull in a thousand and throw the running noose over his horns.

There are a few Indians about Nevada. They go skulking through town with their bow and arrows, their hair stuck full of feathers and porcupine quills, and some miners old shirt on as proud as Lord Chesterfield. They are a low thick set dwarfish tribe very different from the tall manly warrior looking fellows we saw when crossing the plains among the Pawnee, Omihaw,[1] Sioux and other tribes. In some parts of California the red men are more numerous and sometimes troublesome, but in general they are friendly.

We don't exactly eat dry bread. We get beef at 30 cents a lb smoked pork ham and bacon same price and we bought some honey the other day at five dollars per gallon, plenty of molasses (good) at four dollars pr gal. Provisions are much cheaper than when we came here. We now buy the best Chili Flour at 16 dollars pr 100 lb and potatoes good as ever grew in Ireland same price as flour. Clothing is cheaper in proportion than provisions. We get good red or blue flannel shirts at 2 dollars, trousers all most as low as in the States. Last fall I paid 17 dollars for a pair of boots and now can get as good a pair for $\frac{1}{2}$ an ounce (8 dollars) and must have them

1. Omaha.

too before many days. Woolen socks costs one dollar. We bought two pair of good heavy blankets last fall at 16 dollars pr pair.

We have our cabin or boothy fitted up with berths like a passenger ship and we sleep on the soft side of a pine board, with an old blanket and sometimes a little hay between us and it. Hellen guessed right about the washing. We do it all ourselves. We get plenty of soap at 50 cents (2/3) pr lb. Of course we do our own mending and cooking. Put me into a well filled kitchen and I would not thank anybody for a better dinner than I could get up. I forgot to mention we can also get milk here but it is $1\frac{1}{2}$ dollars pr quart about three times as much as you would pay for whisky at Aboyne. I can't get any oat meal or I would treat myself to Potage and milk some night notwithstanding the big price.

Gold dust is the principle currency here sixteen dollars (about £3/4/ sterling) per ounce is the common value. There is also a good deal of gold coin Mexican doubloons (16 dollars) and American ten and five dollar pieces. English Sovereigns pass here for five dollars. In the States they are only worth 4 dollars 84 cents.

There is one Methodist meeting house in Nevada and there is several preachers around who sometimes hold meetings in the largest houses. Preachers here generally follow St Pauls example and work with their hands so as to be chargable to no man. . . .

Although an ocean and a continent at present divides us I hope it will not always be so. If fortune only smiles upon me and I make enough in California to enable me to visit the land of my nativity, depend upon it I will embrace the earliest opportunity to do so.

One of my partners John McCargo has been my travelling companion and partner ever since we started from Chicago. He is from Canada, his grandfather Dr McGaughlan[1] is a great man in the west. He is one of the head men in the Northwest Fur Company. He lives in Oregon City. John and I are going to see him when we make our fortunes and then steer for Scotland by way of New York Canada and Boston. My other partner is from the State of Iowa they are both good fellows.

I must now bring this long letter to a close, for my candle has got a little a head of time and is just about to end its wick (week) although this is only friday night. Please write again at your earliest convenience addressing me at Nevada city

Your affectionate Son

James B. Thomson

Dear Father, you ask if every man does what seems right in his own eyes in this country. In a great many respects he may do so. This is a very free country, but not quite so much so as it was in Israel when there was no judge in the land. We have two sets of judges, the civil law is administered by one set of Judges and Judge Lynch or mob law sometimes does little jobs too at punishing offend-

1. Dr. John McLoughlin (1784–1857), a partner in the old North West Company, who built Fort Vancouver for the Hudson's Bay Company. After 1846 he kept a general store in Oregon City. He is known as 'the father of Oregon'.

ers. You who have never been accustomed to such things will no doubt think that mob law is not very just law, but circumstances alter cases. Judge Lynch inspires more terror into the hearts of evil doers than any other judge in the country. I have never seen any lynching done, but there has been two or three cases in this neighbour hood lately. One case happened last week and I have seen a good many persons who were present at the trial and punishment. A person in town had 2500 dollars stolen, and four fellows who were overheard quarreling about dividing some money were aprehended on suspicion. The civil law took the case in hand and were to send the prisoners to the county jail. In that case their trial would not have come on for some time. The witnesses would probably be scattered all over the mines by that time and difficult to be found. Many such cases have happened and guilty parties escaped. In view of circumstances the people took the prisoners from the officers, appointed a judge, empaneled twenty one citizens as a jury. The prisoners were allowed a lawyer to defend their case. One of them turned States evidence. The other three were convicted and sentenced two of them to twenty each and the other to thirty nine lashes. They were allowed their chance either to take the lashes or be hanged. They chose the former and got it too in presence of a vast crowd. The fellow who executed the sentence is an ox driver and is said to have wealded the whip scientifically. . . .

I mentioned in my last letter that we were making pretty good wages on our bought claim. We still make from ten to twenty dollars a day each. A few

days we did better. On the seventeenth of last month
(which you know is something of a memorable day
in my memorandum book) we three with one hired
man washed out one hundred and fifty dollars and
the day following with three hired hands we made
one hundred and seventy nine dollars. The price
paid to hired hands is from four to six dollars per
day and they board themselves. Some hire by the
month for from seventy five to a hundred dollars and
boarded. You express a hope that I may get some
easier occupation than board making or mining. I
like either very well.

The weather has been so pleasant during the
winter working in the open air gives me a noble
appetite, and after a hard days work I can sleep far
more soundly and sweetly on my board bed than the
sons of luxury and ease can on their beds of down.
The labouring man alone knows how sweet is rest.
We do not work so hard as I did ten or twelve years
ago in Aberdeen. We take breakfast about sun rise
go to work between seven and eight take an hour at
noon for dinner and work till five or six as we feel
inclined. In the evenings we bake bread, clean our
gold and weigh it and make a dividend Saturday
nights after paying our provision bills out of company purse. We get United States newspapers for
twenty five cents.

Until the fire there was a good book store in
Nevada, they gave out books in library fashion. By
paying twenty five cents we get a reading of a dollar
book. I have had five or six numbers of Harpers New
York magazine a very good work contains 144 pages,
matter similar to Chambers' Edinburgh Journal.

The population of this country is a strange mixture of races and professions. You will find ministers doctors lawyers and all sorts of tradesmen digging gold on this same ravine or stream. Americans Canadians Mexicans Chilieans Sandwich Islanders Chinese Dutchmen Irishmen Welchmen Scotchmen Englishmen Spainards Peruvians and Jews may all be found digging within a circle of two miles. I have made a mistake I beg pardon, Mr Jew, we cant catch you digging in this country nor any other. He would rather eat pork than dig a days work. But go to town on Sunday and you will see his Hebrew countenance behind a counter covered with ready made clothing for which he will ask twice the price he expects to get.

Fully one half of Nevada city was burnt down about three weeks ago. The loss was estimated at a million dollars. Some merchants lost about twenty thousand dollars. The houses were entirely built of such boards as I described. They were so thin and dry that they burnt with fearful rapidity. The burnt district is now almost entirely rebuilt.

To Helen and Alexander Thomson
27 July 1851

Nevada City Cal July 27 1851

My Dear Sister

I have this day received your highly esteemed
favour of May 12th. You can imagine better than I
can describe, the feelings with which a letter from
home is received by an exile like myself thousands
of miles from home with few friends and in a country where the state of society morally and religiously
is widely different from what he has been accustomed to. Yours is the third letter that I have received since my arrival in California the first being
Fathers of 30th December which reached me in
April and which I answered a few days after receipt.
My other letter I received from McPherson about
two months ago in answer to one I wrote him on
Christmas day.

Dear Helen I am sorry that the news contained in
your letter is mostly of a gloomy cast, the loss of our
dear sister. I hope we will all be enabled to bear
with christian resignation and may we profit by
affliction as the Psalmist of old did. . . .

Helen, you mention that Elizabeth Middleton is
one of that number [of friends who remembered
him]. I thank her most kindly. I thought she would
have long ago forgotten the little boy whose head
she used to pat and to whom she gave pieces of
bread well loaded with red berry jam. If there is a
good crop of berries next summer tell Lizzie to put
up an extra gill of them for me and if I should have
the good fortune to get back to Scotland she may

154

depend on a visit before I am many days at home
and as a token of respect I send her in this letter a
small piece of california gold. . . .

I think I have now done about my share of ram-
bling through the world, but Dear Helen I cannot
give you any hope that I will settle in Scotland.
Dearly as I love my native land my dear relatives
and kind friends, still I cannot make up my mind to
return to Aberdeen. Even if I had money enough to
buy out the best baking establishment in that fine
city and were assured that I would do a good business, still I would not agree to engage in that trade
which cost me years of toil to learn. This I know is
talking rather independently for one of my size but
I have reasons for disliking that calling and I am
aware that giving up one calling and adopting
another is much more common and much less
thought of in America, than in Scotland. My highest
ambition at present is to realize enough money to
purchase a farm or start some business that may suit
my fancy and I know of no place at present that I
would prefer to Edwardsburg, Canada. There I have
many kind friends and it seems more like home than
any other place but more of this when I have more
time. . . .

James B. Thomson

Augt 1st
Dear Father
I am happy to inform you that we were not among
the sufferers by the great fire that destroyed our city
last march. We live about a mile and a half from
town although we are within the limits of the cor-

poration. You can form some idea of the rapidity
with which Nevada burnt when you consider that it
was built almost entirely of such boards as I described in a former letter. All traces of the fire have
now disappeared and a more showy although still
temporary class of buildings have taken the place of
those destroyed. Some of the stores are well filled up
and keep quite a variety of articles.

I think I mentioned in a former letter that I intended to go up north this summer to the Feather
river mines. There was so many big stories told of
the northern diggings that we were induced to start.
We left Nevada about the end of April and went
ninety miles up Feather river. Time prevents at
present giving you a detailed account of the journey.
Suffice it to say we spent two weeks and a good few
dollars and found nothing but returned to our
diggings satisfied that it is better to make a little
every day rather than spend what we had hunting
for a big pile, as hundreds have done and been unsuccessful.

We are still at work within a few hundred feet of
where we commenced December where by working
hard we make five or six dollars per day each. I have
now got nearly fifty ounces of the yellow ore worth
here sixteen dollars per oz. I should like to know
what it is worth at the London mint. At the United
States mints in Philadelphia and New Orleans it is
worth two or three dollars more than here.

Provisions are still getting cheaper. Our provision
bill now averages about an ounce a week for three
of us. There is three stores near us. They keep some
cows and milk is down to fifty cents per quart. I

have had pottage and milk several times only the meal is made from Indian corn instead of oats.

We have had no rain since april and do not expect any for two months more. The weather I might call very warm although I do not feel any more inconvenience from the heat than I have often felt in Canada or Chicago. There is generally a light breeze during the day and the nights are cool. We are considerably above the level of the sea. The drought is affecting our ditch. I am afraid it will fail before long. In that case we may be unable to wash for some time unless we can get some other diggings, and this section of country is pretty well dug over.

I and my friend McCargo at present talk about starting home next spring and here dear Father I would like a little of your advice as I can hardly bring my mind to the deciding point, whether to remain longer in California supposing I can make four times as much as I could any other place, or to return to more civilized society with my small savings and strugle through the world with a smaller income. I know that men in business often pass weary days and anxious nights when they have bills falling due and no funds to meet them, and farmers who owe part of the price of their farms generally have pretty hard times. Whatever business I may engage in I want to keep clear of debt. I have always avoided it yet excepting probably a week or a fortnights board. Now you can learn from this letter my situation, and I would be very thankful for your advice on the circumstances at your earliest convenience.

JT

Dear Father, I wish to send home a little cash and would have done so in that letter if I only knew that you could get it without too much trouble. The way I intended to do was to purchase a draft on the Rothschilds (they have a banking establishment in San Francisco), and have it payable at some of their houses in Great Britain. What I want to know if you can inform me is have the Rothschilds an agent in Aberdeen and if not would any of your bankers or merchants cash such a draft without charging too much discount. I have not very much money yet but I can spare fifteen or twenty £s well enough and as I understand that Sandy is still a plough man or engaged in some other employment but little more lucrative, I can nearly "guess" that his income is barely sufficient to maintain a family. I would therefore like to send home a little. You are now old and can't be able to do much hard work. I hope you will take the world easy keep yourself comfortable, and so long as God grants me health and strength and opportunities of making money as I have at present I shall ever be most happy to share with you for I feel that I shall never be able to repay the toil that you have undergone for me during my early years.

I remain your affectionate Son

James Thomson

To Alexander Thomson 25 November 1851

Nevada City Cal. Novr 25th 1851

My Dear Father
... I am sorry to say that one part of your last letter
has caused me considerable uneasiness. As however
you have hopes of being able to give a better account
next letter I shall not at present say what my feelings
prompt me to say of the conduct of a certain individual. In reguard to those dear little ones who are
now under your care I have only to say that I am
perfectly satisfied so long as you and Helen are their
guardians and if their natural protector neglects to
do his duty towards them I trust you will train them
up as the scriptures of truth direct, and allow me the
privilege of defraying the expenses of their bringing
up, for so long as my Creator enables me I shall
never see her childern want, who was to me both a
sister and a mother.

Dear Father, Inclosed I send you a draft on Adams &
Co or their agents in London for £20-Twenty pounds,
which I expect you can get cashed at some of the
Aberdeen banks. When you get the money I wish
you to give Sandy five pounds to help him to educate
his family. The balance will be for yourself, Helen,
and your little grandchildren. Please write me as
soon as convenient after you receive this, and let me
know whether you had much trouble in getting
the draft cashed. Perhaps I could remit money to
you through McPherson or some of my friends in
Canada, that you could draw more conveniently.

Do not be backward in calling on me for whatever
supplies you may want.

I cannot at present state any definite time when I
expect to leave California. Since Augt. we have been
able to do but little in the way of making money.
Not having water to wash more than an hour or two
each day, the balance of our time we occupied in
stripping and throwing up ground so as to have it
more convenient when we do get water. We have
fixed up our ditches and built a larger reservoir to
hold water during the night.

We have also built a new cabin close by our dig-
ings, and cut up a good pile of firewood. Our Cabin
is fourteen by sixteen feet built of logs and daubed
with clay. We have a window two feet square and a
large chimney with any quantity of wood for the
cutting. We have our beds ranged round the wall
like the berths in a ship. Two poles six feet long
thirty inches apart with a sheet of canvas stretched
between them makes a capital bed-stead. Our roof
is shingled with boards and is rain proof. Hundreds
of families in the back woods of Canada and the
Western States have less comfortable dwellings than
we now have.

Several of the provision dealers of Nevada have
now got wagons driving all round the city and
vicinity supplying their customers. We have only to
order today what we want tomorrow and it will be
delivered at city prices. Flour at present 12 dollars
pr 100 lbs Potatoes the same Hams 30 cents pr lb
fresh Beef 20 cts Butter in small kegs 60 cts pr lb
Onions 30 thirty cts Tea a dollar coffee 25 cts Sugar
12½ cts Molasses $2 pr gallon.

We can now buy good shovels steel blades long handles for 4 or 5 dols picks from 3 to 5 dols. For laying or steeling a pick a dollar each point, for sharping do. 25 cts. For use of grindstone to sharp an axe 25 cts. For use of cross cut saw a dollar pr day. Sheet iron 30 cts per lb inch bands 8 dollars pr 100 ft. at mill. We have put up a sluice lately for washing gold which took a thousand feet of boards. There is now four or five sawmills about Nevada.

In answer to a question in your last I have to say that in reguard to the banking institutions of California there is still great room for improvement. In San Francisco & Sacremento there are several respectable banking institutions such as Adams & Co who are connected with no [one] in the U. States or England. I suppose it would be perfectly safe to deposit money with them. They have agents in the principal towns throughout the mining districts, who are authorised to give drafts and receive deposits. There are also several merchants in Nevada who have fireproof money safes, and who take in money either coin or dust for safe keeping. They charge one pr cent pr month. They don't or at least have no right to use the money but merely keep it for you, and they return the same identical purse and money you deposited. There are also plenty of merchants and speculators who would borrow money at five pr cent pr month but unless one were well accquainted with the partners it might be difficult to get back the principal as it would be running great risk to take property as security.

I and my partners have hitherto kept our money by us. We don't go from home much unless to town

on Sundays and two or three lbs of gold dust is not
very bulky. If I conclude to remain in California
longer than next spring I shall endeavour to have
my money deposited in some safe place where it
will bring me interest. If I had it in Chicago it
would bring eight or ten pr ct pr annum. This will
leave by the steamer of 1st Decr. I am sorry you
cannot get it as a christmas present but I hope it will
reach you soon after your Aboyne new years day or
Handel monday.[1] With prayers for your welfare and
happiness I remain

Your affectionate son

James Thomson

We have had no rain yet to do any good only a
shower or two about fortnight ago but it will certainly come soon. The last few nights we have had a
slight frost. The days are still warm and pleasant,
but we look for signs of rain with as much anxiety
as the Jews of old did when the prophet ordered his
majesty Ahab to drive to Samaria lest the rain should
stop him.

There are now two churches in Nevada one
Presbyterian and one Methodist. I see by the papers
that there is a great many murders and roberies
throughout this country. Society about Nevada is
now pretty well civilized considering the mixture of
races, tongues and complexions of which it is composed. The Indians around here are friendly. They
seem afraid of the pale faces and unlike most Indians

1. Presumably an annual church music festival in Aboyne or
Aberdeen.

162

they neither steal nor beg much. Bands of them pass our house frequently but they seldom stop unless we talk to them. They can all say 'how do' and some can say 'good morning'. They mostly carry bows and arrows. Some few have got fire arms.

I can give you no information about the two men you mention from Birse. We are not very particular about names here. Dozens of men have worked for months within half a mile of me whose names I do not know. Besides you must recollect that California is a larger country than Great Britain and miners generally move about a good deal. . . .

J.T.

To Alexander Thomson 26 March 1852

March 26 [1852] Nevada Cal

Dear Father

... I sent you a letter by the mail of 1st of Decr.
inclosing a draft for twenty pounds on Edwards
Sandford & Co London agents of Adams & Co of
New York and San Francisco, which draft I hope
you have received and got cashed. In case it should
have been miscarried however I now send a dupli-
cate of it, which will be equally good, if No 1 has
not reached you.

You will think me a strange fellow when I inform
you that I am again a baker. Such however is the
case. I have personally given up mining for the present, although I still own interests in several mining
claims. On the 16th of last month my friend McCargo
and I bought one undivided half of the American
Bakery Nevada city. It is one of the oldest and most
extensive establishments of the kind in Nevada. I
hardly know how it will pay yet but we are doing a
pretty good business. I attend to the baking and
McCargo manages the mining claims. They are a
mile and half from town. We have invested all our
surplus money in mining claims, and have hired
some hands to work for us. The other half of the
Bakery is owned by two young men from the eastern
States. One of them stays here, the other is engaged
in mining along with McCargo.

Since the first of this month we have had a tremendous rain and snow storm. It commenced on
28th Feby and lasted nearly three weeks during the

first of march. It rained very hard day and night, the rivers rose rapidly and carried away many bridges and some houses and in the valley a great many cattle were carried off.

... The Oelt [?] although usually only a small brook rose to the magnitude of a mighty river. It carried away two bridges and two houses, and damaged several other buildings. We sustained but trifeling damage although the water stood ankle deep in our bake house one day. In consequence of the loss of bridges on most of the rivers we had no communication with the cities of the valley. The weather is again fine and the mail stages are commenced running.

By last mail I had letters from Mr & Mrs McPherson Edwardsburgh. My friends there were all well, railroads and canals are all the go in that section of country. Mac is doing a pretty large business. . . .

You will probably see by the newspapers that there is still a great rush of emigration to this state. A great many of those who have returned home are comming back and many of them bringing their families with them. Gambling is rapidly disappearing from our cities and the country generally is assuming more and more a settled and civilized appearance. . . .

James Thomson

To Alexander Thomson 24 June 1852

Nevada City Cal. June 24 1852

My Dear Father

By your last letter I am happy to learn that you were
all enjoying ordinary health and that the draft I sent
had arrived safe and that you had little trouble in
getting it cashed. I now inclose another draft on the
same parties (Adams & Cos. agents in London) for
fifty pounds, payable to your order. When you get it
cashed I wish you to send five pounds to Christina
Scott as I wish to make some presents to my Auchinblae friends. I had a letter from her two days ago
and I answered by the same mail this goes with. If
Sandy would rather rent a small farm than to follow
his present occupation, and could find a place to
suit him, where he could make a comfortable living
I wish him to have the balance of the draft and if I
succeed well in business I may probably be able to
send him a little more before next whitsunday. . . .

Today the Free masons are celebrating St. Johns
day. In the forenoon they walked in procession to
the church. They are now getting supper in the
Nevada Hotel and are to finish off with a grand
ball. . . .

I mentioned in my last letter that I had quit mining and gone to baking; I think I can do fully as
well at the latter occupation, and it is not so hard
work this warm weather, as I am not so much ex-
posed to the rays of a burning sun under a cloudless
sky. We do not get up so early as Aberdeen bakers,
but work more like white folks. We have a first rate

baker hired to whom we pay nine dollars per day.
He has been in this establishment two years although the place has changed proprietors two or
three times. McCargo & I own one half of the
bakery. I am most of my time in the bake house.
The young man who owns the other half attends the
shop. McCargo is still engaged in mining. I get half
what he makes mining he, half what I make baking.
We paid eleven hundred dollars for our half of
bakery. Up to this time we have got back the
money we paid out and pretty good wages for my
time besides, and the establishment is worth as
much as it was when we bought in.

We have bought several mining claims, some of
which will pay pretty well after a while. One lot of
claims we bought are on a hill side. They are from
thirty to forty feet deep. This spring they have
washed the whole hill side from top to bottom. It
pays very little until within three or four feet of the
granite or bed rock. Now the water is giving out
and they are going to run a tunnel into the hill and
drift out only the gravel that will pay well. McCargo
and I own one fourth of eighteen claims each thirty
feet square. We paid seven hundred dollars for our
interest and could now sell the same for two thousand dollars so there is a prospect that they will
pay pretty well for working them only we can't get
the gold out until next rainy season.

There is a great deal of mining done about Nevada by tunneling into the hills. The tunnels are
about four feet wide and five feet high. They run
them on a level until they strike the granate of bed
rock and then follow that taking out the gravel

167

immediately above the granite. They lay rails in the
bottom of the tunnel and run the gravel out in small
cars. This is found to be a cheaper plan than Sinking
shafts and hoisting by windlass. . . .

James Thomson

Address   American Bakery, Nevada City,
California, U.S.A.

To Alexander Thomson 9 September 1852

Nevada City Cal Sept 9 1852

. . . I wrote to you in time to go by the Steamer
leaving San Francisco on 28th of June or 1st of July,
inclosing a draft on Adams & Cos agent in London
for fifty pounds (£50) which I hope you have received and found all right. At same time I wrote to
Miss C. Scott. . . .

I am still baking in Nevada. In consequence of
want of water in many places for mining purposes,
a great many miners have gone to the rivers. Trade
is consequently somewhat dull, and flour is very
high in price at present. Two months ago it was
selling here at seven and eight dollars per 100 lbs or
sixteen dollars per barrel. Now it is worth thirty
eight dollars pr bbl and still tending upwards. In
consequence of foolish opposition on the part of
some of our neighbours we have not been able to
raise the price of bread in proportion to the advance
on flour, but I think the high price of flour will not
hold long as it is now about time for Chili flour of
present season to be getting in. We get some beautiful flour from Valparaso, Chili equal to the best
American brands. It comes in 100 lb sacks. We get
barrel flour from New York. It comes around Cape
Horn and is generally of excellent quality.

We came pretty near having another big fire in
Nevada a few nights ago. A hotel in the lower part
of town caught or was set on fire and completly
burned down, also four or five houses adjoining
including Adams & Cos Exchange office. Their vault

169

lately built stood the firey ordeal and saved their treasure, books & cc.

Deer Creek runs between the place where the fire broke out and the town, that and a light breeze blowing favourably was the means of saving Nevada.

We have just finished building a new oven cost five hundred dollars. We had to get the brick and lime from Sacremento City. Cartage three dollars pr 100 lbs.

My mining partner is this summer running a tunnel under a hill forty or fifty feet below the surface, they lay rails as they go along and wheel the gold bearing earth out in railway cars, to be ready for washing next winter.

Dear Father, excuse a short epistle this time as I have had sore eyes for the last few weeks. They are not yet entirely better, and reading or writing by candle light is rather unfavourable. . . .

I intend to leave California next spring, if every thing goes favourable till then, and if Providence permit. I will visit Scotland in the summer. . . .

James Thomson

To Alexander Thomson 20 January 1853

Nevada City Cal. Jany 20th 1853

Dear Father

. . . I want to know if you still climb the Cairn or cross Bulg and wade the water of Bervie when visiting the How o' the Mearns. I suppose, when the Deeside railway is in operation the iron horse will take you to Fordoun by way of Aberdeen much quicker and easier than you can go by the overland route. . . .

I have . . . had a letter and some Canadian papers from McPherson.

It is still my intention to return home next summer. If Providence favours my intentions I will leave California about the first of May. I intend to go to Canada. I wish you would write to me about the middle of May and address care of K. McPherson Edwardsburgh C.W. I expect to be there early in June.

We Californians have had a very severe winter. Provisions of all kinds have been very high. Flour has been up to fifty cents pr lb. one hundred dollars pr Barrel. We paid that figure for several Barrels. During last week we were almost at the starvation point, the weather and the roads were so bad that no supplies could be brought from the valley. The stock of provisions at the commencement of the rainy season was very light had the rain continued much longer we would have had pretty tight times. As it was, All the Bakeries in Nevada except the American had to suspend for want of

Flour, and last Friday we had the last of our Flour made into dough before the arrival of a new lot. The way the hungry miners crowded into our shop when the bread was comming out of the oven, it was something like old times in Egypt during the second seven years that Joseph was Prime Minister in the Land of Pyramids. During this week the weather is again fine, and the roads are improving. Flour is down to $30 pr 100 lbs. Board at the Hotels is twenty dollars pr week. A great many miners had to leave their mountain homes, and retreat to the lower regions.

You say you have to pay postage when you receive my letters, I am not sufficiently accquainted with the postal arrangements of G.B. and the U.S. to say that it is wrong to charge you anything on letters that I send, but it is my opinion they have no right to do so. Our postmaster never pretends to ask postage on prepaid letters from England or any other place. When I mail your letters I pay 29 cents (or as near to it as we can make change having no copper currency in this country) which is the same as you pay $1/2\frac{1}{2}$ sterling.

McPherson tells me that times are good in Canada they are to have a railroad the entire length of the province. They are beginning to imitate their go-a-head neighbours south of the St. Lawrence. I have written to Wm. Scott, Toronto but have never received any letter from him. I will write to my Auchinblae friends by this or next mail, two weeks hence. . . .

James Thomson

To James Thomson 26 February 1853
From Julia A. Akin, Edwardsburgh

Edwardsburgh, Feb. 26th 1853

Mr. Thompson

Dear Friend
It was with much pleasure that I received yours of
the 25th Dec yesterday morning, as I am always
happy to hear from a friend. You were no doubt not
a little surprised on hearing of the death of my
mother. We have met with a sad loss. Our home
seems lonely now. You say we have the sympathy
of all who knew her. I can assure you Mr. Thompson
that no one knew her but those that knew her well.
She seemed only to be happy when she could make
every one else the same. Ah! little did I think on that
bright Christmas morning when your letter came
and we were all enjoying ourselves so well that it
would be the last one she would spend with us. The
last letter she received from you was read times without number and even after she was taken sick I read
it several times for her.

I did think of writing to you as it was her wish
and again I thought you would think very strangely
of it. Mrs. McPherson is a naughty girl for telling
you. You say we may look for you home soon. I for
one would most gladly welcome you home but if
nothing happens more then I know of now to prevent me, I shall leave home for the Western country
about the time that you leave California and in all
probability will never have the pleasure of seeing
you again.

Your friends in this place are all enjoying very good health. We attended a temperance meeting in the school house on Thursday evening. There was some of the gentleman from Prescott there and Mr. McPherson gave us a speech. Mr G. Anderson also. In his speech in speaking of the ladies he said he had once heard it remarked that one lady could do more for the cause than $13\frac{1}{2}$ gentleman. So you see your temperance lecture is not forgotten.

I suppose Mr McP. will write you all the news. As I am not much accustomed to writing, anything I can write will not be very interesting but as you said a 'few lines would be welcome' I thought I would do the best I could.

Good bye

With many kind wishes for your safe return, I am Your Friend

Julia A. Akin

To Alexander Thomson 14 March 1853

San Francisco, Cala March 14 1853

My Dear Father
Enclosed I send you a draft on Adams & Cos Agent,
London for (Five Hundred Dollars) one hundred
pounds payable to your order. Please get the check
cashed and take care of the money for me till I
come home.

I am now homeward bound two hundred and fifty
miles from Nevada. I left the Mountain City early
on Tuesday morning last per stage couch and
reached Sacremento City (75) miles same evening,
left Sacremento at 2 p.m. on wednesday pr steamer
and arrived in this city same evening at 10 p.m.
distance 180 miles.

I have not yet taken my passage to the East. One
boat the Pacific leaves tomorrow morning for San
Juan, the Nicaragua route, and the Mail boat Golden
Gate leaves the following day by way of Panama.
The fare either way is pretty high this trip, the
opposition Line to Panama having no boat going
this time. I would prefer the Nicaragua route, but the
Panama boat is far the best. The Golden Gate is the
finest boat on the Pacific Ocean, she is 2500 tons
burden 1600 horse power, and is a regular floating
palace. The fare on either boat is 350 dollars first
cabin $250 second $175 steerage, that is for through
tickets from San Francisco to New York. My Friend
John Allan who crossed the Atlantic with me in "44"
is to accompany me home. Wheeler my partner in
the American Bakery is also along with us. He goes

175

to State of New York, also several other accquaint-
ences. Some are in favour of one route some the
other, we must decide this evening. . . .

Tell my Auchenblae friends that I have not forgot
them although I have not answered their letters. I
am taking the Irishmans plan, bringing the letter
myself to save postage.

Please write to me on receipt of this, at Edwardsburg, C.W.

James Thomson

4 Oclock p m   We have just purchased our tickets on
board the "Pacific" $275 : 00 through to New York
including transit from ocean to ocean accross
Nicaragua.

My Friend McCargo could not arrange his business so as to go home. He is to stay another year.

If all goes well I will be in New York before this
letter.

As I do not think it advisable to carry much
money with me I have purchased drafts on Adams &
Co & Wells Fargo & Co and sent duplicates of them
to McPherson with instructions that if I should step
accross the narrow line that divides time from
eternity, he will forward my worldly possessions to
you.

Hoping however that we will yet meet in this
world, I am as ever Affectionately, Your son

James Thomson

A VISIT TO SCOTLAND

To Alexander Thomson 12 April 1853

New York City April 12th 1853

Dear Father

As I learn that the English mail leaves here today, I
thought I would write you a few lines to let you
know that I had got this far all well.

I sailed from San Francisco on the 15th March on
board the Steamer "Pacific". Arrived at San Juan del
Luce on the 27th, crossed the Isthmus of Nicaragua
in $2\frac{1}{2}$ days, sailed from San Juan del Norte on the
31st, put in to Charleston S. Carolina for coal on the
7th April and arrived in this city on the 10th. We had
a pleasant passage on both oceans, and no sickness
beyond that common to land sharks, when they
travel on Neptunes dominions. My friend Allan is
along, we are going to Canada tomorrow.

I wrote to you from San Francisco (by the mail
Steamer which left same time as I did) enclosing a
draft on Adams & Co for one hundred pounds which
I hope you have received. I cannot say exactly when
I shall sail for Scotland. I want to stay a few weeks
in Canada. I will go and see Wm. Scott. I shall probably be at Aboyne some time in June.

James Thomson

[Enclosure ?]

New York   April 13, 1853

Mr. J. B. Thompson

To Robert Rait Dr.
JEWELLER
No. 261 Broadway Cor Warren Street

Gold Patent Lever Watch
Hunting Case 5 prs Jewels Chro Ball
18 K No 627-36540   125.
Solid Gold vest chain   28.

                                           $153.

Received paymt

R. Rait

JK

Warranted

To Alexander Thomson 15 June 1853

Steam Ship Europa at Sea June 15th 1853

Dear Father

At noon today we are seven days out from Boston.
The officers of the ship calculate that we are nine-
teen hundred miles from that port and nine hundred
from Liverpool. We came by way of Halifax N.S. So
far we have had a very pleasant voyage, wind favourable most of the time and nothing like a storm.
During the last twenty four hours we have made
302 miles. If the weather keeps favourable we will
be in Liverpool on Saturday afternoon or Sunday
morning.

I intend to mail this on my arrival at Liverpool
and shall probably get to Aboyne 24 hours after this
letter. . . .

Your letter of 2nd May arrived at Edwardsburg on
the 23rd and I left that place on the 25th intending to
have sailed from New York on the first of June. But
when I got there I found that the Steamer sailing on
that day had her full complement of passengers engaged, so the next best move for me was to go to
Boston and secure passage on the Europa for the
8th of June. She also has a full complement of passengers, among the number is two clergymen Rev
Mr. Irvine of Toronto and Rev Mr. Kirk of Boston.
The former read prayers and the latter preached
twice last Sunday.

We have also Chief Justice Shaw of the U.S. and
Mr. Anderson the Wizard of the North. We have
several Canadians on board a good many Americans,

some English Scotch French and Jews. Although made up of a mixed multitude we have so far been an agreeable social party. Right at my elbow just now there is a jew and a christian playing a game of chequers (damboard). Out on the decks a party of Americans and English are playing against each other at a game similar to curling. On the opposite side of the table from me, sits a Sister of Charity (Nun) reading her rosary and counting her beads. Others are employed various ways, some reading, some writing, some playing cards, some chatting and some walking the decks.

Since we sailed the weather has been quite cold.

Thursday June 17 Noon.   Since noon yesterday we have made 291 miles, wind still favourable. Hopes are entertained that we will make Liverpool by noon Saturday. We are to run the north channel that is keep to the north of Ireland, and go down the Irish channel between Ireland & Scotland Friday noon. Since this time yesterday $23\frac{1}{2}$ hours we have sailed 310 miles, having fair wind. This morning we had some rain but soon after breakfast it cleared up and we have had a stiff gale since at present there is a pretty high sea running. We have one Lady on board who has got her face washed today for the first time since we left Boston. I mean Madame Europe, the figure head of our gallant vessel. She has kissed the Atlantic more than once this forenoon, but she is walking through the white capped billows at the rate of fourteen miles an hour. Before sun down we expect to see land.

Emerald Isle Friday 7 p.m. Two hours ago we

hove in sight of land. We are now running in between the Irish mainland and the small island of
Torry.

Saturday noon.   This has been a very rough morning. I enjoyed once more the luxury of Sea Sickness.
We have got out of the rough water. It is high water
at Liverpool at $\frac{1}{2}$ past 8 this eve and it is doubtful if
we will get in before that time. I hope to be home
on Wednesday.

Your affectionate Son

James Thomson

To James Thomson July 1853
From John Macpherson, Dingwall, Scotland

Dingwall July 1853

Dear Sir

I was favoured with your kind and obliging letter
dated 18th and return you most affectionatly my
most sincere thanks for the very explicit detail that
you gave me respecting my Son Kenneth his spouse
and young promising family and the improvement
in the way of his business which gave me infinite
pleasure. And I am happy to intimate that my dear
Son from his Infant days was a great favourite of
mine. His disposition was so very agreable to me
that I never remember to give him so much as a
reprimand as from his Infancy. Untill he parted
with me to his destination presently in Canada he
always returned my Silent love and regard and it
gives me infinite pleasure that Providence was
graciously pleased to provide for him such a suitable Companion as she indeed writes an excellent
and gramatical letter so that I understand that she
got a Liberal Education.

My affectionate Son writes me in as dutifully
manner as any Parent could wish from a Child.
Happy would I be to see one sight of him but that I
never expect while upon this side of time as my few
remaining days is now drawing near to a close.
When you return to Canada very probably you intend to commence for yourself and if so is your de-
termination it is my most ardent wish that prosperity may attend your undertaking. And I am most

happy to understand that you and my dear son were on such friendly terms while you had been together. When you arrive at Canada you will please remember me in the kindest manner to my dear Son his worthy spouse and my dear and promising young Grand Children. The wellfare of all of them is my esential request at the Throne of grace.

My hand is now getting very nervous but I have great reason of thankfullness that my faculties is not in the least impaired. It was a day that I could write a pretty good letter for myself and others but there is many infirmities attending old age. But it surprises many that a Person of 81 years of age would be able to write a single letter.

As I have nothing further of any importance worth to communicate at present I therefore conclude with my greatest regards and esteem and I ever remain, Dear Sir, your's very Sincerely

John Macpherson Senr

Please excuse an old nervous hand of write

James Thomson: Diary Form
12 October 1853

Aboyne. Aberdeen-shire October 12th 1853

Left this morning at 6:30 pr coach, arrived at Banchory at 8. Left pr Deeside railway at 8:30 and arrived at Aberdeen at 9:30. Had breakfast at Wm Ewens, called on James Dunn, Mr F Patterson—Miss Shanks—North of Scotland Bank—met David Scott had dinner went to Ferryhill station and left for Fordoun per railway at 2:33 p.m. arrived at Fordoun Station at 3:30 walked to Auchinblae called on Miss Walker Messrs Annandale Mr & Mrs Scott stopped all night with Aunt.

Oct 13th.   Bade adieu to Auchinblae friends walked to station, goodby to Sister and cousin and at ten a.m. started for Glasgow arrived 3 p.m. Put up at Albion Hotel Argyle Street, went to the office of Messrs Burns agents for Cunard Mail Steamers was told they could engage no more passengers as the berths on the 'Niagara' for Halifax and Boston to sail on 15th inst were all engaged—didn't know very well what to do under these circumstances.

New York.   My previous calculations were now knocked on the head, and I had to choose one of three courses either go to Liverpool and wait for the next Steamer return home till I could get a Steamer. Or take the first sailing vessel from Glasgow.

The former of these would be very expensive as the next mail steamer would go to New York 2nd

cabin £20. The second course I could not think of as
I had so lately parted with relatives and friends to
return home and in a week or two have another
farewell scene was out of the question. So I resolved
on adopting the latter course and looking over the
Glasgow newspapers I saw by advertisement that
the Harlequin, Capt. Logan was to sail on the 15th
for New York. As the time would suit me I went to
the agents and engaged my passage.

From the time I left the Fordoun station all along
the railway I felt very low in spirits. I felt as if I were
again alone in this cold unfeeling world, and even
the bustle and excitement of crowded streets of
Glasgow could not rouse me from my lethargy. I
then wished for 'a lodge in some vast wilderness'. I
felt more lonely in those crowded streets than ever I
did in the backwoods of Canada. Happy they who
live a country life enjoying the pure air of heaven
and beholding the beauties of Nature, far away from
the din and bustle, the squalor and misery of great
cities. Let me not envy the rich or great for there is
splendid misery, as well as squalid misery. But if
Providence will bless me with competence as the
fruit of my labour, and with health to enable me to
labour, I shall endeavour to be contented, and surely
contentment is happiness as far as happiness can be
obtained in this ever changing world of ours.

Went to the Theatre regal in the evening to see
'macbeth'. The largest company of performers I ever
saw, the witch scene done with splendid effect
scenery very fine and combat between Macbeth and
Macduff well done.

Friday 14th. Got luggage on board Harlequine,
bought Siberian coat 34/ and some other small purchases, wandered through the streets of Glasgow
Argyle Buchanan Union Jamaica Fren Gallowgate
Saltmarket Greene & co. In order to pass time and
drive away dull care visited the circus performing
very good burlesque political speech by the clown
excellent, house crowded.

Saturday 15th. Settled bill at Albion hotel, wrote to
father. Got on board, sailed about eleven a.m.
Towed down to Greenock by steamer. Had fine
opportunity of seeing the numerous shipbuilding
yards on the Clyde. Immense numbers of iron
vessels.

To Alexander Thomson, 15 October 1853

Glasgow Sat. morning 15th

Dear Father
. . . I have now engaged to go with a Sailing vessel
from Glasgow. She sails at 9 oclock this morning—
she is a large vessel called the Harlequin and has
only about a dozen passengers. I have written this so
you might not be expecting a letter from America so
soon as if I had gone by Steam.

I remain your Affectionate Son

James Thomson

To Alexander Thomson 17 October 1853

Fritto of Clyde Oct 17th 1853

Dear Father

On Saturday morning I got on Board the Barque
Harlequin and sailed from Glasgow. A steamer
towed us down to Greenock but the wind was blowing strong from the west and we could not get out
of the Clyde. We anchored off Greenock until this
morning at daylight. The weather is now fine we
are a long way down the frith. There is a boat comming along side, by which I intend to send this. I
am the only cabin passenger on board I have a comfortable room and all my luggage beside me. The
captain and mate seem very fine steady fellows. The
captains wife and child came down the river with us
and staid aboard till this morning. The Harlequin is
a very good sailer and if we get good weather, I
trust we will make a quick passage. For these and all
other blessings we must look to Providence. The
captain is a strick observer of the Sabbath, as far as
his profession will allow and we have a library of
good books on board.

No more time at present, but remain Your
Affectionate Son

James Thomson

To Alexander Thomson 18 November 1853

At Sea Lat 41° Long. 72°

Novr. 18, 1853

Dear Father

As we are now within about 130 miles of New York, and the Harlequin not quite so much disposed to roll as she has been during the greater part of the voyage, I resolved on writing a little this afternoon as I may not have much time in N.Y.

We have had a very boisterous and in some respects rather disagreeable passage although considering the season of the year not more so than I expected, and to all appearance it is not likely to be a very long one. At present we are almost becalmed but if we get anything of a favourable breeze tonight we expect to get into N.Y. tomorrow (Saturday). That will be five weeks from Glasgow.

The Harlequin is a large barque and a pretty fast sailer. She has 650 tons pig iron aboard which is a bad cargo in rough weather. She rolled and pitched about awfully nearly the whole time. We have not had half a dozen fine days since we left Greenock. I suffered a good deal from sea sickness but am quite well now. I suppose I deserved a little extra touch of sickness for being so foolish as to cross the north Atlantic at this season of the year, and that too in a vessel loaded with pig iron, but if I was unfortunate in regard to time and cargo I was fortunate in having a very agreeable Capt. and mate. They are both young men the former a Scotchman and the latter a Welchman. We have a library of religious books

189

furnished by the Glasgow Seamens Friend Society,
and the Capt has a good many fine books of his own.
To hear some shipmasters a person would almost be
inclined to think that sailors could not be managed
without a daily allowance of grog and an hourly
allowance of swear[ing], but Capt. Logan and Mr
James can manage their crew nicely without having
recourse to either of those practices.

We have a second mate, carpenter, steward, cook
and eighteen seamen, twelve steerage passengers
(Irish). They pay £3.10/ each adult, and get each 5 lb
oatmeal 3 lb flour 2 lb Rice 1 lb Sugar (2 oz Tea or
4 oz Coffee) weekly and 3 quarts of water daily.

Two children under fourteen years of age are
considered as one adult, children under one year of
age are charged no passage and get no allowances
from the ship. There is an act of Parlement regulat-
ing all these things. Each passenger gets a contract
ticket from the owners of the vessel, stating what
allowance they are to receive and the law imposes a
heavy fine if the contract be not fulfilled. If Sandy
sails from Aberdeen he will have to find out whether
the ships from there give any provisions. Even if
they give the same as the Glasgow ships, still passengers would want some of their own, and if they
give none, the price of passage will be so much less.

For a voyage from Great Britain to North America
the law requires each ship to have a suficient quantity of provisions and water for all on board for eight
weeks for a summer voyage and for ten weeks for a
winter voyage. The latter includes vessels sailing
between the middle of October and middle of March,
and where passengers furnish their own provisions

I suppose they will be required to have a suficient quantity for the same length of time. If the Aberdeen ships are the same as when I sailed from there, Sandy would have to engage four passages and would receive three gallons of water daily. He would require to have about 400 lb. provisions. They will know better than I can how much they will eat in eight weeks (the voyage may not be so long, but it is better to err on the safe side). I think something like the following would be a pretty good assortment

1 Boll[1] Oatmeal, $\frac{1}{2}$ cwt Fine Ship Biscuit, 2 Bushels Potatoes $\frac{1}{2}$ cwt Beef Ham & Fish, 28 lbs Butter Cheese & Treacle, some Tea, Sugar, Salt, Pepper. Medicine of some kind, some jelly or jam such as cranberries if they are sour all the better, some cream of tartar or vinegar helps the water a good deal, some bannocks or cakes baked thin and well fired would keep nicely. The white iron flask or can to hold 3 gallons water. A tea kettle to hook on front of grate to be got in any tin smiths shop about the shore. Most dishes to be used on board will have to be got at the tin smiths or ship chandlers.

Saturday Novr 19th 4 o'clock p.m.   Since noon yesterday we have had thick foggy weather. From the soundings (yesterday 50 fathoms today 14 and green grass at the lead when hauled up) we must be near land and are now knocking about in hopes of its clearing up so we can get a pilot.

In exchange for the heather I carried off I send you a small piece of grass from the bottom of the Atlantic forty five miles from N. Y.

1. A Scottish measure.

Monday 21st.   Yesterday we got a pilot but have
had a head wind since so that we have made very
little progress. . . . I intend to make my way to
Edwardsburg as soon as possible

James Thomson

To Helen Thomson 21 November 1853

[Nov 21, 1853]   Aboard Harlequin
off New York

Dear Sister

. . . Monday evening 6 o clock.   We have just taken
tea, a little after dinner we got in tow of a steamboat
and are now close to the city, we can see the lights
plain and could see the steeples before dark. I will
stay aboard tonight and be ready for a fresh start
tomorrow. Five hundred miles of railroad will carry
me to Ogdensburg, two miles steamboat across the
St Lawrence to Prescott, nine miles by perhaps a
farmers waggon to Edwardsburg where I will feel
myself pretty much at home.

I have got some oat cake yet for Lilly, but it was
all I could do to keep from eating it when I was sea
sick, I could not look at anything else unless Agnes'
brandy. It is all done long ago but I have saved the
bottle for the good it did. Mrs. Ewens present was
also very good, it helped to take the bad taste out of
my mouth. I would have given a good deal for some
of Lizzy Middletons billberries. The Capt had some
jelly but it was too sweet. We are now moored at
New York and I trust the balance of my journey will
be completed in ten days. . . .

James Thomson

SETTLING IN EDWARDSBURGH

To James Thomson 31 December 1853
From William Scott, Mimicoke

Mimicoke, 31° Decr, 1853

We have received your epistle of the 5th inst and are
right glad to hear that you are again safely moored
in Edwardsburgh,—not having heard from you
directly since you wrote us from Boston on the eve
of your departure for Europe per the Europa. . . . We
received a letter from my sister . . . which informed
us that you were then rusticating in the Highlands.
. . . Now my dear James, if you come here, which I
hope you will do soon, try and make arrangements
for more than a flying visit.

With regard to taking you as an apprentice I suppose there is not a farmer in Upper Canada, I mean
a real farmer who would not be proud of such a
recruit. If you determine to follow that profession all
assistance in my power to give shall be willingly
rendered. I am not acquainted with the country in
your immediate vicinity but from what I hear as
well as the little I have seen of it I should not chose
it for farming in. I should not take the course of the
St. Lawrence further down than Kingston. The
prices you mention for land however is very low
(which is certainly some consideration provided
there is a fair prospect of their advancing in value).

There has been quite a land fever in this part of the
Province this year. . . .

Your affectionate friends,

W & Mary Scott

N.B. If you are not coming up the country immediately, write and say when we may expect you. The
children are all in a fervour to see this man that has
been to Scotland and back again.

W.B.S.

To Alexander Thomson 4 January 1854

Edwardsburg C.W. January 4th 1854

Dear Father

... On arrival at N. York we had to cast anchor some distance from the wharves as the Capt had some difficulty in getting a berth for this ship on account of the crowded state of the harbour. I spent one day in the City, visited the Crystal palace,[1] and the following morning got my luggage ashore and to the railroad depot and started at noon by way of Troy, Rutland, Burlington, Rouses Point, and Ogdenburgh. From the time I left Fordoun until my arrival at Ogdensburgh I had not seen a kent[2] face. At O. I met an old friend who gave me a nights lodgings, crossed the St Lawrence with me the following day and drove me down to McPhersons where I was received with the utmost kindness and hospitality. I am still living with Mac.

I had no trouble with my luggage. The Custom House officers both at N.Y. and Prescott took my word that I had nothing to sell so that I did not even have to open my chest at each of those places. I went to the Custom House and reported my luggage and had no more trouble.

Shortly after my arrival here I wrote to Wm Scott and have just received an answer. They are all well

1. The Crystal Palace in New York was built for an exposition in 1853 intended to rival the Great London Exhibition of 1851, but it was a financial failure. In 1854 P. T. Barnum, the showman, tried unsuccessfully to revive it. The glass structure in New York burned during the 1850s.
2. Scottish dialect meaning 'known'.

and invite me up to stay a while. I wrote to Wm for his opinion as to the best part of Canada to settle. He does not know much about this part of the country but thinks it is better farming land above Kingston. Land in this part of the country is rising in value but it can yet be bought much cheaper than in the Upper part of the Province. There, railroads and land speculation is the order of the day. In the present state of excitement on the subject I do not think it would be advisable to purchase in that part of Canada. Wm says that land is three times the price it is about Edwardsburgh. He says, 'a great part of this estate has changed hands since your last visit at prices varying from £7.10/ to £17 per acre and these are now considered very good bargains and there are farms in this neighbourhood for which £20 per acre has been refused.'

Now about here good farms nearby all cleared can be bought for £5 pr acre. The farmers here certainly do not have so much wheat to dispose of as they have farther up the country, but I think that is as much the fault of the farmers as of the soil, and there is one grand consideration in favour of this place, it is generally very healthy. I have been looking at two or three farms that are for sale in this Township but have not yet made a purchase. My old friends here are all anxious that I should settle among them. Last week I was down at Cornwall (forty miles below this place) visiting my old employer Mr Elliot Contractor. He is now Mayor of Cornwall and has fine mills at that place. He wishes me to go to store keeping there, but I would prefer owning a farm, and as I have a good many friends about here, I would rather incline to settle in this part of Canada.

We have only a few inches of snow yet just enough to make good sleighing, and the jingling of the merry sleigh bells along the road gives proof that many holiday parties are taking that mode of enjoying themselves. I have had my share of sleighriding. That you may have some idea of how some folks drive on the winter roads I may mention that Mr Elliots son came up here from Cornwall on Saturday 24 Decr with a pair of horses and light sleigh. On Monday 26th he and I went down to Cornwall. Tuesday and Wednesday afternoon, we drove about Cornwall ten or twelve miles out and back. On Thursday morning at day light Mr Elliot and I started for Edwardsburgh with the same horses and sleigh. Drove to Matilda 36 miles in four hours, left the horses there to feed. Got some breakfast before we started and some at Matilda where Mr Elliots brother resides. Got fresh horses to Edwardsburgh. Mr E. stopped a few minutes here went back to Matilda, got his own horses and got home same evening. On the following Saturday he was here again by the middle of the day and same evening drove to Brockville 21 miles above this. There are few people in Canada keep better horses than Elliot and none that drive harder, but he feeds well and keeps them in good order and never allows them to go beyond a trot. Would not have them to gallop in harnass for all they are worth.

Times are good in Canada, and I think will continue so for some time. At any rate there will be plenty of employment next summer for all that are

willing to work. I have no doubt from what I have
seen and heard from all classes in this country that if
Sandy were out here and liked the place he would
do better than in Scotland, and I have never seen any
person who has been here three or four years but
what likes Canada, and if he decides on comming
here I shall see that he has a house to go in to on
arrival. . . .

James Thomson

We had a very severe visit from him, [John Frost]
last week. When comming from Cornwall I had my
cheeks a little frost bit they are now better.

To James Thomson 12 February 1854
From William M. Halsey and
John McCargo, Nevada City

Nevada City Feby 12th 1854

'Friend Jamie'
Your Most Welcome Letter bearing date Dec 12th
was by Mr McCargo Recieved Yesterday and being
very busy himself, and Knowing you Would be very
anxious To Recieve The answer He was depudised
—or I may say, in his usual goode natured Way
Wheedled me into Answering for him. I will therefore in his Name give you all The news wich at
present is Considerable. . . .
    Nevada is still the same old Town, that is about
Main Street. Since you Left there has been a great
Many improvements—for instance, Wells Fargo &
Co W. H Davis & Co Now do business in Brick
Stores built on the site of their old Places also
Espincide, who has a very Pretty Brick Corner.
Frisbie has added a Large Building called the Con-
cert Hall, also a Small Brick Store House, to his old
place. We also have a Large Number of New Frame
Houses on the Outskirts Besides a Number of New
ones in Town. The Town Folk have complained
Bitterly for the Last 3 Month, at the harde times. For
the Rainy Season this year did not Commence
Untill within 8 weeks. However Mony is somewhat
scarce yet. To day We are in the midst of a Heavy
snow Storm. Evening Before Last, we Experienced
a very hard Rain storm. 2 Weeks ago we had about
3 feet of snow, and if it continues on in this Way—

for a month or two More, there Will be Water a
Plenty for Every Purpose. John, George Warren and
Myself Expect to Leave for home in July next, at
Least I am sure of going—and as John will add a
Postscript to this. I will leave him to speak for him-
self.

Before I close I must tell you of an Effort that has
been made in this Place Within the Last few weeks.
To organise a City Government, an Election took
Place, and Trustees appointed at the same time—
Foster of Candy celiberty was appointed asseser, and
King the Gambler, City Marshall. The City Limits
are one Mile Square—How Much further The thing
progressed I am not at Present aware—I will now
close and you must not be vexed although I dare say
you will Laugh at the idea of John making me his
Medium—Wherby To Communicate To you—You
Know That Spiritual Manafestation are all the Rage
Now a days and I suppose John thought the Effect
would be the same with you—as if he had indited
this with his own Hand—The Boys all Beg to Be
Remembered

Your Truly

Wm M. Halsey

P.S Thompson you will have to excuse me for not
writing to you myself. Bill Halsy has given you more
news than I possibly could. We washed out this
week eight hundred dollars in two days and half. I
trust we will keep doing so and then for home in
June or July. If you see Mother before that time, you
can tell her she will see [me] then if living. I seen

Allen but did not speak to him and as for Lewis
boys I will make all enquiries and let you know
   Give my best respects to McPherson and family
and not forgeting yourself old Friend John
[McCargo]

To Helen Thomson 25 February 1854

Edwardsburgh Feby 25th 1854

My Dear Sister

. . . This is the season of the year for making visits
in this country but not in Scotland, at least some of
the Glasgow folks who were about to visit Aberdeen
found that to be the case, when they ran into a
twenty foot Snow bank at Laurence Kirk. I see by
the Herald which comes regularly and for which I
thank you, that you have had a very severe snow
storm. We in Canada have had very little snow as
yet, just enough to make good sleighing. We have
had very hard frost since Christmas in fact some of
coldest weather that has been in many years but I
have stood it about as well as those who never were
out of Canada. I had a slight cold last week but got
all right again in a few days. I am in very comfortable lodgings this winter and all my old friends are
very kind. . . .

I have been looking after several farms in this
neighbourhood but have not yet made a bargain for
any. I offered 650 pounds for a hundred acres fronting
the river St Lawrence about two miles below this
place. There is a good stone house and a fine orchard of apple and cherry trees on the farm. My
offer has not yet been accepted. The place could
have been bought for less money a few years ago,
but Land is rising rapidly in this country and at
present the people are all excited on the subject of
railways so that very few along the front of the river
are disposed to sell farms. I have the offer of a

hundred acres about one half of it cleared lying
about 6 miles back from the river, for £200 Sterling,
and I have been looking after two or three other
places, but I think I will let them alone for the
present.

I have, in company with an accquaintence, taken
a contract on the Grand Trunk Railway, to be built
through this part of the country next summer. We
have taken three miles and if we can succeed well
with that we have the promise of as much more
as we can do. Our Section is in the Township of
Matilda, seven or eight miles down the river from
this place, and from a half to three quarters of a mile
back from the river. We closed the bargain last
night, and we must commence work immediately,
at least must get out fencing timber as that can only
be done to advantage when there is snow on the
ground. . . .

About Sandy bringing bedclothes or such articles
as would not be damaged by crushing in pack sheets
I should think it would do well enough, at anyrate I
think there would be little risk in an Aberdeen ship
if the passengers were as honest as when I came.
Write on receipt of this and let me know when and
what vessel Sandy intends comming with &c. . . .

James Thomson

To Mary Armstrong 2 April 1854
From James Thomson, Edwardsburgh

Edwardsburgh April 2nd 1854

Miss Armstrong at Mr. Raymond's, Ogdensburgh,
N.Y.

Dear Mary[1]
I thank you for a newspaper just received and especially for the kind wishes for my welfare which
accompany the paper. I hope you are enjoying good
health and every other blessing.

I cannot hope that thou be freed
From woes to all since earliest time decreed;
But may'st thou be with resignation blessed
To bear each evil howsoe'er distressed.

May Hope her anchor lend amid the storm,
And o'er the tempest seal her angel form;
May sweet Benevolence, whose words are peace,
To the rude whirlwind, softly whisper cease.

And may Religion, Heaven's own darling child,
Teach thee at human cares and griefs to smile,
Teach thee to look beyond that world of woe
To Heavens high fount whence mercies ever flow.

And when this vale of tears is safely passed,
When deaths dark curtain shuts the scene at last

1. The daughter of Henry Armstrong, a farmer of Edwardsburgh,
and later Thomson's wife. Armstrong owned a small farm and saw
mill at the head of the Galops Rapids. His grandfather, said to have
served with General Burgoyne, bought land in Upper Canada in
1801.

May thy freed spirit leave this earthly sod
And fly to seek the bosom of thy God.

Mary, I ought to give you some Edwardsburgh
news but really you must excuse me as I have been
living in Matilda lately and only came up here last
night. I hope you will also excuse me for writing
letters on Sunday.

The Sons of Temperance Edwardsburgh Division
held a grand Soiree here on the 15th of last month,
but as circumstances prevented me from attending I
cannot give you the particulars only I believe it went
off well. For some time before it took place we were
all anticipating the pleasure of spending a happy
evening in promoting the cause of Temperence. I
had a letter written to you soliciting the favour of
your company on that occasion, when an unexpected
dispensation of Providence took place, which prevented me from attending, and forcibly reminded
me of the vanity of all human calculations in regard
of future happiness. A few days before the Soiree
took place sickness and death entered the family in
which I reside and took away one of its members in
the morning of life like an early flower blighted by
the frosts of spring.

I am sorry to inform you that Mr McPhersons
eldest boy died on the 13th and was buried on the
15th of March, aged five years.

Mary, I trust you will write to me on receipt of
this. Don't take example by me in regard to writing.
I have been very lazy but trust for pardon to your
forgiving disposition. Say how you are, when you

intend comming home &c. You know what to say
well enough.

I expect to be in Matilda most of the summer, but
will visit Edwardsburgh occasionally.

Hoping the time for your return to Canada will
soon arrive, and wishing you health and happiness.
I am

Yours respectfully

James Thomson

Address   Matilda, C.W.

To Alexander Thomson 11 April 1854

Edwardsburgh April 11th 1854

Dear Father

A few weeks ago I received a letter from Sandy
stating that he was short of money and as he wished
to come to Canada by the Spring vessels, I wrote to
him to try and borrow ten pounds on my account.
As I could not then conveniently get a draft, to
reach him in time to be of use in April, I hope he has
been enabled to make raise of the necessary funds
and I shall expect to hear of his having sailed in a
short time.

I now enclose payable to your order a draft on
Anderson, Fordyce & Co. Glasgow for ten pounds,
for Sandy, or to pay what I authorized him to borrow
if he has done so. You will see their address on the
draft. Write your name on the back of the draft and
send it to Glasgow. They will remit the money or an
order on some of the banks. Perhaps Mr Ogg will
be kind enough to assist you in the matter.

Since writing to you last I have purchased a farm,
within $\frac{1}{2}$ a mile of this village. The farm contains
one hundred and fifty acres, fronting on the River
St Lawrence. There is a pretty good house and barn
on it. I will give you a more lengthy description of
it some other time. I have got the deed, and took
possession the third of this month, but as I am busy
with the Railroad, I do not intend to live on the farm
this summer, nor do much with it farther than having a few acres ploughed and put under crop. I pay
for the farm at the rate of five pounds fifteen shillings

209

per acre in all £862,10/ of which I have paid £500 and the balance in three equal yearly instalments.

For the last few weeks I have been most of the time back in the woods in the Township of Matilda, getting out Cedar timber to fence the Grand Trunk Railway. We have the fencing as well as grading of five miles, and as we could not do anything at the Grading until the frost gets out of the ground, we have been getting out all the materials we could. . . .

James Thomson

To James Thomson 22 May 1854
From Alexander Thomson, Bridge End, Aboyne

Bridge end Aboyne May 22nd 1854

My Dear James
I received yours of the 11th April in due time with a
draft for ten pounds. I aplied to Mr Ogg and he sent
it to Aberdeen to there head office and they sent it to
Glasgow and Anderson & Co have remited an order
on the North of Scotland Bank and Mr Ogg received
a letter requesting him to pay me the money and I
have deposited it with him in the North of Scotland
Bank untill such time as Sandy may need it.
    I suppose before this time you have received
Hellens letter leting you know that Sandy could not
get money to take them all out with the April ships
and I much dout he will not be able to start with the
August ships. About the time that you left Aboyne
when he was resolved to go to Canada I thought he
had been possessed of fifteen or twenty pounds of
the money you give him before. But when it came
to be needed he had none of it to produce and I was
not able to give him so much as to take him out. I
do not think he can save much through the summer
as provisions of all kinds is very dear at present and
I do not think that he takes very good care of money
when he has it, for I cannot see how he could have
spent so much money in so short a time. But I shall
endeaviour to keep this ten pounds in the Bank till
such time as I see that he has as much collected as
will take them out when the ten pounds is added to
it. If its not needed it can be returned.

I am glad that you have got such a large farm so
near your village and so many of your acquantance.
If it is a good one you may do very well with it but
if a bad one you have too much of it.

I take it to be pounds sterling you payd for it per
acre which I calculate to be about six years purchess.
The nixt thing you have to doo is to look out for a
good wife to help you manage the farm. If there were
any of our Scotish ladys that you thought would sute
you let us know and we shall inquire if they would
come. You will also need two or three servants in
order to cause the work go on in a regular form.

A few weeks since we had a call from Mr Shanks.
He says he has a son and Daughter going to there
uncles some where on the river Misurie. . . .

This Russian war[1] is causing a great many things
to get up in prices, so many taxes going on particu-
lary malte and spirits taxes. The 2 lb loaf is 7 pence
here some places $8\frac{1}{2}$, oat meal from 28 to 30 shillings
per boll.

David Bell Blacksmith Aboyne left for Canada in
April with the ship Arura and Dr Fuller with the
same ship. Report says there is nearly one thousand
old and young left Aberdeen this spring for Canada.

I do not remember any news in this place worth
the while of troubling you to read.

I am still enjoying ordinary good health and able
to doo a little work every day just as when you ware
here for which I cannot be too thankful to an all
good and merciful providence and although you be
in a distant land from us I hope you will still re-

1. The Crimean War.

member that the same God watches over us all and
may he still watch over you and all of us is the
earnest prayer of

         Your affeconate Father

              Alex[r] Thomson

I have not heard of Smith[1] since you was here so I
think I may call him a deserter of his family.

1. The husband of Thomson's deceased sister, Mary Ann, whose
children were in the care of James's father, Alexander, and his sister,
Helen.

To Alexander Thomson 22 June 1854

Matilda C.S. June 22nd 1854

My Dear Father

Yours of 22nd Ult reached me yesterday evening and as we have had a heavy shower this morning so that we can't do much on the railroad I thought I might as well reply to it at once.

I see you have got the money I sent to help Sandy to get to Canada. When he wrote to me for money he did not say how much he wanted and I thought ten pounds would have been enough as I had no idea but what he must have had considerable left of what I gave him before.

I have no money on hand at present and don't expect to have any until the beginning of July.

If I can spare it then I will send some more to assist Sandy to get to this country where I think he can at least make a living, as I cannot afford to support him in Scotland at the rate I have done the last two years.

We are getting along pretty well with the railway works. We have fifty men and twenty horses at work. We will have a mile & a half finished about the first of July. The Engineers have not yet made an estimate of the Amount of work done so we cannot tell exactly how it is paying. They are to take measurements at the end of this month. We have been to a good deal of expense so far for horses waggons and tools. I have worked pretty hard since we commenced the road, and I thank God for the health and strength which enables me to do so. I never felt

214

better in my life than I do this spring and summer.
With keeping things straight on the railroad and
occasionally seeing after the farm I have not much
spare time. I board with my partner near the
section we are working on now, but I make my
home at McPhersons. I go there Saturday nights and
sometimes through the week. We have a Sunday
School in the Methodist Church at Edwardsburgh,
there is eight or ten of us teachers and when we get
through with the little ones the teachers and larger
Scholars form a Bible class and take lessons from an
old Methodist exhorter. The Sons of Temperance
have a Society in the village. I intend to join them.
I have not drunk a pint of whisky since I came to
Canada. By joining the 'Sons' I think I can induce
one or two hard drinkers to join too.[1]

There was a grand Temperance demonstration
yesterday at Spencerville a village twelve miles back
from Edwardsburgh. It was an open air Soiree, the
place where it was held is a beautiful spot in the
woods where the tall and graceful Maple trees form
a delightful shade, a spring of cold water (the drink
God furnishes his creatures with) bubbles up free to
all as if Nature had intended the place for such an
occasion. A platform decorated with banners and
with flowers was erected for the speakers and the
band seats were set for the hearers and a table spread
for the visitors. A thousand persons partook of
dinner in that cool retreat. The speakers (one of
whom is a clergyman) did ample justice to the

1. Among his fellow-workers in the vineyard may have been
James Thomson's future brother-in-law, George Armstrong, author
of several manuscript temperance poems in the collection, including
'The Landlord's Pet' (see Appendix C).

cause, the Edwardsbg Brass Band (eighteen in number) did ample justice to the Music. At least those who are judges say so, and I speak from personal experience when I say that some of the visitors did ample justice to the dinner. Yesterday was a regular jubilee in the back woods, as it was a pretty place to go to, a good cause to support and one of the nicest little girls in Edwardsburgh to go with me.[1] I hope you will excuse me for leaving the railroad one day, and taking a drive out there.

I have not done much on the farm this summer as I could not attend to it myself. I took up some of our horses in the spring and ploughed and sowed ten or twelve acres with wheat and oats, and planted a few potatoes, expecting that Sandy would have been out to take care of them. I have now got a man who lives near the farm to take care of the crops. My house is unoccupied. I have rented my pasture and I will have ten or twelve acres of Hay. About one half the farm is still covered with wood, principally Maple and Beech. The Grand Trunk Railroad crosses the farm about 2/3 of the way to the rear. I mean there is 2/3 of my land in front and 1/3 in rear of the Railroad. The railroad crosses through the woods. The Company have purchased eighty feet wide, making nearly two acres of land for which they paid me at the rate of fifteen pounds per acre, and for the timber and other damages they paid me twenty five pounds.

The rain is now over and I must bring this hasty scroll to a conclusion. . . .

James Thomson

1. Probably Mary Armstrong, his future wife.

To Mary Armstrong 27 August 1854
From James Thomson, Matilda

Matilda August 27th 1854

My Dear Mary
This has been a lonesome day for me. It is the first
sabbath in a long time and I hope it will be the last
that I will spend out of your society. I hope you are
well and happy.

I thank the Almighty Ruler of the Universe for a
continuance of good health and pray that the light
of his countenance may ever shine on you and all
who are near and dear to you. I suppose you have
been at sabbath school today and joined in singing
praises to Him who created and sustains all things,
who guides the rolling planets in their spheres, and
yet condescends to watch over us poor sinful mortals.

May He bless the sabbath school and make it the
instrument however humble of spreading a knowledge of the truth and of advancing the interests of
Messiahs Kingdom. May the Great Teacher teach all
connected with it.

Mary, Did you miss me away from sunday school
today? If so I hope you will forgive me and believe
me I wish I had been there and had the pleasure of
walking home with one of the teachers as usual, and
had you a lot of proofs that were applacable.

Dear Mary, the following lines copied from an old
newspaper contain in my opinion beautiful senti-
ments and if you think so too, and derive any
pleasure from reading them, I shall feel happy that

I have copied them. I have some more clippings
from papers but this will be enough for this time.

Father I know that all my life
Is portioned out by Thee,
And the changes that will surely come
I do not fear to see—
But I ask of Thee a patient mind
Intent on pleasing Thee.

I ask Thee for a thankful love,
Through constant watchings wise
To meet the glad with cheerful smile
And wipe the weeping eyes—
A heart at leisure from itself
To soothe and sympathize.

I would not have the restless will
That hurries to and fro
Searching for some great thing to do
Or secret thing to know
I would be dealt with as a child
And guided where to go.

Wherever in the world I am
In whatso'er estate
I've fellowship with other hearts
To keep and cultivate,
A work of holy love to do
For the Lord on whom I wait.

I ask Thee for the daily strength.
To none that ask denied,

A mind to blend with outward life
While keeping by Thy side:—
Content to fill a little space,
So Thou be glorified.

There are thorns besetting every path,
That call for patient care,
There is a crook in every lot
And a need for earnest prayer;
But a lowly heart that leans on Thee
Is happy everywhere.

When I commenced writing I entended to have told
you why I did not go to see you today. What I have
been doing and what I have been thinking & . . .
But it would be such a long string I don't think it
would pay to put it on paper especially as this is the
only sheet I have got and besides the moon which
when I commenced was shining beautifully young
and lovely as yourself just over the Gallops has long
since gone to rest and I suppose you have too and so
must I, but I do love to sit up at night and read or
write when all around is still. . . .

Mary, this will be a very long week for me judging
by the length of this day, and I do not think that I
can get up to Edwardsburgh before next sunday,
but supposing you were to devote half an hour to
my service some evening and send me a few lines
just to say that you are well &c. Send the subject
and a few proofs for next Sunday and as much else
as you please to write. It will all be welcome, but I
must stop. I think it will take you one hour to read

this cross ploughing, it is nearly as bad to read as
Chinese or Greek. You will perhaps require a
Governess.

Good-night, yours while this heart throbs.

James Thompson

To Helen Thomson 22 September 1854

Matilda C.S. Sept 22nd 1854

My Dear Sister

I have been a long time in answering your last letter,
but I hope you will excuse me as I have been quite
busy through the summer. It was only last night
that I returned from a short trip up Country. We
staid a couple of days at Wm Scotts. They have had
a very sickly summer about Toronto. Mary Ann and
little Mary[1] have both had the ague, and their
servant girl and some of their hired men were shaking with the same disease when we were there. The
others are well and send their kind respects to all
friends in Scotland.

But Helen, I must explain a little so that you may
know who my travelling companion was that I
speak of as visiting at Cousin Scotts, and in doing so
I must go a little round about. I must tell you what a
pic-nic party is. A Pic-nic is a meeting of neighbours and friends assembled in some shady spot in
the woods for the purpose of enjoying a days recreation or amusement. Each individual or family furnish something in the shape of provisions, some one
thing some another. When they get to the ground
they have varieties enough to set out a good table,
and as there is generally music and some speaking
the day passes off very agreeably.

On Wednesday the 13th inst we had a Picnic in
connection with our sabbath school. It took place

---

1. Probably William Scott's wife and daughter. The combination
name Mary Ann occurs on both sides of Thomson's family.

on a beautiful green shaded by apple trees. The
teachers and scholars met in the church, formed
into a procession headed by the Edwardsburgh
Brass Band and marched to the ground, where the
old folks had a table spread and loaded with good
things. The seats were ranged in a large circle
around the table and the provisions handed round.
We invited two neighbouring Sunday schools to
join us on that occasion, so that there would be
probably two hundred present, old and young when
all had assembled.

Before distributing the refreshments, the Revd Mr
Coleman rose and said that he had the pleasure of
informing them that they were to be witnesses of an
interesting ceremony. He was about to unite in the
bonds of Matrimony two of the teachers. After a few
introductory remarks, he called on the bridegroom
and bride to come forward. They did so each accompanied by a friend and in a few minutes the indisol-
uble knot was tied. They received the congratula-
tions of the assembly and all partook of the good
things provided for the occasion, and all present
enjoyed a few happy hours.

At the close of the picnic the wedding party drove
off for Prescott where the newly married pair embarked on a steamboat, went up the river St Lawrence, the American (United States) side of Lake
Ontario, visited Niagara Falls, went by way of
Hamilton to Toronto, staid a couple of days in the
neighbourhood of that city and got back to Edwardsburgh all well after a weeks absence. The bride is
now at home and the bridegroom working on the
railroad.

222

I suppose you can almost 'guess' by this time who one of the pair was. I am happy to inform you that the writer of these lines was the bridegroom on that occasion. The bride is a lovely young woman Mary eldest daughter of Henry Armstrong, Farmer of Edwardsburg. By my marriage, I have got a great many Uncles Aunts & Cousins. I have never seen one half of them. Mary and I have been accquainted for five years. She was then a little school girl 'just entered in her teens'. She is not twenty yet. Perhaps Wm Scott will tell you how she looks.

When on our way home from Toronto I was very agreeably surprised to find among our passengers Dr Fowler[1] late of Aboyne. We had quite a pleasant evening together. The Dr has been travelling a good deal since he came to this country. He thinks of settling in Kingston. He has a brother there.

William Fiddes and another young man from Kincardine called on me on their arrival in this country. I was up at my farm when they came, and as the little grain I had was then about ripe, I got scythes for them and set them at work for two or three days. As they thought they would rather follow farming work than railroading they went up country intending to try about Hamilton. . . .

James Thomson

1. Dr. Fife Fowler, M.D., son of a Scottish dentist, educated in Aberdeen, joined the Queen's Medical School at its inception in 1854 and was for many years its Dean.

To Alexander Thomson 25 September 1854

Matilda Sept 25th 1854

My Dear Father

. . . We have had a good deal of sickness. At one
time the cholera was bad, the angel of death spread
his gloom inspiring wings over the community and
many of our fellowbeings were called suddenly away
to the spirit world. The cholera was worst among
the newly arrived emigrants, although a good many
old settlers fell victims. . . .

Dear Father, I was writing to Helen when your
letter arrived. You will see by what I have written
to her that I have changed my position in society. I
have got out of the old Batchelor list.

My wife is young, kind and amiable. She is the
daughter of loving affectionate and christian parents.
They are members of the Wesleyan Methodist
Church.

Her Father Henry Armstrong belongs to this part
of Canada, his father I believe was one of the early
settlers. Marys Father commenced the world a poor
man. He has been industrious and persevering. He
is now the owner of 200 acres of land, fronting on
the St Lawrence about 2 miles above my place. Mary
has two brothers and a sister[1] all younger than herself. They are a happy family. As I am most of my
time at Matilda and have not got my house furnished
yet, Mary is still staying with her parents.

1. Their names were Lora Ann (Sissy), Anson, and James. There
were six other children.

I am afraid the Railroad will not pay very well, I
have no money to spare this summer or I would
have sent some to Sandy. . . .

James Thomson

To James Thomson 15 November 1854
From Alexander Thomson, Aboyne

Bridge Aboyne Novbr 15th 1845 [1854]

James

We received yours on the 16 Octbr and we were very
happy to see that you was still enjoying good health
and also that you have had the good fortune to meet
with such a kind amiable and loving partner for life
and I pray to God that you may both injoy hapy lives
togeather and may prosperity atend you both in all
your undertakings. And when death shall divide
you may it be with the blessed asurance that you
shall again meet in the mansions of bliss when you
will be enabled to sing the song of moses and the
lamb for ever and for ever.

I can say very litel about Sandy coming to Canada
as he is often complaning of weaknes in his legs and
knees. I understand he wrote to you last week but he
did not tell us anything concerning what he was to
write, perhaps seeking more money. . . .

I am very glad that I have got another Mary for a
Daughter. You know that I lost one Mary I very
much estemed but I much doubt that I will not have
the pleasure of seeing the other Mary, it is too long
a journey for her to come and see me and I am too
old to come and see her but I hope we shall meet in
a hapier land than either yours or ours.

We have got our Bridge now covered this season
and it is now as good as at first. I was very hard
wrought some times but thanks be to God I got
through pretty well and I am still injoying ordinary

health. We have had a fine season and a fine crop
but it is still high in price. Meal 22/ Bear 29/. I must
now stop as it will soon be post time. . . .

Alexr Thomson

To James Thomson November 1854
From Helen Thomson, Aboyne

Bridgend, Aboyne, Novbr [1854]

My Dear Brother,
I am glad you have got a Wife and I wish you and
her long life and happiness. . . . And I have been bid
send you as many compliments and kind wishes as
would fill a whole sheet. . . . Agnes[1] says you might
have sent a littel bit of the Brides Dress. . . . Elizabeth Middleton maketh me to send her compliments
to you both. She would like to rock the cradel for
you and [']God bless Jamie feen man for he wis the
geed cheil[']. Aunt Scott at Auchenblae is very much
failed . . . sends her kindest wishes to you and Mary.
She bids you be very kind to her and give over railroading and stay on your farm and mind it and not
take up your head with so many things. Do not work
too hard. . . .

   O Scotts sister showed the Revd Dr Buchan[2]
your letter. He was quite delighted with the idea of
your being married at such a meeting. He wishes
you and your sabbath school every success. . . .
Mary Ann thinks uncel James will not need her
now. She is anxious to know if Dr Fowler would
need her. If she were near him she would be all
right for fear her eyes get sore again. Is your eyes
well now ? Mr Neil Wreaton had a letter from Dr
Fowler lately. He is a Proffessor in Queens College

   1. Agnes [Ogg ?] is mentioned frequently in the letters from
Scotland.
   2. The Reverend Charles Forbes Buchan, Free Church minister at
Fordoun from 14 June 1846.

Kingstown. He was delighted at being recognised
by you and says you have got a beautefull hansome-
wife and spoke very highly of her. He thinks a great
deal of the country and the young ladies. James I
hope you will write us pretty frequently through the
mails.

Your ever loving sister,

Hellen Thomson

To Alexander and Helen Thomson
31 December 1854
From James and Mary Thomson, Edwardsburgh

Edwardsburg Decr 31st 1854

My Dear Father

Yours of 15th Novr reached us a fortnight ago. . . .

I have quit railroading for the winter. We worked at it till the beginning of this month when the frost set in so severe that we had to give it up. We will not do anymore untill Spring when we can finish our Section in about two months.

Mary and I are still living with her parents but we intend to move into our own house in a few days. I think I will take Aunts advice and go to farming next summer. . . .

James Thomson

My Dear Sister

We thank you for your kind wishes. . . .

Tell Agnes that I did not think about sending a piece of the brides dress and even if I had I dont know that I would have got the chance as I never saw any pieces of it and never saw the dress but once. However Mary knows best about these matters and she says it is not worth sending. It was a plain white one. When Agnes changes her name to Mrs W. junr or some other name we shall be happy to see what her taste is in selecting a dress.

I thank Lizzy Middleton for her compliments and kind wishes and for offering her services, although

we do not want her for that job yet. You may tell her
to keep practising her old songs *Hush ba* &ca in
case I should send for her for if I want any one to fill
the situation she speaks of I dont expect to get a
kinder one than Lizzy. But I mean not say any more
on this subject as Mary is blushing and pulling my
ears, and threatning to burn the letter. . . .

I see Mary ann has not yet forgot me, I hope she
will be a good girl and go to school (next summer)
and if she learns her lessons well she may get out to
Canada yet to see Uncle James & Dr Fowler.

But I must come to a close as Mary wishes to write
a piece. . . .

James Thomson

Dear Sister
I thank you for the welcome you give me as a member of the family. And as you say James is a kind
faithful and affectionate brother & I believe he will
be as kind and affectionate [a] companion. He has
been this far and I trust he will until death shall
divide us. I should like very much to go to Scotland
and see you all, but there is a wide stormy Ocean
between us which we must not think of crossing at
present. I think James is rather cowardly on the
water or I think he might be coaxed to return to his
native land once more. I would dearly love to go for
I like travelling very much. I enjoyed my trip off
west very much this summer *especially* at the
falls of Niagara. They are a wonderful sight to
behold.

Dear Sister I think a great deal of your Scotch

Laddies, and you can easily guess that I think a good deal of James. I am not acquainted with many more. One gentleman from your part of the country, Dr Fowler, I got acquainted with on Lake Ontario. And Mr Scott and family. They were very kind to us and we spent a very pleasant time with them.

I think Dr Fowler has licked the blarneystone pretty well by the description he has given of me, and I dont know as it would do for me to send my likeness to you for I am afraid you would be sadly disappointed when you would come to see it. But if you would like to have it, why I would like to favour you that much. I hope Dear Sister that you will write often to us, and we will try and answer your kind letters. I should like to see you dearly, but if it is so that we cannot meet in this world I hope and trust we may meet together in a better world, a world free from trial and sorrows and where parting is un-known. I pray to God that it may be our happy lots.

I remain your affectionate Sister,

Mary Thompson[1]

1. Mary introduced the spelling 'Thompson', which became family usage thereafter except for James.

To Helen and Alexander Thomson 4 April 1855

Edwardsburgh April 4th 1855

Dear Sister

Your kind favour . . . along with a Herald arrived last night for which accept our thanks. We have got quite a lot of Heralds lately. We would send you some of our papers if they would be interesting to you. We take the Montreal Transcript, the Toronto Globe and the New York Tribune and some smaller papers. We are happy to learn by your letter that you are all in ordinary health. We thank God for a continuance of the same blessing and pray that of His infinite mercy He may ever bless and protect you all. I am happy to learn that Mary Ann has commenced going to school. I hope she will soon learn her A.B.Cs and get to the a.b. ab. B.O. bo[s] & C. You say John is pretty hard to learn. Perhaps he will remember well what he has learned, and be a smart boy yet. He is young yet and will study better by & by. I hope Hellen will be at the head of her class this summer. She will be some help to you in the House now. . . .[1]

You ask the name of my Farm. Farms in this country dont generally have names as in Scotland, although some individuals give a name to their place. There is an old Gentleman my second nearest neighbour, close by the village, has a cottage and large garden with a row of spruce trees along the side of the road in front of his house and garden, he

1. Mary Ann, John, and Hellen Smith, were the children of James's deceased sister, Mary Ann.

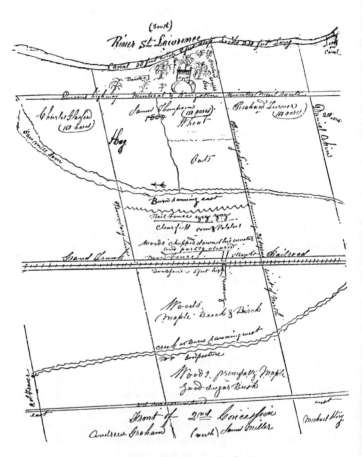

James Thomson's Lot

calls his place Spruce Grove, and that is the only place I know of in this neighbourhood that has any particular name besides that of its owner. When a place changes its owner it changes it name. Canada is divided into Counties, Townships and Concessions. A County consists of several Townships, a Township is ten miles square, and a Concession is a strip from one end of a township to the other, a mile and a quarter wide, and is divided into forty Lots of 200 acres each. In the Deed of Sale which is my title to the property my farm is described as the West quarter of Lot No 3 and the East half of Lot No 4 in the First Concession of the Township of Edwardsburgh, County of Grenville and Province of Canada. I will try to make a rough map of it some time. . . .

Dear Father

If the accompanying rough sketch[1] will assist you to form an idea of the shape of my farm it will have accomplished all that was intended.

You will see that my house is situated about half-way between the road and the river. The land here is about fifty feet above the level of the river and canal. The house is about the same distance from the river St Lawrence that your house is from the river Dee. The bank is fully as steep and about twice as high. We have a beautiful view of the Steamboats passing up and down the river. The canal will be completed in about a year. It is expected that the railway will commence running from Montreal to Kingston next autumn.

1. This sketch map shows the lay-out of the farm at Cardinal. See p. 234

Mr Waddel my partner in the railroad contract
wishes to purchase a small farm and as he will make
a good neighbour I think I will let him have fifty
acres of mine. I think a hundred acres well cultivated
will keep me busy.

Mary has sent her likeness, I hope it will get there
safe. . . .

James Thomson

Edwardsburgh April 10th [1855]

Hellon

If you are in want of any money at any time please
let me know and I will endeavour to let you have
some as I wish to do something towards bringing
up the children committed to your care. Time prevents me saying more at present.

J.T.

May 31st 1855

Helen, Dear Sister, will you be kind enough to
forward the enclosed letter to Sandy. I am unable at
present to give him any assistance towards helping
him out to this country, in fact I hardly think it would
be advisable to come the way times are just now. . . .

James Thomson

To James and Mary Thomson
12 September 1855
From Helen Thomson, Aboyne

Bridgend Aboyne September 12 1855

Dear Brother,
I received yours in [due] time and glad to see you
was all well as this leaves us. The only apology I
have to make for being so long a writing is that I
have been so busy working out all summer and then
at night I found so much to do in the house. John
Davidson gae up the farm of Mr Hough and a
doctor, Dr Gennel took it and he hired people by the
Day to do the work and I have been engaged the
most of the summer[1] and by working hard I can get
on pretty well. So James I am not in any want of
money just now but I must tell you some of the
troubles that afflict us as we have no hopes of getting
any thing from Smith. We have not heard of him
since the month of April passed.
Mr Duncan the factor[2] speaks of withdrawing
fathers wages and giving him nothing but house
and garden for attending to the Bridge[3] so if that is
the case I do not know how we will get along. Father
is very thoughtfull about it but if they do not say
more about it he will not mind them. He thinks
sometime he would like to go to America and I
should like very much to go to if it were to be any
advantage to the children. Now James what I would

1. Helen was working as a casual farm labourer.
2. The estate agent or bailiff of the Marquis of Huntly.
3. Alexander had ceased working as a blacksmith and was employed as a toll-collector on the bridge at Aboyne.

237

ask you is if you would think it advisable for us to
go or not. So I hope you will think the matter over
and write me at your convenience but do not troubel
your seilfe sending money as I will let you know
when I am in want of it.

I hope you have a good crop and that you will succeed well with the harvesting. We see by the paper
there is a good crop generally in Canada. Do you
employ any female day labour in your part of the
country and how are they paid. Here we get 10d per
day of labours for working turnips and 2 sh for
harvest work with no vituls. We are busy at the harvest just now it is about half done in our neighbourhood and a fair crop. Some more of the potato
disease but other ways a fine crop.

We have the queen at Balmoral just now and word
reached this today that Sebastapool is taken. We
have the Marquis[1] and the whole family at Aboyne.
He gave a grand ball at the castel to all his tenants
and there was a great turn out. Soon after, the
Marchoness invited all the scholars at both the
schools to tea and they amused themselves about
the grounds for a time and come home quite proud
of the supper.

Mrs Ogg and Agnes desires to be remberd to you
both. . . . All the rest of your acquantances send
compliments to you. We had old Balfour in one day
and we showed him your likenesses and your
[wife's]. He think yours a very good likeness and
said he did not think they had been so good looking
dames in cannada. Heard from Auchenblae not long

1. Charles, 10th Marquis of Huntly, had succeeded his father in
1853.

238

ago. Your friends were all pretty well. Aunt thinks
you might write to her some time.

When you write me if you make any remark about
Smith I hope you will do it on a sheet by it self as
father gets so out of humor when he hears his name
mentioned. I never could have thought he would
have turned out so bad.

The children are all quite well. Mary Ann speaks
of her going to Canada and she is getting on pretty
well at school you would be astonished how well
she can read the new testament. Sandy's folks are
pretty well they had got a little Maggie in their
family. He has taken on a harvest at Slure. I remember not news here worth writing. Provisions of all
kinds are very lean. Please to write soon and I shall
not be so long again.

Your affectionate sister

Hellen Thomson

Dear sister,
You will think me over careless in not thanking you
for your kindness long ago but as I am not a good
hand at the pen I put it off always as long as possibel.
Accept of my best thanks for the liknesses and I am
proud to have them beside me for many a time when
I am brooding over the ills I have received from
them that ought to have treated me otherwise I look
at them and proud that I am connected with some
that takes notice of me. However James will explain
to you what I mean, but he has been the cause of me
working many a day when I otherwise might have
been sitting in ease and comfort but I pray that God

would enable me to be content with my lot. Whatever it may be I will be glad to hear from you soon or any time when convenient.

Father wishes to be rembred to you. The children often speak of Auntie Mary. We all live in the hope of seein you but let that be as it may. I do pray that the grace of our Lord Jesus Christ may be with you all way henceforth and forever,

Your loving sister,

Helen Thomson

To Alexander and Helen Thomson
26 September 1855

Edwardsburgh C W Sept 26th 1855

Dear Father
Yours of 27th May reached us a month after date
and ought to have been answered long ere now.
But I hope you will excuse me this time as I have
been kept pretty busy this summer. . . . I have charge
of the Junction Canal Office. There is about two
hundred men at work and as I keep their Time,
assist in paying them besides finding Pork Potatoes
& other provisions for the greater part of them you
will see that I have not a great deal of time to write
letters or attend to farming.

The office is about as far from our house as the
village is from yours. I take breakfast before going
to the office in the morning and go home to dinner.
The canal will be completed this next winter. It is
two miles in length and connects the Matilda and
Edwardsburg Canals viz fifty feet wide at bottom,
ten feet deep. It is necessary in order to surmount
a small rapid opposite my house. It has been a very
expensive job. It has already cost twenty five
thousand pounds besides breaking down two or
three sets of contractors. The work has been going
on nearly four years. Mr Elliot took it in hand at the
commencement of this year. There is two pumps
driven by steam power at work day & night and a
horse power pump going occasionally.

We finished our contract on the Railroad several
weeks ago but have not yet got settled with the Com-

241

pany. The cars are now running opposite this place
carying Ballast & c. The Line from Montreal to
Brockville a distance of 125 miles will be open for
traffic this Fall. It is only eighteen months since
the work was commenced. It runs mostly along
the front through cultivated land, and generally
very level. For instance through the townships of
Williamsburgh Matilda and Edwardsburgh a distance of 30 miles I do not think there is a cutting of
more than eight feet in depth. A single track is all
that is laid at present. The intention is to have a
double one when we get able to build it. The land
purchased is wide enough for both viz 80 feet and
in some places 100 feet.

The following piece of domestic inteligence
ought to have communicated sooner but was neg-
lected viz on the 25th June a little stranger made his
appearance at our house. He is a fine stout boy and
growing fast. We have named him Henry Alexander
as a small token of respect for both Grandfathers.

We have got through harvest. Oats are good wheat
rather poor having been greatly damaged in spring
by a worm or grub that cut off the braire[1] just below
the surface of the ground. Our potatoes are good and
we will have quite a lot of apples. Although the
canalers are carrying off a good many we have some
Indian corn and our garden vegetables grow fine.
Altogether we have much cause of Thankfulness to
a Bountiful Providence for prospects of plenty. Our
Barns are filled with plenty. May our hearts over
flow with gratitude.

In regard to the money I sent to assist Sandy and

1. Braird, the first sprouting of young grain.

242

about which you make enquiry in your last letter as
to how you will dispose of it, I have only to say that
if agreeable to you give Sandy half of it to help him
along through the winter as he is not very strong
and you keep the other half to pay the childrens
school Bills & c. That arrangement will be perfectly
satisfactory to me. As to sending the money back to
Canada you must not think of that as you must want
it more than I do. I have been a little hard up for the
last twelve months, but hope soon to get over all
that. . . .

James Thomson

Ellen,
I hope you will write us soon. Mary would have
written to you but she has no news to send as I have
already told you the most interesting piece of information that she had to send, viz that she has got a
fine little boy. An Indian woman has made a cradle
for him of Basket work and painted off in native style
and now you may tell Lizzy Middleton that we are
ready for her to rock and sing. Tell Mary ann that
her little cousin in Canada laughs and kicks and
squalls. . . .

To Helen and Alexander Thomson
9 October 1855

Edwardsburgh Oct 9th 1855

Dear Sister

Yours of 12th September arrived here on the 5th inst
and I hasten to reply. As there is now no prospect of
Smith doing anything for his Childern it becomes
our duty to provide for them the best way we can.
And it is my decided opinion that we can do so
better in this country than in Scotland. You cannot
work for their support. Father is old and cannot long
continue to work. Sandy has enough to do at home,
and what means I could send from here would not
go far. But if you were all here, each could do a
little and make it light for all. I have a farm which
only requires labour to make it produce enough for
all and if God in this good Providence bless us with
health and strength we need have no fears for the
future. If Sandy could only manage to get out here,
there would be work enough for all and there is
better prospects for his family here when they grow
up than at home.

J.T.

Dear Father

In Helens letter lately received she mentions that
there is some word of the Factor depriving you of
your small salary and giving you only House and
Garden for attending the Bridge. And I suppose in a
few years more, when you get a little older they
would deprive you of that too. For reasons already
stated in this letter and which I need not again mention, it appears plain to me that the time has now

arrived for you to leave your native land and sojourn
in a strange country.

In the mysterious dealings of Providence you have
been subjected to many losses and many crosses in
this world, but it is consoling to think that there is a
day coming when that which is now dark and mysterious, will be made light as noon day. We must
wait with patience till that time for surely the God of
all the earth doeth right. I believe Providence has
sent me here before you, to provide a home, where
you might spend the evening of your days in comfort; to be the means of securing your comfort and
happiness shall ever be the highest object of my
ambition. My wife will do what she can to make you
happy. She is not very strong in body but she has a
gentle loving, christian spirit, well fitted to soothe
the ills of life.

I know it will be a serious undertaking for a man
of your advanced years to bid adieu to native land
and cross the ocean. I would not want Sandy to come
here and leave you behind. I would not want you to
come and leave him. I would rather that you would
all come together. My advice is just take passage in
the next spring ships for Quebec.—However you
may see Sandy and decide the matter among yourselves. Form some idea of what assistance Sandy
will require, and write to me as early as possible.
I will do what I can, and if you decide on comming
I shall endeavour to provide some accommodations
for you on your arrival. Hoping this will find you all
well as it leaves us at present.

I remain, Your affectionate son

James Thomson

To Alexander Thomson 4 January 1856

Edwardsburgh Jany 4th 1856

Dear Father

Yours of 4th Decr reached me a few days ago. I am
happy to learn by it that you have resolved on comming to Canada next Spring. It will no doubt be hard
for one of your advanced years to leave home and
native land and seek a new home among strangers
in a strange land but I hope and trust that you will
be contented and happy in this country and I am
sure Canada affords a far better prospect for the
children than Scotland does.

In reply to your enquiry as to the cost of comming
up the St Lawrence from Quebec to Edwardsburgh
I cannot say exactly how much it will be but I think
it will not exceed two dollars (eight shillings sterling) for each person calculating the childern at the
same rate as on shipboard viz up to a certain age at
half price. . . . The price from Quebec to Montreal is
one dollar and from Montreal to Matilda (the landing place below this place) about the same . . . that is
for passage alone exclusive of meals.

The passage from Quebec to Montreal generally
occupies about from twelve to sixteen hours and
from Montreal to Matilda about twenty hours that is
by the mail and other large Boats. There is a smaller
class of Boats that go through the Canals that take
longer time. Any of those comming through the
Matilda canal could land you within half a mile of
my house. We have also the railway open from
Montreal. I do not know what their fares will be for
emigrants but I think travelling will be pretty cheap

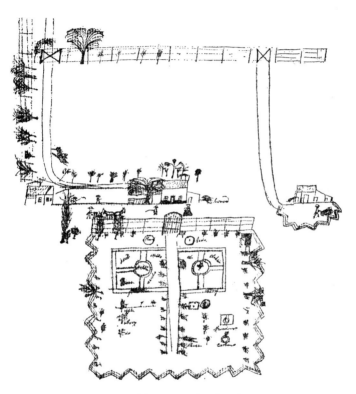

Mary Thomson's Garden

next summer. However, I will write to you again in regard to this subject. In regard to your outfit for the voyage I dont know that I can give you any information more than what you know. If Sandy has a letter that I wrote some two years ago it might help you some in making your calculations. If you think you are likely to be short of funds you can let me know. I will forward some to Quebec, to Mr Buchanan Government Emigration Agent there, collect, receive and pay over. . . . It is part of his duty to give advice and information to emigrants and if they have been imposed upon or ill used by ship capts or others, it is his duty to enquire into the matter and see that they get justice.

Please write on receipt of this and I will then have time to write again before you leave. Dont address my letters (via Canadian Steamers) as there is none of that line running. They dont commence their service till April or May.

If you have a chance to choose places in the ship you ought to secure your berths pretty well 'aft' towards the cabin, as when the ship is pitching there is less motion amid ships than near the bows. And another thing to be attended to is having your chests made fast to something or other so they will not move with the rolling of the vessel.

By the Blessing of God we are still enjoying good health and we pray that the same great blessing may attend you all and may you have a safe and prosperous voyage. I wish a happy new year to all my friends in Scotland.

Your affectionate son

James Thomson

I am getting out timber for a house for you and when
we get a little more snow I will go to drawing it.[1]

1. This house can be seen on a small sketch map drawn by Mary
Thompson in 1862. See p. 247.

To James Thomson 5 February 1856
From Alexander Thomson, Aboyne

Bridgend Aboyne Febry 5th, 1856

Dear James

Yours of the 4 January came to hand on the 29 and
we were happy to see that you were all well.

I am under the necessity of informing you that it
will be out of our power to leave for Canada in the
month of April for various reasons. One in particular
is on account of Sandy being in a weak state with
pains in his back and knees but he is getting better.
Another reason he has two of his children fast[1] with
masters and I am fast myself till Whitsunday and
I do not think that Mr Duncan would let me free
before Whitsunday term. And Hellen thinks that she
would be unabel to get ready by the first of April.
For these reasons we will be under the necessity of
puting it off till the month of August when the
Aberdeen ships takes there second voyage unless we
get an opportunity of a ship in June or July. There
was one last year in the month of June. We are not
willing to come away and leave Sandy and famely
behind if he were able to come. But if he does not
get better than he has been through the winter he
would be of no use in Canada. But I trust God that
we will be blessed with a portion of good health to
enabel us to accomplish our voyage in the course of
the summer and meet with you all enjoying health
and happiness.

You mention sending money to meet us at Quebec

1. Apprenticed, or contracted.

but I think you may delay till I see if we need any.
Perhaps we may have as much as will answer when
we get all our efects sold off. There will be time
after Whitsunday to let you know before we reach
Quebec. You say that you are preparing to build us
a house. If you can have it near a well or barn with
the door south or south west and windows that will
give plenty of light. . . . God bless you all, so prays
your affectionate father

Alexr Thomson

To Helen Thomson 1 April 1856
From James and Mary Thomson, Edwardsburgh

Edwardsburgh C.S. April 1st 1856

Dear Sister

Fathers letter of 6th February reached us in due time.
We are sorry to learn that you cannot come out as
soon as expected and particularly as the delay is
partly occasioned by Sandys weak state of health.
I hope however he will soon get strong again. Perhaps a voyage accross the Atlantic Ocean may help
him. Seeing you cannot be ready to start with the
April vessels I think it would be well to come as
early in the summer as possible, that is if there are
any vessels sailing in the months of June or July, as
you would be more likely to have a pleasanter voyage in summer than early in spring. I remember
when I came out first our greatest trouble was cold
weather but as your time of sailing will depend on
circumstances we will wait patiently till we hear
from you again when you will probably be able to
give us some information as to time. At all events
when you do start we hope and pray that you may
be favoured with gently breezes to waft you in safety
accross the dark blue sea.

Dear Sister

Seeing Thompson is not inclined to write a very
lengthy epistle to you, I think I will put in a few
words. I had very hard work to get him to write at
all. He has been a little inclined to be lazy today.
He has left the store where he has been for the past

year, and it being the time a year that there is not much a doing he cant find anything to imploy himself with *but* I have just given him the boy to take care of. I must tell you what a fine lad he is, he weighs 20 pounds and a half and he can sit alone, and tries to creep, he has got two teeth, and he says da, da, as fast as anybody, and making a long story short he is a remarkable fine child, (Thompson thinks so at least).

We are going to make Maple sugar this spring. We have the trees tapped, but the sap has not begun to run yet on account of its being so cold. I wish you were here to have some sport with us making it for it is nice fun to be in the woods this time of year.

I hope you may have a safe and pleasant voyage coming out to this country, & give my love to all enquiring friends. I think I will finish and let Thompson write the rest. You will please excuse this scratching of mine, no more at present excepting I remain your sincere and affectionate Sister

Mary Thompson

Mary has told you what a fine boy we have got. He has been quite healthy so far. I have got some oat meal. He sups his pottage like a Scotchman. We have plenty of milk yet, and the pottage goes well.

We have had a very cold winter an unusually steady cold, we used always to have a thaw and some rainy weather in January but this winter the January thaw has been postponed on account of the weather, for since the first of December we have had

steady frost and not a drop of rain so far. The sun in
the middle of the day is now settling the snow some
on the roads so that sleighing is about done although
there is a great deal of snow yet in places where it
drifted deep.

We have given up the store on the Canal. The
works are now nearly finished. There will be very
few men kept on after next pay day, so that this
spring I will have a chance to try my hand at farming. Last week was the first leisure time I have had
at home since we commenced keeping house. Our
next pay day is on the 10th after which I will be done
with the Canalers. I have got along well with the
Paddys. My kind love to the childern. Does Mary
ann still talk about Canada and Dr Fowler—by the
by I have never seen the Dr since that time we met
on Lake Ontario. . . .

I wish Lizzie [Middleton] was here now to rock
the cradle and sing, as I find it rather hard work to
write and rock at the same time, and if I take the
boy up he tears my paper and pulls my hair and
pushes my hand every way. . . .

James Thomson

To Alexander and Helen Thomson
24 June 1856

Edwardsburgh June 24th 1856

Dear Father

Yours of 27th May has arrived. I am sorry to learn by
it that Sandy is still so weak as to be unable to come
with you to Canada.

I am also sorry to inform you that on your arrival
in this country you will not see your little grandson.
He who while on earth took little childern in his
arms and blessed them, has called the spirit of our
little boy home to heaven before it had time to be
tarnished by sin. We bow with humble submission
to the Divine will knowing that the Judge of all the
earth will surely do right. Our loss will be his eternal
gain. Henry Alexander was a fine healthy child, I
may say he never had a days sickness until the third
of this month when he was attacked with Scarlet
fever, which terminated fatally on the morning of
the eighth. Had he been spared he would have been
twelve months old tomorrow, but he is gone. He
cannot return to us but we shall go to him.

By the time this reaches you, you will likely have
your arrangements for crossing the Atlantic pretty
nearly completed. At all events I do not think that
I could tell you anything about that but what you
already know. I shall therefore say nothing about
that but endeavour to give you some information as
to how to proceed when you get to this side of the
ocean. On your arrival at Quebec it may be that your
ship will not at once get to a wharf but may have to

anchor in the river. In that case if there are many
passengers it might be well for one or two of them
intelligent and active men to go to the office or go
on board some of the Montreal Steamboats and
make arrangements for all those who wished to go to
Montreal. By so doing it is probable that they might
send a Steamer alongside your ship to take off passengers and Baggage which would save going ashore
in small boats and carting to Steamboat wharf. The
Captain of your ship might do something in this
matter as it is his duty to see you landed.

If you want any information or have any grievance
to complain of you best apply to Mr Buchannan
Emigration Agent. He or some of his clerks will
likely come on board your ship on her arrival. When
you get to Montreal you will find plenty of Steamboats ready to carry you up the river. The Kingston
Mail boats or the Ogdensburgh boats are either of
them good and come from Montreal to Matilda in
from sixteen to twenty hours. As they do not come
through the Matilda Canal, they do not have any
stopping place here. Those boats that come through
all the canals and stop here are a smaller and slower
class, unable to go up the rapids, whereas the fast
Boats go up all the rapids except at two places. I
think it would be well for you to have a few lines
ready addressed to me and when you get to Quebec
and find out when you are to start for Montreal,
pencil down the time and drop in Post office. You
might do the same at Montreal and it is probable
that I might get word in time to meet you at Matilda.
If not, on your arrival at the latter place you might
put your luggage in the Store house on the wharf

and go to Gordon Brouse or some other Tavern
Keeper and they would bring you up here-about five
miles.

When you leave the ship you will require to have
your luggage in as handy a shape to lift about as
possible. Keep them as well together as you can and
recollect how many pieces or packages you have.
You will be one night between Quebec and Montreal
and one between Montreal and Matilda So that you
will want some of your bed clothes as the night air
may be cool. You will probably have to sleep on top
of your luggage, or among boxes and barrels, that is
if there is a crowd of Passengers. Write when you
engage your passage and know when you are to
leave Aberdeen. Wishing you a safe prosperous and
pleasant voyage I must bid you good night
                    Your affectionate son

                              James Thomson

Dear Sister
In reply to your enquiry about bringing blankets
and pillows, Mary thinks you had better bring what
you can conveniently unless you can dispose of
them to good advantage at home, as such blankets as
you have would cost high here and feathers are
scarce. Only mind and not burden yourselves with
too much luggage. When at sea you will require considerable bed clothes as it is sometimes very cold.
Your chamber and cooking utensils will have to be
tin ware as far as possible, and you will have to keep
your provision chest well packed in case of rough
weather. A tin can (with narrow mouth) large enough

to hold your daily allowance of water would be very
convenient. The children will likely be sick at first
but they will soon get over it.

Hoping soon to see you I remain your

Brother James Thomson

BY PANAMA TO THE CARIBOO

James Thomson's Diary[1]

Entry 31 March 1862

James Thompson, Edwardsburgh, C.W.
March 31st, 1862.

Met the boys who intend going to British Columbia
and agreed to go to N. York to secure passages for
them and myself, to San Francisco, also to telegraph
to S.W. Smith Prescott [erased and replaced by
Ogdensburgh] at 2 o'clock on Saturday 5th April.

April 1st

    Thomas Harbottle.

    By cash $100 for tickets

James McIlmayl	$100
Wm. Rickmer	$100
S.W. Smith	$100

1. James Thomson's Diary is a leather-covered loose-leaf book,
$4'' \times 2\frac{1}{2}''$ containing 216 pages. It was kept primarily to record the
accounts of the 'partnership' or 'company' of friends who went
together to the gold-fields. Many pages are lists of purchases of
provisions or lists of contributions from the partners. As much of it
was written in pencil, it is in some places illegible. There are also
many quotations from sermons and religious papers. The pages are
not in order.

Anson Armstrong[2]	$100
John Lawrence	$100
Joseph K. Irwine	$100
James Ferguson	$100
George Adams	$100

April 2nd   Left Home 7 a.m. [travelled via Prescott, Ogdensburgh, Malone, Rouses Point, St Albans, Burlington, Vt] Car load of US soldiers from Plattsburgh en route for Washington [Rutland] Very romantic scenery. Marble quarries. Damp Foggy morning, Slate Quarries [Troy] ice breaking up on Hudson river. Further down ice and snow all gone. [Arr. New York]—Came across one of the Bogus Ticket sellers—put up at Lovejoy's Hotel.

2. Anson Armstrong was Mary Thompson's brother.

To Mary Thompson 7 April, 1862

Lovejoys Hotel
N.Y. City
April 7th 62

My Dear Mary

Since I left you I have often felt that Good-bye is a
bitter word to say. I feel very lonesome and sad
amidst all the thousand of human beings that crowd
the busy streets of this modern Babylon not one
familiar face. But I thank the Great giver of all our
mercies for the health that I enjoy and for the pre-
cious hope of meeting again. Oh that the Holy
Spirit may keep us and guide us till we meet in that
better land where parting is unknown. Mary I hope
you got home safe and found all right. After I left
Ogdensburgh, I got along as well as I expected as
far as the journey is concerned. I felt no disposition
to enter into conversation with my fellow passengers
and they seemed quite willing to leave me to my
own thoughts, and I need hardly say that every
revolution of the wheels was increasing the distance
between me and the objects of my thoughts.

I took but little notice of the scenery along the
road in fact it was nearly the same all day wednesday, Snow and woods and the top rails of fences. At
Malone[1] we stopped twenty minutes for dinner. In
summer I should think Malone would be a very
pretty place, situated on the high banks of a winding
river. We got to Rouse's point about 6 o'clock
changed cars, and crossed the Lake just before dark.

1. Malone, Quebec.

Got to Burlington Vt at 10 and Rutland about 2 a.m. Thursday. Slept 3 hours got up at 5. Had breakfast and started at 6. Rutland is a very romantic city hemmed in on all sides by steep rocky mountains. To look from the Hotel one cannot imagine how a railway train could ever get in, or how we were to get out. But the bell rang and away we started. Yankee ingenuity and enterprise aided by Irish bone & sinew had made a way, up the hills and down the valleys now accross a deep ravine now along a mountain side. One could almost imagine himself in the Highlands of Scotland. We passed several large marble and slate quarries, and many little villages and pretty cottages situated by the sides of rippling mountain streams. Still the deep snow covers the ground.

We got to Troy at $\frac{1}{2}$ past Ten a little behind time, changed cars and started on the Hudson River Road east side of river. When opposite Albany stopped and got addition to train. Got to N.Y. City at 5 p.m.

My kind respects to all friends. I will write again soon. Be as cheerful as you can. Pray for me and teach the dear little ones to pray for PA. I wish the boys would come that I might hear from you.

Your loving and devoted husband

Thompson

LOVEJOY'S HOTEL
On the corner of PARK ROW and
BEEKMAN STREET,
opposite City Hall Park and Fountain
NEW YORK
John P. Huggins, Proprietor

The convenient location of LOVEJOY'S HOTEL,
is without a parallel in New York being near
the principal Mercantile Houses, and convenient
to all the Railroad Depot and Steamboat Landings.

This Hotel is conducted on the EUROPEAN
PLAN for the accommodation of both Ladies
and Gentlemen

Prices for rooms, as follows:
Room for One Person, 50 cts. per day.
Gentleman and Lady, $1.00 per day.

Adjoining the LADIES PARLORS is a PRIVATE
RESTAURANT, for Gentlemen and Ladies,
where Meals will be furnished at all hours—
guests paying only for what they order.

Guests arriving by the New Haven Railroad
trains, can take the small horse cart and ride to
the door of Lovejoy's Hotel, for five cents.

BEWARE! Of a house in Greenwich Street
Called "FALLON & LOVEJOY'S HOTEL,"
and falsely represented by Hackmen and
Runners as a branch of this Hotel! Said house
is not, and never was, in any way connected
with this Hotel. BEWARE, also, of hackmen
and runners who will meet you at the depot or
landing, and tell you we are full. They do so,
to get you to houses which they represent, for
the purpose of defrauding and cheating you.

To Mary Thompson 7 April 1862

Lovejoy's Hotel
New York April 7th 1862

My Dear Mary

The small sheet brings my travels down to my arrival in N.Y. on Thursday afternoon. I left my Bagage in the Hotel and went to the shipping office, but found it closed for the day. I went to bed early, and slept soundly not withstanding the incessant rattling of carrages on the street. The Hotel fronts the City Hall park. From my Bedroom window I can see the time on the city clock at all hours day or night.

Friday morning I again went to the shipping office, could get no satisfaction about Tickets, was told to call again at one oclock. They will take no money at the office except American gold or N.Y. city Bills. I went to a Broker and had my money changed. I had to pay $\frac{1}{2}$ per cent discount on Canada Bills. I went to the office again at one oclock and was then told that I could get a ticket for myself but no more as they had adopted the rule to give tickets to none unless personally present, as speculators had formerly bought them up and sold at a higher price. I tried all I could to get them but it was no use. They are very stiff and independent.

On learning the state of matters I wrote to Mr McPherson, hoping that he might receive the letters on Monday, in case the Telegraph might miss carry. I telegraphed to Wesley on Friday afternoon, (with instructions to leave it at the office in Ogdensburgh till called for) requesting the boys to start on Monday. But I cannot tell whether he got it or not as I got no answer on Saturday. If Wesley went to Ogdensburgh on Saturday and my communication had not gone, the Boys would hardly know how to act. I am glad that I wrote to Mr McPherson, as I think he will certainly get the letter today, but to make doubly sure and to let them know as soon as possible, I Telegraphed again this morning, expecting that if Wesley did not get my message on Saturday, some of them would get to Ogdensburgh today. If they got my message on Saturday I will expect them here tomorrow

P.M.   If they get my message today or my letter to Mr McPherson, I will go to meet them on Wednesday. There is no prospect of our getting tickets for Steerage passage on the vessel leaving on the 11th. I believe it is the Northern Light will go, but she came in Friday last. There is another called the Champion at the Wharf, but the Northern Light is the Largest vessel and will likely go this time. I cannot tell whether I will get away or not until the Boys come, as of course I did not buy my own Ticket till I would see if they could get theirs, and I believe the only course now open is either to go in the second cabin or wait till the 21st. I wish the Boys would come soon for I am very lonesome.

On comming here after getting below Albany the snow began to disappear and was only visible in spots on the mountains. The ice on the Hudson was breaking up and the Boats just beginning to run. When we got in to the city the streets were dry and

265

dusty the water carts going about sprinkling them.
Friday evening I took a walk out to Central Park, a
field of about 800 acres beautifully laid out with
carriage roads and foot paths, Hills, ravines, Lakes,
rocks, Trees and flowers (to be). I felt far better here
than in the crowded streets. Saturday it rained all
day, and as I could not hear from Ogdensburgh nor
walk out much I felt pretty lonesome. Sunday morning brought sun and bracing air, I feel lighter
hearted. This morning went to church St Johns.
Dont know what minister. I have enjoyed Mr
Walkers sermons fully as well. May the God of
Heaven & earth bless you all

Thompson

April 10. Had likeness taken on cards—1/2 doz.

To Mary Thompson 10 April 1862

New York April 10th 1862

My Very Dear Mary
It is now past 6 oclock a.m. I have just got up and
dressed. Some of the Boys are up and some are not.
While waiting for them I thought I would commence
another letter to you. I wrote to you on Monday. At
that time I did not know whether Wesley had
received my Telegraph message or not, but soon after
mailing your letter I received a reply from Ogdensburgh. It came to N York at 5 o clock on saturday,
but had been mislaid by the Clerk of the Hotel. I was
very glad when I received it. The Boys got along all
right on tuesday pm. I waited for them at the Depot
in the City. There was such a crowd and a rush
when the Train arrived, some of them lost sight of
me and the others, they got led away by some
runner for some other Hotel. They suspected that
he was taking them too far and left him. By enquiring of policeman they found Lovejoys after a
good long chase. One man Smith from Mountain
who came on the Cars with them got led away
from all the others and got shaved to the tune of
$10 or $12. He found his way here after a while. I
think he is the greenest travelor that I ever saw. By
the time the Boys got in and straighted up the
shipping office was closed for the night. Yesterday
morning we went to the office. There was a great
crowd. All the steerage tickets were sold and we had
no alternative but to get second cabin or stay for
next boat. The Boys were all agreed on going ahead
and I was glad of it for staying here doing nothing

is hard work and poor business. We accordingly
bought Second Cabin tickets @ $150, and it was by
hard pushing that we got them. We got about the
last that were sold with berths. The Steamer Northern Light that goes out with us is the one that the
complaint was made against, on a former trip for
poor provisions. Yesterday we had a few inches of
snow in the morning and the streets very slippy all
day. We spent the afternoon in Barnums Museum.
He has a living whale, a sea lion, a Hippopotamus,
a Giant 8 ft high and a pretty little dwarf, less than
Tom Thumb.

I believe the Boys are now ready to go to breakfast.

Mary I thank you for the kind letter you sent me, I
am sorry to hear that Jamie[1] was sick, and in all
probability I shall have to sail without hearing from
you again. I think you ought to write by the first of
May and address to New Westminster. I will be so
anxious to hear, and will try to get letters from that
place. I will endeavour to write to you from Aspenwall.

Mr McPherson wished me to Telegraph from San
Francisco. If we stop there any time I will try to do
so, to Mr Merrill of Prescott Telegraph. But you
need not feel uneasy if you do not receive any message from these, as in such a long distance and so
many offices the message might miscarry. I called
on Mr & Mrs May on tuesday. Mrs May has been
quite sick and is still confined to bed. She is getting
much better. Mr May is quite well. I promised to call
again and take James McIlmay and Anson to see

1. Jamie was James Thomson's eldest surviving son, born 26
September 1856, died 1895.

them. They were very glad to see me and to hear
from their Boys. If they had known we were comming through they would have sent for them.

5 o clock p.m.   We have just returned from paying a
visit to Mr & Mrs May. They live six or seven miles
from the City Hall. We rode out in the 3rd Avenue
cars and walked home by way of Central Park 5th
Avenue and Broadway. The snow of last night has
all disappeared and the sun is shining bright. Mrs
May looks better today. We took dinner with them
and spent a couple of hours very plesantly and our
walk home through the finest streets of New York
was very agreeable, and we are now just tired
enough to sit down and write. I thank you for my
nice neck tie. I have been sporting it in Broadway
today. In accordance with your suggestion I have
purchased a pair of Carpet slippers cost 50 cents.
I have them on now very comfortable. I feel much
lighter hearted since the others arrived and got
tickets secured. The vessell sails tomorrow at noon.
There will be a great crowd on board, and I am glad
we have got in the S. Cabin. I do not think that I can
give any instructions about managing the farm. Do
the best you can with it among yourselves. Do not
undertake too much, so as to have to work too hard.
Tell Grandfather not to work any more than is
agreeable to him, and I pray the good Lord to prosper my exertions that I might be enabled to place
you all in more comfortable circumstances. May we
meet in that better land where all tears are wiped away.
  My Dearest Mary yours ever

James Thompson

James Thomson's Diary

Entries 11 and 17 April 1862

April 11. . . . Mailed cards to Mary and 1 pictorial paper to Jamiee. . . .

April 17.   Pass one of the Bahama Islands, surrounded by reef. During night passed Cuba. . . .

To Mary Thompson 20 April 1862

Aspenwall, New Grenada April 20th 1862

Mary,

It is now nine o'clock Sunday morning. We landed
about an hour ago. I am sitting in the shade of a
Telegraph pole on one side of the main street of
Aspenwall, within six feet of the water of the Bay.
There is no house on this side of the Street. The
little waves are rippling in with gentle sound at
my back. In front of me is the Railroad office, with
the Hotels and stores, with any quantity of stalls
attended by natives black as Erubus, selling all
kinds of fruit and cakes, Oranges, Bananas, Pine
apples, Cocca nuts, Lemons and I don't know now
all what. We (that is the Port Elgin Boys) instead of
going to a Hotel have piled our baggage around a
pole and I am now sitting by the side of pile keeping
watch and writing to you while the others are stroll-
ing about. . . . The Train with the steerage passengers will leave at one o'clock and that with the Cabin
passengers at 3 p.m. . . .

Mary—you will please excuse me for not writing
Dear, Dearest or something of that sort before your
name, but believe me no amount of adjectives that
I could write would express my love nor make you
dearer than you are, therefore when I say Mary, I say
as much as if I ransacked the whole dictionary. . . .

We had a prosperous voyage of eight and 1/2 days.
We had favourable winds and fine weather. Our ship
was very crowded, some 1200 or 1400 passengers,
but beyond sea sickness there was no disease and

all seemed friendly, no quarrelling as far as I am
aware. I had a pretty tough time with seasickness.
. . . Anson was pretty sick for some time but he was
not so long away from the table as I was. . . . I should
think three fourths of all on board were sick the
first few days. . . . They say the vessel (Golden Age)
we go on board of at Panama is much larger than
the Northern Light so we will have more room. We
had berths in the second cabin but most of the time
we slept on deck as it was too warm below. . . . I
have not shaved since leaving New York but as none
of us thought of bringing a looking glass I don't
know how my beard looks. Did you get my Photo-
graphs ? Do you think they are good ? How do you
get along ? I long to hear from you. How are the
boys and Minnie. Who gets first dressed now ? It
seems to me as if it were three months since I left.
Cheer up Mary, be happy, be cheerful, pray for me
and believe me, Ever your loving Husband,

James Thompson

To Mary Thompson 20 April 1862

Steam Ship Golden Age, Lat. 16° Long. 98°
Saturday April 26th 1862. 10 Oclock am

My Dear Mary, when writing to you from Aspinwall
I intended to send the letter back to N.Y. by the
Northern Light but before doing so I called on the
British Consul and he took charge of the letters and
would send it by the first British Steamer by way of
St Thomas, Bermuda & Halifax. The cars with
steerage passenger started at $\frac{1}{2}$ past one oclock, a
long train 15 cars each holding about 60 passengers.
At 3 oclock the train for Cabin passengers was ready.
We got aboard and started at a rapid rate.

The road is very good but very crooked winding
in all directions some very sharp curves, through
swamps and over ridges. Sometimes along the
Banks of the Chagres river and sometimes along a
rugged mountain side, now passing a native village
with its Bamboo huts thatched with leaves, and its
sable inhabitant in their Holiday attire (Easter sunday) some with shirts & some without. The younger
portion of the community seem to be entirely independent of Dry goods merchants. We saw some
very good looking Cows a few horses, and any
number of miserably poor pigs. The Station Houses
are built in the American style and some of them
have really pretty gardens. They would suit Mr
Ramsford, with tropical fruits and flowers all around
and the lovely Cocoa nut with its feathery branches
waving like a gigantic plume right over the houses.
We only stopped twice, drove at the rate of 20 miles
an hour and reached Panama a little before 5 oclock

distance by railway $47\frac{1}{2}$ miles. In a straight line . . .
the distance is less than 30 miles. Country very
warm.

On arrival at Panama we immediately embarked
on board a small Steamer and were conveyed out to
Bay about 3 miles where the Golden Age was lying
at anchor. We got on board and had supper about
10 p.m. When all the passengers and Baggage were
got on board we started. The *Age* is a splendid
vessel much larger than the N. Light, so that we
have plenty of room. On the main deck is the dinning
Saloon with staterooms all around. Up one stairs is
the first cabin parlour, with state rooms, and above
that is the Hurricane deck covered with canvas
awning. Our sleeping apartment is below the dining
Saloon but up to the present time the weather is so
warm (90 degrees in the shade) that the majority
prefers sleeping on the decks.

The waiters are coloured gentemen from Dixie-
land and are kept pretty busy as they have a dozen
tables to set every day. Meal hours are 2nd cabin
breakfast $\frac{1}{2}$ past 6. (3 tables) dinner 1 oclock (3
Tables) Tea $\frac{1}{2}$ past 5 3 Tables First Cabin Breakfast
8 oclock 1 Table Lunch 12 and dinner $\frac{1}{2}$ past 4. We
have very good provisions, Tea & Coffee, Beefsteak
& potatoes, and sometimes Fish for Breakfast, Soup
of different kinds Roast Beef do Pork Pudding or
Pie for dinner, Hot rolls dry Beef good bread &c for
Tea. The water is pretty good but very warm, and
we get no ice without paying for it 25 cents per lb.
We generally club together and get a lb in the forenoon put in a pitcher of water which makes a tum-
bler for each of seven or eight of us. We avoid eating

much salt meat and drink a good deal of Tea. A glass
of Lemonade or Sarsaparella with ice in it costs 25
cents at the Bar. Whisky I believe is the same price.

On taking observations at noon each day the
Captain puts up a ticket giving Latitude and Longitude and distance runs for 24 hours. We expect to
be at Acapulco, Mexico this p.m. to take in coal &
water. Yesterday we were in Lat. 14:57 North &
Longitude 94:33 West, distance run last 24 hours
233 miles. Total distance from Panama 1097. In a
few minutes we will get the result of todays obser-
vation.

p.m.   We have now had dinner. Our Latitude and
Long is just about what I guessed it at when I
commenced writing. The distance run is 228 miles
Making the total from Panama 1325. So it will be
night before we get to Acapulco as it is about 1500
miles from Panama and about 1800 from San Francisco. From San F to Victoria is 812 miles. I think I
mentioned that we had no looking glass on the N
Light. Here we have plenty. Every time we go up or
down stairs we have a full length view of ourselves.
We have to wash with salt water. Sometimes we
Hook a little fresh water to wet our hair. The ship
furnishes towels.

The passengers generally are quite sociable, some
read their Bibles some read novels, and other books,
some play cards, checquers and other games for
amusement. No gambling allowed on board. The
Ladies read and sew & embroider, and knit and
dress and promenade. The childern run about and
play and some times squall. Thursday & Friday we

were out of sight of land crossing the Gulf of Teham-tepea.[1] We came in sight of land again this morning. Yesterday morning a Mr Chamberlain from Na-panee, above Kingston, who got one of his hands badly hurt about the engine of the Northern Light and had some of his fingers cut off, died of mortifica-tion. His body was sewn up in sheets, weights put to the feet, the engine was stopped a few minutes and the body lowered into the deep. The deceased was pretty well advanced in years. He has two nephews on board, and leaves a large family at home. A few days after he was hurt, a collection was got up and $160 collected for him.

With the exception of one morning the Pacific has done credit to its name. It has been delightfully smooth and nice. I feel quite well now and sometimes all most wish that you were here, with the children to play with, but I am afraid if you had been on the N. Light you would have been poorly attended to the first few days.

Sunday April 27th.   We reached Acapulco last night between 10 & 11 oclock and commenced taking on board coal, water, Beef cattle, Hogs and their pro-visions. Scarcely was the ship anchored when a number of Boats came out from shore with fruit of all kinds for sale. They did a large business. They had lanterns and torches, by the light of which the swarthy Mexicans, half naked looked like the pic-ture of a gipsy camp. They were not allowed to come on board and the decks of our ship was high above them, but they are prepared for that. They

1. The Gulf of Tehuantepec, Mexico.

throw up a line with a bag or basket tied to it in
which the money is passed down and the fruit
passed up. They know enough English to tell the
prices of their goods. Twelve oranges for a quarter.

The entrance to the harbour is narrow. It is well
sheltered by high rocky mountains. There is four
Men of War ships (2 British and 2 French) lying in
the harbour. . . . We sailed this morning at sunrise,
weather still very warm, passengers all well. I
bought a dozen oranges, nice ones. If you were here
I would share with you. We must be cautious about
eating fruit in this climate.

To Mary Thompson 28 April 1862

Monday April 28th 1862
3 o clock p.m.

My Ever Dear Mary

We have another very warm day we have had dinner and I began to feel sleepy. In order to drive away drowsiness I have got my paper & pencil and will write a few more lines to you. Just as I commenced writing a large school or drove of Porpoises came alongside the ship and tried a race with us. There must have been more than a hundred of them. They kept up for a mile or more. They seemed to be five or six feet long, with long sharp noses and thick bodies. Occasionally they would jump high out of the water and fall down with a great splash. We see some of them almost everyday jumping and playing. They always go in droves but they have never followed us so close and so long as those we have just left.

Since yesterday morning we have been running pretty close to shore. At noon today we ran into a harbour at a little town called Manzanillo, landed a naval officer and letter bag for the U.S. Ship of War St Marys, lying in the harbour, took on board a few Mexicans passengers to San Francisco & $100,000 in Silver from the Mining town of Coloma in the interior of the country. We stopped about $1\frac{1}{2}$ hours.

I suppose you will expect to hear about more fruit, but there was a poor supply of that, only one boat and they had nothing but watermelons. We are still coasting along perhaps two or three miles from

the shore, which in some places is low and sandy
but generally steep and rocky with high rocky
mountains in the distance. We expect to get to San
Francisco this day week. I am afraid these letters of
mine will puzzle you to read them you must excuse,
read what you can and guess the rest. We expect
soon to meet the Steamer from San Francisco.

Tuesday April 29th 1862 8 o clock a.m.
Good Morning little wife, how do you do ? Another
lovely morning has dawned upon us. The sun in all
his tropical glory is shining upon us. We are now
crossing the mouth of the Gulf of California, out of
sight of land, so that on either side as far as the eye
can reach there is nothing but one calm blue expanse
of water, with nothing to disturb its glassy surface
save the paddle wheels of our noble ship which
leave a streak of sparkling foam behind them like
the Milky way on a clear winter night.

   I have had breakfast and am now sitting in an arm
chair on the upper deck at the stern of the vessel
with my book and paper on my knee. My fellow
passengers are variously occupied some reading
some writing some talking others walking but none
interfering with me so that my mind is at full liberty
to roam, and I need hardly tell you that my thoughts
often wander to where my friends and loved ones
dwell. I can imagine that lovely spring will now be
paying you a visit, that little feet will be running
about and little hands will be digging in the sand.
Is Jamie going to school next month ? Does Colin
know S. from O. yet ? And what is my Bonny Lass

doing ? I hope they will all be good and mind what
ma tells them.[1]

Mary we have very much to be thankful for in
regard to our family. One family on board this ship
have a little boy with a contracted leg who cannot
walk without a cane, and another family have a boy
about Jamy's size whose feet are turned in so that
he can hardly walk and whose mind does not seem
to be very bright.

I am very glad to see so many reading their Bibles
every morning. We had a prayer meeting on Sunday
afternoon, and I feel that God is present here as the
hearer and the answerer of Prayer. It is a consoling
thought that we can pray for each other. May the
Lord Bless you all and keep you and guide you.

Steam Ship Golden Age. Friday May 2nd 1862.
Latitude 27.55. North. Longitude 115.34 West.
Distance from Panama 2586 miles

Mary, since I finished my former sheet, day before
yesterday, we have had a strong head wind and the
sea a little rough, a good many of the passengers
have been sick again. I have stood it first rate this
time. The wind has now gone down a good deal and
the white caps on the waves have disappeared. Still
the ship pitches considerably so that you must excuse my pencil if it does not always go in the direction it should.

Yesterday morning we were off Cape St Lucas the
southern point of Lower California at the 23rd de-

1. Colin H. Thompson, born, 26 May 1858, died 1944, and Lora M.
Thompson, born 29 December 1859, died 7 May 1877.

gree of N. Latitude which you will remember as
the boundary line between the Torrid and Temperate Zone. We have experienced quite a change of
weather since we passed that point the wind is quite
chilly.

Linnen coats have been laid aside and over coats
taken their place.

There is some cases of measles among the childern on board, the first case was the child of a Canadian Lady. Up to the present time they are confined
to cabin passengers. I was forward through the
steerage this morning, to see Mr Lane from Augusta,
(they are not allowed to come among the cabin
passengers.) He has been sea sick the last two days,
but is getting over it now. They are very much
crowded, but he says their provisions are pretty
good. When on the Northern Light they were not so
closely watched so that he could often get aft to the
quarter deck, and when I was sick I gave him my
table ticket so that he got several meals in the cabin.
He does not intend to go farther than San Francisco
at present, but expects to go to British Columbia
before the first of August. We expect to get to S.F.
on Monday.

Mary, I hope you are writing to me now or have
written. If I keep on much longer I will be able to
surprise you with quite a large letter. It will give you
something else to do besides *sit and think.* If it gets
much rubbed it will be as hard to make out as a
rebus.[1] I hope you will give me a long one in return.
Write often and number your letters so that I will

1. A rebus is a puzzle in which words or their syllables are represented by pictures, symbols, or figures.

know whether I get them all. Let the one Anson
brought to New York be number one, this will be
my number five, three from N.Y. and one from
Aspinwall. I would be very happy to receive a letter
from Lora Ann[1] occasionally and if I did not reply
I would tell you what to say to her. As there is so
many of us from the same neighbourhood, if all do
their duty in writing we ought to keep pretty well
posted up. It is now getting near dinner time and
I will hold on for a little.

Saturday morning, May 3rd.   My Dear Mary. The
wind has gone down this morning and the weather
is pleasant just like a May morning, but there is a
heavy ground swell on the ocean which makes the
ship pitch *fore* and *aft* slowly and steadily. I am now
on the hurricane deck near the centre of the vessel
so that the motion is not so great. I feel quite well
but very lonesome wishing I could hear from home
and hoping you may soon receive my letters from
Aspinwall. I hope you are all well. If I were only
sure of that I would feel lighter hearted, but I will
trust Providence and wait patiently till I get word.
I have another likeness to send, one of them that I
got in N.Y. It would have made the letter to heavy
to send with the others. If my letter from San Francisco is not too large I will enclose it from there and
you can dispose of it as you think best. Anson intends
writing from San Francisco, and I believe all the
other boys will do so too. It is our intention to Telegraph from that place to Mr McPherson or to Mr

1. Probably Mary Thompson's sister.

Merrill and perhaps to both. If we get in on Monday
it might be in time for next Wednesdays Telegraph.

San Francisco Cal. May 6th 1862

Mary, My Beloved Companion. It is with feelings of
profound gratitude to The Almighty Disposer of all
events that I now announce to you my safe arrival at
this place. By His kind Providence we are enabled
to raise our Ebenezer[1] and say, 'Hitherto Hath the
Lord helped us, Oh that He may guide us all
through the voyage of life amidst the waves and
rocks and quicksands of temptations in this world
and bring us in safety to the harbour of Eternal
Felicity.'

Mary, as I kept pencilling along while on the ship
I have but little more to say regarding the voyage.
We had a very interesting meeting on the ship on
Sunday in which Mr Smith of Mountain took a pro-
minent part. He is a very *green Traveller* but I
believe he is a very sincere christian. From Saturday
morning when I last wrote, till the close of the voyage, the weather continued pretty rough. We arrived
in port at 4 o clock Monday Morning, and landed
soon after daylight. We are stopping at the Clinton
Temperance House Pacific Street S. Francisco.

After breakfast went to Shipping Office and paid
for steerage passage to Victoria $20 per steamer
Pacific to sail on Thursday the 8th at 4 p.m. We then
went to the Telegraph Office and telegraphed to Mr
McPherson the arrival of Port Elgin party all well.

1. 'Ebenezer' was a Puritan's exclamation of rejoicing. It was much
used by George Eliot.

283

We thought you would hear from us sooner from
him than by sending to Mr Merrill. The charge for
a message of ten words is six dollars and seventy 5
cents. It affords us much pleasure to think that if the
message has gone right you will today know that
we are here.

In the afternoon took a walk through the city and
up to the top of Telegraph Hill, commanding a
splendid view of the city & Bay Contra Costa and
surrounding country. We also had an opportunity of
seeing the annual review of the firemen, a great
many companies with their beautiful engines decorated with garlands of flowers and accompanied with
Bands of music, Flags & c. On the top of one engine
was a little boy, dressed in the style of George
Washingtons early days, knee breeches white stockings swallow tailed coat cocked hat and white curled
wig. On another were two little girls dressed like
nymphs, seated in a bower of splendid flowers. I
know you will wish that you had some of the flowers that now bloom so lovely here and I wish so
too, to ornament your pleasure grounds but if the
Californians beat you in raising flowers and plants,
you can match them when the boys and girls come
to be showed without the flowers and fine trappings.
The music by the Bands I suppose was splendid. It
seemed to tickle Anson and as he is writing he can
tell you about it.

I send a newspaper to Mr McPherson and one to
you. The Overland Mail leaves tomorrow morning
so I want to mail this today. Give my kind wishes to
all. Kiss the children for me. Be cheerful, be happy,
pray for me, and may God enable us to meet again

284

and praise Him for his goodness. I am ever your
loving companion,

James Thompson

Messrs. Rothschild will remit by Bills on their
London department any money given to them at their
House in San Francisco, California, and you will
receive instructions there how to forward the Bills to
me and your Brother.

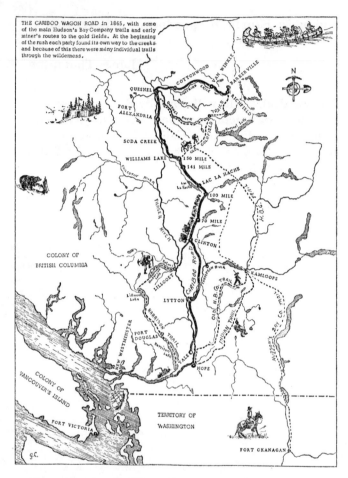

Route to the Cariboo (from *Wagon Road North*)

PROSPECTING IN THE CARIBOO

James Thomson's Diary
Entries 8 May–25 July 1862

May 8. . . . got on Board 'Pacific' and sailed at 4 p.m. Ship dreadfully crowded with passengers, oxen mules, Horses and sheep. Passed out at Golden Gate strong head wind. . . .

May 13.   Arrived at Esquimalt Harbour at 4 a.m. Got ashore and walked to Victoria $3\frac{1}{2}$ miles, put up at the Globe Inn $1 per day. . . .

May 14.   Rented house at $2 per week . . . Board cost $2 each.

Fort Yale, at the head of navigation on the Fraser, is a village of two streets and a few stragling cottages. There is two churches (E. & W.M.) a dozen or so of stores and several Taverns. It is completely surrounded by steep lofty mountains. (May 27th met Dr Easton[1] yesterday at Ferry) Above Yale the river is narrow and during high water rushes through the cannons at a rapid rate. The trail[2] lately made by the Sappers and Miners runs along the side of the

    1. Dr. Easton has not been identified.
    2. The first six miles of the Fraser River Road were built by British Army engineers in 1862.

mountain, in some places blasted out of the face of perpendicular rock. 12 miles above Yale the trail crosses the river by ferry boat, Fare 25 cents. The trail from 4 to 6 feet wide runs along the left bank of the river, some times 400 feet or more above the stream. The mountains are very steep and rugged and perhaps 2000 feet or more above the river. The trail in some places very steep going zig zag up & down.

Left the Boys at noon, camped 2 miles beyond Forest House (dis 15 miles)

May 29. . . . camped at Lytton.

May 30th.   Soon after starting passed Edwin Brouse & Mr Bissell from Augusta. They intend starting when Dr Easton returns from Yale. Camped on left bank of Thompson River about half way from Lytton to Ferry.

May 31.   Reached Ferry 2 p.m. crossed & camped 2 miles beyond. . . . Distance from Lytton to Ferry 25 miles. . . .

June 2.   Started at 5 a.m. travelled 20 miles. Left Thompson river, followed small creek, passed small lakes, killed rattlesnake, camped by a little creek. Mosquitoes very troublesome. . . . Flat grassy hills, alkali water, four miles between creeks.

June 3.   Started at 5 travelled 17 miles very warm dry dusty road feet blistered, camped at junction of

Grave Creek & Bonaparte. . . . Passed McLeans @
2 p.m. Scotts Junction of Lillicott[1] Trail, 17 miles.

June 4. Left Bonaparte creek followed small creek
to left, chain of small lakes, Trail very crooked.
Alkali water, followed creek down, south-east, struck
Bonaparte creek, turned north passed log house
camped 1 mile beyond. Distance travelled 17 miles
feet blistered.

June 5. Trail following Bonaparte camped by small
creek near house at Junction of Scotties cut-off and
our Trail. Distance travelled 15 miles, Juniper
berries.

June 6. Left Bonaparte followed small creek and
ridge between Lakes, through timber, poor water,
camped by north shore of Green Lake, cool night,
travelled about 18 miles. Large Lake, fine sloping
shore, fine scene at sun rise.

June 7. Started at 5 a.m. Trail winding along Lake
shore through Timber, many fallen trees and numerous Sloughs to cross. Part of road a natural highway, camped on a low island in swamp, mosquitos
very bad. Distance travelled 16 miles.

June 8. Started at 5 a.m. travelled 9 miles through
woods mosquitoes very bad reached Bridge Creek
at 7 a.m. and camped for a day on nice green knoll

1. Lillouet on the Fraser River. Scott's Junction seems to have been
in the neighbourhood of Clinton.

between road & Creek and about 1½ miles from
Bridge Creek house. . . .

June 9.   Passed Bridge Creek House and took
dinner at Creek, went Fishing. Picken caught 5
trout. Soon after dinner struck Lake La Hache, a fine
sheet of water 12 miles long & 1½ miles wide.
Trail good. Camped near north end of lake. Dis.
travelled 20 miles. Caught trout in lake. . . .
June 10.   Blue Tent at noon. . . . Camped at La
Hache Creek 10 miles beyond Blue Trout. Dis
Travelled 16 miles.

June 11.   Followed La Hache creek passed Jone's
ranch, struck Wms Lake at noon. Lake 8 miles long
2 miles further to Lake House, Camped at Lake
House, dis 20 miles. . . . Met returning Caribouians.[1]

June 12.   Rain this morning started at 7 a.m. Trail
up hill through timber and sloughs. Fell in with
Mr Ross, Ballalar. Dinner at Deep Creek. Met 30
returning from Cariboo. Met 20 more returning this
p.m. Trail through burnt timber, water good, camped
at Round Tent. Distance 22 miles. . . .

June 13.   Started at 6 a.m. pretty good road. Reached
Beaver Lake House at 4 p.m. . . . Went five miles
past House and camped by creek in Burnt Timber.
Met 42 returning at Beaver Lake 2 Trading Houses,

1. From this point Thomson and his companions struck directly
northeast on the old gold-field trail to the Cariboo country. Thomson's route was shown on a sketch map which is among his letters.
See p. 299. The Cariboo Road, built later, followed the Fraser to
Quesnel and then went east to Barkersville.

several fields fenced & sowed to grain. Dis travelled
22 miles.

June 14.   Trail through timber very thick. Dense
forest and trail for 4 miles very bad with mud holes
and fallen timber. Reached Little Lake House at
10 a.m. Took Dinner last of our bread. Reached
Forks of Quesnelle at 3 p.m. Rain. Saw Leckie,
McGregor & Duncan. Met 40 returning Caribooites.
Dis travelled 18 miles. . . . Quesnelle City,[1] consisting
of some 30 or 40 Houses & shanties & 70 or 80 Tents,
stands on a small Flat at the junction of the south &
north Forks of the Quesnelle. It is surrounded by
lofty thickly wooded mountains. A small space has
been chopped and burnt off. The south Fork is
crossed by a very good wooden bridge. It is the
Depot where the Cariboo mines are supplied. Discouraging accounts from the mines are causing
many to return home and throw a gloom on others.
To the upright there ariseth light in the darkness
may it be so with us.

June 16.

Paid for Shovel $7.00
   ,,   ,, Pick   3.00. . . .

Prospected creek on south Fork of Quesnell. . . .

June 17.   Prospecting Creek 5 miles up S. Fork of
Quesnell. Got few specks. Ottawa Smith & Duncan
arrived yesterday many going and many returning

1. Thomson meant Quesnel Forks, not the settlement at Quesnel
on the Fraser river.

from mines rather gloomy accounts. Saw Irmie &
Dinwoodie in good health and spirits. . . .

June 20.   Left Forks of Quesnell for Cariboo with
heavy Packs and bad roads. Crossed north Fork at
Bridge 8 miles above Forks. Miserably bad road.
Camped at creek 3 miles beyond bridge in Brush
shanty. . . .

June 21.   Started at 7 a.m. Trail pretty good, some
very bad spots, followed river Trail arrived at
Louck's Ferry Cariboo Lake at 3 p.m. Paid Ferryage
$3.00 camped at Keithleys Creek.[1] Dry all day.
Tired with heavy packs. Loucks away Fishing

June 22.   Camped at Keithleys. Frequent Showers.

June 23.   Went up hill 4 miles down 1 mile. Prospecting in creek Turned creek.

June 24.   Commenced sinking hole in bed of creek.
Gravelly clay very hard.

June 25.   White frost this morning, quite cold, rain
P.M. hole down about 6 feet.

June 26.   Hole full of water. Bailed out and got
down about 10 feet from bed of creek.

June 27.   Hole half full of water. Bailed out enlarged
and timbered. Got no lower than yesterday. Very
hard picking. Dry all day.

1. Keithley's Creek flows into Cariboo Lake. The Cariboo creeks
lay to the north and could be reached by going up Keithley's Creek.

June 28.   Got down about 12 feet. Still hard clay
and gravel. No gold. Fine dry day.

June 29.   Beautiful morning. Sun shining bright
and clear. Tent pitched in beautiful spruce grove,
Elgin Creek[1] rippling past in new channel we have
made for it. Lofty mountains on each side, thick
timbered towards summit. Sides green with willows,
grass wild rhubarb, weeds gooseberry bushes spruce
pine & poplar trees. A good many travellers camped
on Trail $\frac{1}{2}$ mile above, this being a regular recruit-
ing station for animals, being the only good feed
from Forks to Antler. Gloomy accounts from above.
Provisions very high, some say $1.50 at Antler. Our
stock getting low, but we trust by the guidance of
providence soon to find means of replenishing.

June 30.   Picken & Tom started for Forks of Quesnell for Grub. Smith & I worked away at Hole. Getting too deep to shovel out of. No appearance of
bed rocks. Weather fine. *Sound Boys* quit their Hole
and that discouraged us.

July 1.   Very heavy thunder and rain nearly all day.

July 2.   Hole caved in last night and filled with
water. P & Tom arrived from Forks before breakfast. Abandoned hole and started after dinner for
Antler. Camped on SnowShoe mountain. Snow

1. Elgin Creek was probably a name given by the partners, who
called themselves the Port Elgin Boys. Port Elgin was an early name
for Edwardsburgh. Elgin Creek may have been either Four Creek
or Weaver Creek.

during night. White around the Tent this a.m. Camped beside Dr Easton. Tom shot grouse with revolver. Picken & Harbottle Paid for Provisions at Forks $72.75.

July 3.   Camped at foot of Hill 3 miles from Antler village. Road very bad.

July 4.   Got to Antler about 10 a.m. . . . . Prospected creek p.m. Saw Dinwoodie.

July 5.   Started for Wms creek. Dinner at Maloneys. Picken thought of going to meet Boys and return to roads. Camped on Flat above Maloneys (Mr Big called and cooked supper. Looking for garden spot). Many returning from mines very discouraging a/cs.

July 6.   Camped as above Micah 4th & 2nd.

July 7.   Went over mountain 8 miles to Wms Creek. Took up 2 claims alongside Dr Brouses.

July 8.   Went to Antler got Mining License for self cost $5. Judge could not *record* claim, his Books not having come. Paid for Pick & Handle $5. . . . Tom paid Sharping pick $4.

July 9.   Commenced digging in Wms Creek.

July 10.   Digging ditch.

July 11.   Digging hole on claim P.M. struck bed rock 4 feet down, water comming in very fast. Gave

up. No prospect. Camped beside Dinwoodie and
Fairbairn.

July 12.   Sold Pick & Shovel for $12.00 and started
for Antler on way to meet Boys at Forks of Quesnell.

July 13.   Camped at Antler saw Ross Rayside &c. . . .
Psalm 40th & 17th. . . .

July 14.   Started at 6 a.m. for Keithlys. Rain P.M.
got to K at 7 p.m. . . .

July 16.   Left Keithleys and arrived at Forks of
Quesnell at 4 p.m. Met Anson and Joe and resolved
to go below to roads. Trail very muddy. Bridge
Keeper says that 4400 passengers have come up and
1700 have gone down 500 of whom passed without
paying.

July 17.   Started at 7 a.m. dinner at Little Lake slept
at Beaver Lake. Square supper $1.50 drink milk.
Rain at night. Sold Pick $2.00. Sold pan $1.00. Sold
shovel 1.00

July 18.   Started at 6 a.m. Travelled 5 miles mostly
up hill stopped and cooked pancakes, had breakfast
reached Big Lake at 11 a.m. good Trail deep black
loam soil. . . . Passed Round Tent at dinner, came on
5 miles and camped in woods.

July 19.   Dinner at Deep Creek, took new Trail and
reached Davidson new Ranch at 6 p.m.

July 20.   Remained on, camped at Davidson Lake Valley House Milk $1. . . .

Spence[1] contract for $7\frac{3}{4}$ miles of road $47,500.

Trees at Westminster 36 cords wood. 1 Log 16 standards.

Thomas Harbottle cr. . . .

[Other accounts apparently settling of the affairs of the company]

July 21.   Agreed to stop with Davidson[2] to get out Lumber & Shingles.

Davidson Cr. By – – – – – $47.37

Mr Davidson Dr July 28th To 23 feet Lumber for Bread Trough @ $120 $2.70.

July 29.   To 47 ft Lumber 2 Slabs.

July 21.   Digging Clay for oven.

July 22.   Built oven size 3 ft 8 in $\times$ 5 ft 8 in. Hunting for timber.

July 23.   Built saw pit & cut saw Logs.

July 24.   Fixed Sawpit & commenced sawing. Boys gone to cut Trail.

July 25.   Sawing.

1. Thomas Spence, a road builder and contractor.
2. Davidson had a farm, a store, and a tavern.

To Mary Thompson 27 July 1862

Williams Lake, British Columbia.
July 27th 1862.

My Ever Dear Mary,
I have so much that I wish to say to you that I really
hardly know where to commence. It is now two
months and a week since I wrote to you from Victoria. Since that time till a week ago last night I have
never been a week in one place. Part of the time 480
miles and am now 360 miles from a post office. An
express messenger is expected to pass this place
some time this week and I intend to embrace the
opportunity of sending this by him. No doubt you
will be looking anxiously for a letter before you
receive this. But Oh Mary think of my feelings in
that respect. Not a word have I heard from the loved
ones at home since the morning of the 7th of April.
Amidst all the toil and anxiety and privations
experienced in this country that is hardest of all to
bear. Would to God I knew how you all were. I expect to hear soon as I have made arrangments to
have my letters forwarded from New Westminster
to this place as I expect to remain here a few weeks.

By the mercy of a kind providence I have enjoyed
uninterupted good health and amidst the scarcity
and high prices of provisions I have still had enough
to eat. I suppose before this reaches you you will
have heard of many a disappointed Canadian returning from this country with hard news from *Cariboo*.
We too have had our share of toil and disappoint-
ment, but in order to set your mind at ease concern-

ing us I will now give you a short sketch of our travel since I last wrote to you from Victoria May 20th.

We left Victoria at noon on 20th May, reached the mouth of Frazer River at dark. On account of the high water and drift-wood floating down we anchored all night and ran up 15 miles to New Westminster next morning. There we changed Boats and had to wait till next day at noon for a steamer to Yale, distance 100 miles. The river is very rapid. We got to Emery Bar 5 miles below Yale on the morning of the 24th. Here the passengers and horses went ashore and walked to the town, while the boat, lightened of part of her load managed to stem the swift current with the freight. We got to town about noon. They were celebrating the Queens birthday by music and horse racing. We remained in Yale over Sunday. Rev Mr Browning preached twice. He called at our tent, after service and was very friendly.

Yale is at the head of steamboat navigation. Above it the river rushes at a rapid rate through a narrow channel of almost perpendicular rocks. The Trail of foot path winds along the mountain side sometimes at a fearful height above the river. We had 600 lbs of provisions on board the Boat, expecting to get it packed from Yale but when we got there the mules were all engaged. So we each took what we could carry, sold the balance and started on foot for a journey of 380 miles. We travelled 13 miles that afternoon and 22 miles the next day which brought us to Boston Bar. Here they had commenced work making a waggon road which is intended to run from Yale to the mines. As it was still early in the season to go to the mines the roads bad and pro-

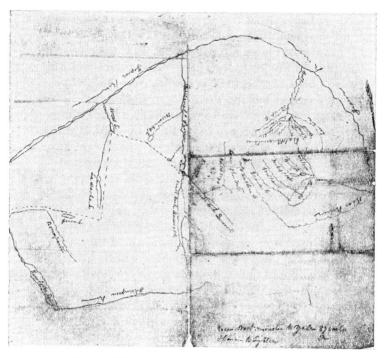

James Thomson's Map of the Cariboo

visions scarce and dear, we concluded it was better
for some of us to remain. Accordingly Anson, James
McIlmoyl, Irvine Raney and Smith from Mountain
hired with the contractor for one month while Picken,
Thos Harbottle and myself should go on to Cariboo
and prospect.

I find that I have not paper enough to give you an
account of my journey. Three weeks travel brought
us to Forks of Quesnell (322 miles from Yale). We
went 60 miles beyond the *Forks* to Antler and
Williams Creek where some of the richest diggings
are but did not succeed in finding any gold. We dug
several holes, but like hundreds of others were unsuccessful. The ground is nearly all taken up and
holes being dug but only a few claims are paying
and they are very rich, which has given rise to the
excitement about Cariboo. Every one seems to be
convinced that this country has been greatly mis-
represented both as an agricultural and a mining
country. No doubt new discoveries will be made
and much gold found but this season provisions will
be so dear that very few will be able to stay long
enough to prospect thoroughly. When we were at
Antler Creek, Flour, Beans, sugar, Salt & Rice were
each one dollar per lb. Fresh Beef 50 cents & Bacon
$1.25 6/3 and at Williams Creek a quarter of a dollar
was added to the price of each. Just think of Two
hundred & fifty dollars for a Barrel of Flour and
everything else in proportion. We could not stand it
long.

When we left the Boys the agreement was that at
the end of a month they should come on after us and
we would meet them at Forks of Quesnelle a month

after we got there. Accordingly we returned to that place and found Anson & Irvine waiting for us. The five started to come but when they had travelled three days they met so many returning with bad news about the mines that they concluded to turn back and go to work again and sent Joe and Anson on to meet us. When we met we concluded that it was no use trying to prospect any more at present, but go down where provisions were cheaper and work at any thing we could get to do. Accordingly we left the Forks a week past on Thursday and got here on Saturday night, staid over Sunday and on Monday morning took a job of building a clay oven for Mr Davidson proprietor of a Farm, Store & Tavern. He is newly settled here and is doing business in a large tent. Is now preparing to build a house and we will furnish the Lumber & Shingles. Here Flour is 60 cents 3/ per lb milk 7/6 per gallon Beans 3/3 Bacon 4/ per lb.

By some acquantances who were travelling down with us we wrote to the Boys before starting where we were and requesting them to send our letters here as James had made arrangements to have them forwarded from Westminster to where he was. And Mary while I think of it you better address my letters after you receive this to Victoria, Vancouvers Island as it is likely we will winter there or at all events we can get them from there as early as from Westminster. You can tell the friends of all my partners that they are well. The only sickness we have had in this country is some times an attack of Home sickness, and if we could only get some letters from home would be the best prescription for

that disease. Tell Mr Waddel that Tom will write
as soon as he gets a letter—The weather here very
warm at present and we are very much pestered
with mosquitos and flies. In Cariboo it is quite cold,
rain almost every day, on the morning of 3rd July
there was several inches of Snow on our tent and we
walked over old snow six feet deep.

   With heartfull respects for all I am ever,
                  Your Devoted Companion

                              James Thompson

Mary my Beloved Companion, I have written you
quite a long letter. It may be that you will have to
read some of it to enquiring friends. I would now
wish to have a little talk between ourselves. Oh Mary
were you by my side I have much that I would like
to say. Mary I have thought of you more, prayed
for you more, and if possible loved you more this
summer than ever before. Volumes would not contain all the thoughts I have of Home and the loved
ones there. Mary I often wish that I had more of
your courage and energy and resignation to battle
with the disappointments of life. I sometimes wonder how I ever came to leave a kind and affectionate
wife and all that the heart of man could desire of a
family to sojourn in this land. But then the thought
comes up that we were poor, that you had to deny
yourself many of the comforts of life that a little
money would have secured, and then I think of my
poor old Father toiling and labouring when he ought
to be enjoying the evening of his days in ease and
comfort. Then I pray God to strengthen my arm and

encourage my heart and bless my exertions to pro-
cure the means to make you comfortable. Our prospects at present are rather poor for making much,
yet I cannot say that I regret comming to this country for God has softened my heart and enabled me to
see myself in the gospel glass as I never did before,
and I never yet have been able to get over the con-
viction that God in His providence pointed it out as
my duty to come. If so, good must come although it
may not come just as we would wish. Mary continue praying for me, keep up your spirits, be cheerful and happy. We have much to be thankful for.
May God enable us to be truly grateful.

Mary, I really hardly know what to think about
this country I cannot make up my mind to remain
long away from home and then to think of returning
without making something, to be as poor as when
I left and in debt besides, and it might be to be
laughed at into the bargain is hard to think of. To
think of bringing you to this country unless it were
to Victoria, is out of the question, I cannot say much
about Victoria, but for this upper country if it were
nothing else than mosquitos and bad water I would
never think of settling here to say nothing of bad
roads and poor society. I sometimes think that I
would like to go home, sell half my farm, build a
little cottage for you to live in and stay with you and
Minnie and the boys and let the world laugh and
talk as they please. Then again I think if by staying
here a little longer I would make enough to pay
my debts and build the cottage it would be so much
better. But I will not decide till I hear from you.
I expect to go to Victoria in the Fall, when we can

correspond regularly and I will be able to get your views on the subject.

What troubles me most is how you are to put in the long cold winter in that old house. Could you do anything by papering to make it warmer? Could *Aunty* paper her house to keep out the wind some? I hope to be able to send you some money perhaps by Christmas to help you to rig up for winter. Try to get warm clothing for all.

I suppose the children have forgotten all about Pa. Tell them I have not forgotten them. I have got a Bible lesson for them to learn, I hope to hear them repeat it yet. Oh if God would enable one to return and hear Minnie repeat that verse I would be a happy man. It is the 2nd verse of the 4th chapter of Micah (ommitting the first and the last clause, get down to paths. May God bless all, and bring us to that land, where *farewells* are unknown.

J.T.

Mary, Although we take fits of homesickness, you must not think that we are always downhearted. We are quite cheerful some times. I have not been half so lonesome since I met Anson and Joe at the Forks, and there we see so many that are worse off than ourselves that we cannot but be thankful. We expect to see James McIlmoyl, Raney and Smith in a few weeks. We have seen Mrs Easten & Brown and the boys from Adams Mills, since we came to the mines. All well.

July 28th 1862
Mary, I have just got supper and am sitting on the

smoke to keep away the mosquitos. We do our own cooking and sleep in our tent at the job we have now. We can make about six dollars a day each, but our provisions cost us about two dollars per day each.

Will have several weeks employment perhaps longer. Tell Mr McPherson that I will write to him in the Fall as soon as I can get the name of the season. Great marchers are still passing down from the mines scarcety of provisions is their general cry.

Wes Anson is well and will write in a few days. We all send our compliments to every body. Pa & Lora Ann. Grand Father and Aunty and all friends. I met an old school mate in Cariboo who has been in this country three years. He knew me from my likeness to Grand Father he sends his compliments to him and Aunty and Eluja Ogg. He took up a lot of Cabbage plants and garden seeds with him and was trying to raise them at the mines. See if they can guess who it was he is from Glentanner and remembers carrying his A.B.Cs on a board accross the hill for three years. Name Jonathan Begg.

Good night

J.T.

James Thomson's Diary
Entries 26 July–22 December 1862

[July 26 to August 13 1862. Details of Wood sawn]

Davidson Cr By [Food purchases to Aug 27.]
a/c Rended $242.16

Aug 14 [to Aug 13] 2930 feet.
Company money from Anson $10.00
Mrs Mary Thompson [This entry is in ink—copper-
plate style]

Lake Valley Ranch B.C.
August 31 1862 Estimate of work done for Mr Davidson till do.

. . . .	$501.60
Amt provisions	242.16
	$259.44

[Accounts for wood sawn and provisions for September 1–17]
August.   Geo Freeland (son of Richard) passed
Davidsons Ranch from Cariboo for California.
Bob Harkness of Iroquois, passed Davidsons Sept
16th having come overland route, and down Fraser
river.

[Accounts for Sept 18–22]
Davidson due us $588.28
& Company money in hand   10.80

Statement Davidson . . . .

Amt Davidsons a/c to order	$244.83	
Baldwin Thomp & Co	260.93	
Slabs	50.00	
	$555.76	
Pd Davidsons a/c	$244.83	
Paid Pickens	$72.34	
Paid Anson	52.34	
Paid Joe	52.34	
Pd Harbottle	72.34	
Pd Thompson	72.34	
Pd for Provisions	6.00	
	$572.56	

[The right hand column is on adjacent page]

a/c August 31, 1862
Cr.

1 mo & 10 days at $60	$83.00
Building oven	15.00
2898 ft lumber @ 1 $\frac{1}{2}$	547.76
5 shingles 1 $\frac{1}{2}$	60.00
	505.76
Slabs	50.00
	555.76
Company money in hand	16.80
$572.56	

of which	$599.08
Pickens share is	72.34
Ansons „	121.62
Joe „	121.62
Harbottles	141.62
Thompsons	141.62

Sept. 19   Davidson being unable to pay us for a few
days and no work for us to do we went fishing in
La. Hache Creek head of Wms Lake. Caught 13 fine
speckled Trout

Sept 20.   Fishing this p.m. caught 23 Trout. . . .
Two men of overland party working for Davidson
left Canada in April & got here a few days ago.
Plains, a hard road to travel. Struck Fraser river near
source, rafted down it 400 miles to mouth of Quesnelle. Got wrecked lost provisions & c. Bob Harkness
Capt.

   On 1st Sept Picken withdrew from partnership
and hired with Mr Davidson. Gave no reason for re-
tiring, but left us four to finish sawing and shingles,
which we did on 16th Sept. On 18th Anson hired
with Mr Davidson for 2 mo. and probably all winter,

Sept 22.   Still waiting for our pay. Washing mending
& c. Went Fishing p.m. caught 8 Trout.

Sept 23.   Still waiting. Earl & Pike passed on Sunday from Antler made nothing. Rev Mr Browning
passed down today.
Davidsons Dr To Amt due us $588.28. . . .

Sept 24.   Got our money last night having had to
wait. Davidson charged nothing for grub got from
18th inst. Parted on good terms. Started at 9 a.m.
Took dinner at Irishmans. Got mutton for frying
pan. . . . Do for tin pan reached Blue Tent at sun-
down very Tired slept on floor

Sept 25.   Got to Cochranes 16 miles. Stopped all
night. Cold snow storm.

Sept 26.   Reached Bridge Creek 11 miles at noon.
Pretty tired. Travelled with Swede. Heard that Open-
heimer had failed and run away. Staid all night.
Slept in garret.

Sept 27.   Started at 8 a.m. Trail through green timber showers of hail. Dinner in woods, got to Green
Lake House at 5 p.m. (25 miles) staid all night straw
mattress. Staid over Sunday at Green Lake. Snow on
mountains all around Lake 3000 feet above sea.

Sept 29.   Started at 7 a.m. met Eldridge from back
of Prescott. Had worked 2 months on Openheimers
road along with boys and got no pay & little grub.
Camped on Loon Lake.

Sept 30.   Started at $\frac{1}{2}$ Past 5 a.m. Walked 4 miles
before breakfast. Got to Scottys at 2 p.m. had bread
and milk $3.40. Came to McLeans 25 miles.

Oct 1.   Started at 8 a.m. got to camp on waggon
road at dusk found Boys all well. Got no pay yet,
time up 10th.

Oct 2. Could get no work on road. Smith, Jas and Jack Rennie expect to get paid for 3 months when Mr Moberly gets back. . . . Bot 8 lbs Flour at Ferry and 3rd. Baked. Waggon road follows Thompson river round some tremendous rocky Bluffs. Got to Lytton 5 p.m. Slept at McCulleys. Had square breakfast.

Oct 4. Left Lytton at 8 a.m. travelled with Swiss Frank Bloom. Cooked dinner at 10 mile house. Got to Farrout House 5 p.m. 22 miles staid over Sunday.

Oct 6. Square breakfast started at 7 made Boston Bar at 11 a.m. Met Mr Spence agreed to go to work 4 miles below Ferry. Slept at Nicaragua Slide. Salmon for Supper. Mr Spence's Canoe upset men drowned. Tools lost.

Oct 7. Got to Spences' camp at 2 p.m. no Tent up. Had to go to house one mile to stop till Thursday morning. Rain this P.M.

Oct 8. Went to Mr Spence's new camp 7 miles from Yale. Put up Tent.

Oct 9. Commenced at 9 a.m. to work for Mr Spence contractor on Yale Lytton waggon road at $40 per month and board. Weather fine.

Oct 19. Wrote to Anson Wms Lake. Postage one dollar.

Oct 20. Received four Letters from home.

Oct 23.   Laid off work yesterday and today with
swelled face.

Oct 26.   Divine service. Church of England
minister.

Nov 2–9.   Rain all day very uncomfortable.

Nov 11.   Took our time got order on Trutch[1] Yale
for pay. Snow p.m.

Nov 12.   Started at 5 a.m. reached Yale 8 miles at
daylight snowed 3 inches deep. Stopped at Yorks
Hotel waiting boat, drizzling rain all day. Tom
handed 3 small specimens to take home, total value
$9 dinner at Yorks, bed do.

Nov 13.   Breakfast at Yorks $1 Bread & Butter at
Bakery.

Nov 14.   Brekfast at Yorks. Moved baggage to
Bakery. Dinner at Chinaman's Shanty. Tea at Bakery
50 cts. . . . Sappers went down in canoes yesterday
Turned out of Bakery. Had to look for Lodgings at
10 p.m. Slept at California House.

Nov 15.   Breakfast at do. $1 dinner at Chinaman's
camp. Weather mild. Heard yesterday that steamer
was aground on Harrison River. Had the *Blues*. Tea
at Cal House. Steamer whistled. All jumped up and
hurrahed. No money by Boat. Boat got aground.

1. J. W. Trutch, another road contractor.

Nov 16.   Fine Day. Trying to get boat off. Succeeded at 4 p.m. Took Baggage on board. Slept do. Got order cashed $41.25.

Nov 17.   Breakfast at Indian Rancherie. View Manner Falls [?]. Started at 9 a.m. Crowd of Passengers, mules, sappers & miners tools C.E. clergyman & a Serv. Rain last night and morning. G. Munro on board. Fort Hope 15 miles 11 a.m. Mouth of Harrison river at 2 p.m. Indian Ranchere Fish &c. At 6 p.m. Got aground on shoal. Tried in vain to get off.

Nov 18. 4 a.m.   Tide rose got boat off arrived at N.W. at 5 a.m. Stopped at Colonial Hotel. Met Picken. Moved to Mansion House. Met Gid Fairbairn, Brock Lame, Morrow, Dr Crouse & c.

Nov 19. Beautiful morning white frost last night. Sailed at 11 a.m. per Enterprise for Victoria fare $3. Took in lot of Hay at mouth of river 1 yoke of oxen Gulf smooth. 200 passengers detained by fog a few miles from Victoria.

Nov 20. Got to Victoria at 8 a.m. Went to Miners Exchange. Got breakfast. 3 meals $1. Met Ottawa Smith Lodges with Dinwoodie, Imrie, Ross &c. Drawers $1. Sold gold dust at $15.50 amt $94.50. Bot boots $3. Wrote to Anson saw Daniels. Ferguson Elridge McCullough.

Nov 21.   Made up mind to go home. Received from Joe Imrie $16 being my share and Ansons of amt

due us by Mc Ilmaze, Rany & Smith. . . . Received
five sovereigns from Picken to carry home to his
wife also one letter. Received from McDonavon 1
small specimen for brother John. Three specimens
from [indecipherable].

Nov 21. Left Victoria. . . . Walked to Esquimalt.
Bot ticket for San Francisco $25. Bade adieu to boys.
Went on board. Got mattress on floor. . . . Started at
9 a.m. . . . [Stopped at Astoria at mouth of Columbia
River November 23–26] Cash $77 & 94 $171 and five
sovereigns for Mrs Picken. Kingston & Johnson
from Spences camp only two on board I ever saw
before. No human arm to lean on. May that draw me
closer to the Friend that sticketh closer than a
brother—Mary may he comfort you in your loneliness and speed me on my way to meet you once
more. . . .

Nov 30. 8 o'clock p.m. arrived at S.F. Mr White,
Mr Robt, Emsly Guelph, and myself went to Me-
chanics Hotel Dutch House. Spring bed Fleas &
mosquitos. Slept very little.

Dec 1. Had breakfast at 6 a.m. Went to shipping
office. Paid $107 for ticket. $1 for Lodging & Breakfast $1 for waggon to steamer, to sail at 9 a.m. did
not leave until 2 p.m., felt lonely and sad. . . . Great
many passengers. $1,200,000 in Treasure.

Dec 2. Got up at 4.30 got Collins cup full of fresh
water and washed. . . . Thoughts far away on the
banks of the St Lawrence, little woman there spend-

ing lonely days and wearisome evenings. Sending
often to the Post Office and getting as often disappointed. Poor Mary. . . . 5 oclock is just struck on
big bell it will now be about 8 oclock by your time.

Another long cold lonely evening will be nearly
past. It may be the little olive plants have gone to
rest and you Mary are thinking of me and wonder-
ing why you get no letter. I wish I could tell you
that I am bounding over the briny waves to meet
you & relieve your anxiety. . . .

Dec 4. Bed fellow from Brockville. . . . Overland
Canadians on board. All the passengers seem very
orderly and sociable. There are five or six families in
steerage and that has a great tendency to keep down
vulgarity. . . . Frenchman in strait jacket. . . .

Dec 7. 5.30 p.m. . . . We are passing the place
where the Golden Gate was lost last July. It was on a
Sunday evening too. When we think of the heart-
rending scenes enacted and endured in that ill-fated
vessel on the evening of her destruction, may our
hearts rise in gratitude and devotion to Him who has
been so good to us. And oh may He continue to
protect us and speed us on our way to relieve the
anxiety of many hearts.

Dec 8 1862. . . . Was talked to for taking fresh water.
Colin's cup being so small let me go with it. . . . A
few minutes after midnight, got into Acapulca
moored alongside coal hulk. Soon surrounded by
canoes with torches selling fine sweet Oranges,

twelve for a quarter Pine apples 1/– Bannanas Shells
coral Bread Cigars Cocoanuts & c.

Dec 9.   The scene at Accapulca last night was certainly picturesque and interesting. The moon was
shining down in all her loveliness. The air warm as a
july night. The natives in their light cotton dresses
with their swarthy countenances lit up by the torches in their boats, each shouting at the top of his
voice the qualities of his particular merchandize and
busy passing his basket up and down from the main
or upper deck as the case might be. After taking on
board a lot of coal, water, and some beef cattle we
sailed at 4 a.m. I bought 12 oranges and basket of
coral & shells for 75 cts. At 11 a.m. stopped and
spoke steamer bound up. She had been delayed at
Panama in a/c of a breakdown on the Railroad. Capts
exchanged papers, passengers exchanged hurras.
One shouted from our vessel to forward passengers
in the other. ' 'ow are you off for *groub* in the steerage ?' We have about 450 passengers and the great
majority of them are quite respectable persons. A
good many children. Sat up till near 9 p.m. quite
warm. Brought quilt on deck and slept abaft the
wheel on main deck. . . .

Dec 11. . . . This day two weeks will be Christmas
Day. It is hardly possible to realize the probability
of my being near home by that time. Or that the
burning heat of the tropical sun will be changed to
the biting frosts of winter. Two sick men on board.
French man again tied up for opening trunks.
5. p.m. Tea is over. The sun is getting low. Fine cool

breeze. I was just thinking that it would be about
your bed time, but I forgot that we were a great deal
further east than we were. There is only about one
hours difference in time now instead of three that
I have been in the habit of allowing. Brother David
& a few others are singing. We are homeward
bound. They sing, 'Rest for the weary', and some
others of your pieces. 'Do they miss me at home' by
Murray Spencers Camp. Most affecting piece I have
heard in this country.

Dec 12.   I went to bed last night on a bench on the
upper deck. It is a lovely starlight night. My fellow
travellers are lying in all directions. All around me
all is quiet. The look-out walks the deck like a
sentry in an enemie country. The man at the wheel,
with eye steadily fixed on the ships head and compass, speaks to no one. No one is allowed to speak
to him. It is a head wind. The ship pitches a little
for & aft. The black chimney and the tall masts nod
gently to the comming waves, while the $\frac{1}{2}$ walking
beams of the engines like the skeletons of huge
elephants, with their gigantic trunks, with untiring
regularity keep time with each other and propel us
through the water at the rate of ten miles an hour.
By 3 oclock a.m. the wind had increased to a gale
I then went below and slept till day light. . . .

I wonder what you are doing to night, maybe making
sausages, or peeling pumpkins for to-morrows pies,
or some other useful job no doubt. We are expecting
to get to Panama on Sunday night or monday morning and many are anxious to get to N. York day

before Christmas. May He that commands the
raging waves guide us in safety and accept our
carroled praise.

Dec 13. . . . I hope you will no have more than one
more lonely Saturday night. . . .

Dec 14. . . . 6 p.m. The Steamer Consolation is just
passed. She is a fine looking ship and seems to have
a great many passengers. They called to us to look
out for the Alabama.

Dec 15.   Arrived at anchorage bay of Panama at
9 a.m. Soon after small steamer came alongside and
took passengers to Railway station distance 3 miles.
Got into cars and waited some time in station.
Natives going through cars selling fruit, Bread,
cakes, sardines, wine, ale, lemonade, shells, and
newspaper. Bulletin printed (one page in English)
in Panama. Here we learned that the Alabama had
over hauled the Ariel and made her pay pretty heavy
Blackmail. . . .
   We are now $2\frac{1}{2}$ oclock sitting in the cars (sta-
tionary) about 7 miles from Aspinwall. Something
got wrong with the engine and they have gone to
Aspinwall to get fixed or get another Locomotive.
We are stopped on the bank of Chagres river. On
opposite side there is quite a large native village. I
got off cars and picked a twig of sensitive plant, but
it is raining very heavy and there is lots of mud all
around. At some of the stations we have passed
there is flowers as pretty as if it were june. After
waiting about $\frac{3}{4}$ of an hour another engine came

317

along and brought us to Aspinwall at about 3 p.m.
. . . When we got to Aspinwall we were told at the
ticket office that we could get aboard Ariel at 6 p.m.
and that she would sail at 5 next morning. We came
to the gate at 6 p.m. but could not get in. Didn't
know when they would go or if they would go at all.
The facts of the case seem to be, When the Ariel
was on her voyage from New York to this place on
the 7th inst the Alabama *(Privateer)* came up to order
her to surrender. The capt (Jones) paid no attention.
The Alabama then fired a blank shot accross her
bows still she (Ariel) kept up her flag. The Alabama
then sent a large shot through the foremast of the
Ariel about 3 feet above the top of the Pilot Wheel
House taking about half the thickness of the mast
away. Capt Jones then surrendered. Capt Semmes
with a prize crew took possession of Ariel in name
of the confederate states, took all their sails and
threw them overboard, took away the safety valve of
engine so they could not sail away (took Capt Jones
on board Alabama as hostage), and went away after
a sailing vessel (after disposing of her they returned
to the Ariel), called up the 120 Marines who were on
board, took their arms from them and took their
Parole of honour. They took all the money they
could find belonging to the ship (about $12,000) and
took the best of her stores and made Capt Jones give
bonds for $260,000 or have the ship destroyed. They
did not molest the passengers. Some say that the
marines wanted to show fight but others say that
after the second shot was fired there was not a marine
to be seen, that more than half of them were below
in the ice house. It is reported that the Alabama is

on the look out for the Ariel as soon as she goes to
sea with the treasure. Under these circumstances the
shippers of specie are not willing to risk it in the
Ariel and the Capt advises no one to take any money
with them as he has very little hopes of getting along
without being overhauled, and he thinks if the '290'
finds no treasure on board they might use the passengers rather roughly. The cause of the delay is that
they (the Capt. Consul and other officials) are con-
sulting as to what is best to do. . . .

Heavy showers in the evening. At 9 p.m. the gate
was opened and passengers allowed on board. I got
a berth and slept on board.

Dec 16.   At 6 a.m. steward ordered all hands ashore
so that tickets could be collected at gate as we passed
in. As there would be no breakfast on board got
square meal at St Nicholas, 75 cts, and got on board
at 8 a.m. Fair and very warm. Alabama is all the talk.
Some passengers are undecided as to whether they
will go or remain over till the dreaded pirate is disposed of. Some talk of going by the British mail
steamer via of the West Indies. I called on British
Consul and he told me that my pasport from Dr
Brown would be good in case we got into trouble.
11 oclock a.m., after 3 weary hours we have at last
got under weigh and are standing out to sea. . . .
Three cheers were exchanged between our ship and
a man of war in the harbour, when we were leaving.
The man of war had to throw her guns over board
a few days ago during a hurricane which did a good
deal of damage here. . . .

Dec 17. . . . I am sometimes pretty home sick especially when I think how long it is since we heard from each other. . . . I was always in hopes that Ansons letter to Pa had gone about the first of October and did not know but it had until I got to Westminster when Picken gave it to me to carry home. Then I felt for you in your loneliness.

Dec 18. A few minutes after 4 this a.m. we were roused by the alarm of fire which caused great confusion for some time. At last it was discovered to be some rags and dirt that had been swept into the hawse hole from the forecastle and likely set on fire by cigar or match carelessly thrown down. Another added to the many instances of Gods providential care of us. . . . In order to avoid the Alabama the Capt has taken a different course from that usually run which some say will detain us some days longer. If so we may give up hope of being home at Christmas, as we have some times fondly hoped to be. Still I hope to get home by Saturday night 27th. . . . Dec 21. . . . While eating dinner today the ship gave a heavy lurch and a man (one of the hands) fell overborad, and was drowned. The alarm was given as soon as he fell, the engine stopped and then backed, the boat (the only one left by Alabama) lowered and manned, but the poor fellow who swam bravely for a while, went down before the boat reached him. The boat with a good deal of difficulty returned to the ship. The engine bell rang and we again started on our course over the white capped billows. Such is the way of life, one dropping here another there soon to be forgotten by the busy crowd.

Dec 22. . . . Got fresh water enough to wet end of towel and have a rub for a wash. . . . Still crossing Gulf, seen no land for 3 days. Expect to get to Key West Florida some time today. Saw several vessels yesterday each one supposed to be the dreaded Alabama. We are now considered to be out of danger as we are getting in reach of Blockading Squadron, and last night for the first time carried signal lights on mast and wheel houses.

The Alabama is Barque rigged with screw propeller and when not in pursuit of a vessel can lower her smoke pipe and present no appearance of a steamer. Commanded by Capt Semmy late of the Sumpter. Got in sight of lighthouse and after waiting some time for pilot, passed Fort and anchored near wharf about 6 p.m. About 8 p.m. . . . passengers then got ashore. I went and bought 2 loaves of bread. Mr Emslie bot some cheese & crackers. The stores were nearly all shut and as the place is under martial law we had to be on board at nine or go to the lock up. It is but a small place standing on an island, very low and flat. The fort is a fine one.

To Mary Thompson 23 December 1862

Steam Ship 'Ariel'
off Coast of Florida
Decr 23rd '62

My Dear Mary

You will doubtless be surprized at receiving a letter
from me, from this part of the world, especially if
you have not received one. I wrote from British
Columbia about the beginning of November stating
that I would probably come home about the Holi-
days, which letter I hardly think you have yet received unless it had been sent from California by
overland Mail. I rather think it will be on Board the
Steamer I am now on.

In the early part of the voyage we made very good
time and I had some hope of reaching New York on
Wednesday and would have made every exertion to
reach home on (Christmas) Thursday night. But the
slow progress made by the *Ariel* has blighted that
hope, as there is now no probability of getting to
N.Y. before Saturday or Sunday so that in either case,
I cannot leave there before Monday. I hope and pray
that I may not be delayed on my way home, but I
intend to mail this so that if I should be you would
know that I am homeward bound. I do hope that
you may have received my letter from B. Columbia,
as it would in some measure prepare you to expect
me, for I am afraid that to walk right in without any
previous notice, when you suppose me thousands
of miles away, might be to much for your nervous
system. I must try to send you some word that I am

coming. I do hope I will be home a week from this evening.

Wednesday 24th.   As this afternoon has turned out pretty pleasant, I have got a seat on the forward deck, and although the wind blows pretty strong it is not very cold, and the ship behaves herself remarkably well. Just as I had finished *well,* a wave struck the bows and sent a heavy shower around me. Tomorrow, Mary is Christmas and I am still a long way from home but I feel very thankful that we are nearing it as fast as we are. I feel very sad and lonely when I think how lonely you must be, and how many times you have been disappointed in not getting a letter from me but I do hope you have kept up your courage and borne your disappointments patiently, and with that firmness and energy, which you possess. I wish you had known a month ago that I was coming. It might have helped to cheer you in the long cold evenings. But Oh Mary although I am still many miles away my heart is with you all the time. It is now four months since I heard from you. Oh I wish I knew that you were all as well as when you wrote the last letter that I received. Wouldnt we have a happy meeting. Tomorrow is Christmas, I can hardly realize the fact. A few days ago we were under the burning rays of the tropical sun and even now it is comfortable sitting here on the deck, and yet tomorrow is christmas. I hope you will all enjoy it may you all be happy. I hope Santa Claus, has not forgot to go down chimney Christmas morning.

Decr 25th 9 a.m.   I wish you all a merry Christmas
I often try to imagine what you will be doing at
home. I can fancy to myself that this morning there
probably was some little stockings hung by the
chimney and that the little fat gentleman that drives
the poney team on tops of houses may have put a
fried cake in one stocking a cold potatoe in another
and so on. I hope the turkey is stuffed, the mince
pies made, the guests invited or the invitation to
dine out accepted, and faces washed & cc.

James Thompson's Diary

Entries 23–30 December 1862

Dec 23.   Yesterday p.m. I finished cake of maple
sugar. Some of my cheese I carried to the Cariboo.
I finished my oatcakes at Victoria, a great many of
them went to crumbs. Saw new moon last night
when at Key West. Hope to see you Mary before yon
moon is half round. Making cocoanut rings quite
the rage among the passengers. . . . Butcher killing
Turtles, some very large and would weigh over 100
lbs. . . .

Dec 24.   Felt very lonely, went below, overhauled
carpet bag, read letter from home of 26th April.
Feel thankful that I have such a wife & family. Oh
that we may meet soon, and live happy. I feel lonely
enough but I feel more for friends at home than for
myself. . . .

Christmas morning. Got up at 6.30 being Christmas
I took two cups of water this morning to wash, did
not sleep well last night. Fleas & c kept me awake
great part of night. This is a fine morning, nice
breeze agreeable cool. I have just had breakfast, two
potatoes, 2 slices off my own loaf and small piece of
salt Beef. There is a good deal of grumbling about
the victuals, the coffee & Tea are very poor. I do not
eat much but as we have no exercize I do not require much. What a difference between a breakfast
here, with everybody pouncing into everything like

so many Hyenas, and a quiet sociable meal at home
when all is love. May God speed me on my way and
may He bless us all and make us happy in His Love.
Mary I hope you are enjoying the day and I hope
you have received my letter by this time.
2 p.m.   We have just finished dinner. Although our
grub is not very good sometimes, yet today the
steward has given us a great treat nothing less than
Turtle soup for dinner. I enjoyed it very well. . . .
hoping to get to N.Y. Saturday evening. . . .

Dec 26.   Passed rather dull christmas yesterday en-
livened a little by the hopes that my letter from B.C.
may have got home, and by the favourable weather
and good speed towards home. Some heavy showers,
off Cape Hatteras, weather very fine for the locality,
soft bread for supper.

Dec 27.   . . . Pretty cold but not freezing. Packing
up for travelling. Expect to get to N.Y. some time
tonight. . . . Arrived at N.Y. At midnight got ashore
and to bed at Lovejoys at 2 a.m. on 28th. . . .

Dec 28.   Lovely Day, no snow, streets dry. . . .
Attended Methodist Episcopal Church 44 John Street,
very appropriate sermon for close of our Eccl. 9 & 5.
No time for fretting and repining, up and work, if
unsuccessful try again. Ostentatious display, the sin
of nations. Do that which is right because it is right,
from no other motive. Large respectable congregation, fine comfortable church organ & choir, minister long beard, marble pulpit.

Dec 29.   Got up at day light. Had brekfast at Crooks
Chatham Street—shopping among the Jews. Bot
Pants & vest for one sovereign, price asked $8.25.
Gold worth $3\frac{1}{2}$ per cent premium. Sovereign worth
$6.35 in N.Y. . . . Bot . . . . Dress patterns $3.50 each
U.S. money . . . . Bot R.R. Ticket to Ogden $10.25 at
5 p.m. started per H.R. Railroad. . . .

Dec 30.   I am now within an hours ride of Ogdensburgh and yet I can hardly realize the fact that I may
be at home tonight.
    The Alabama had taken or destroyed twenty four
vessels before taking the Ariel and she is the first
one that the privateer has taken bonds for and
allowed to go.
    The splinters from the mast of the Ariel shot by
the Alabama were eagerly picked up and preserved
as relics by the curious Northerns.

To James Thomson 24 February 1863
From Anson Armstrong, Williams Lake,
British Columbia

Lake Valley Ranch Feb 24th 1863

Dear Thomsson,

I received your kind letter you sent me from Victoria
Nov 21st by Frank the dutchman that sawed here
last summer, and I was almost over joyed in receiving it as I had not heard anything from you or any
of the Boys since I got the letter you sent me from
Spences Camp. I received it about the 10th Dec. The
one from Victoria 10th Feb. You stated that you
intended leaving for home the first vessel & I suppose it is well you did for there has been very hard
times there this winter. There has a few men come
up already and they say there is about 2000 Strapt
men there now & how they are going to get to the
mines I cannot tell unless by begging like some that
have come up already. I suppose you hear some
most fearful exciting accounts about the mines by
this time for there has very exciting accounts gone
down & have been printed in the Colonist & of
course they have reached Canada ere this and will
no doubt cause another great excitement like last
year. It is true there has been a great amount of gold
taken down this winter, but it has all come out of
three or four claims & those Claims have been
working all winter. The Claims that have paid so
well is the Black Jack Tunnel the Canadian Claim
& one or two more. There has different parties gone
down this winter with from two or three hundred

lbs weight of gold that came out of those rich
Claims. Now these stories will be published all
through Canada & people will think of course that
the whole of Cariboo is just as rich. It is true that
Williams Creek is supposed to be the richest Creek
ever discovered in the world but that is not going
to help those that have not Claims there for it is all
claimed now & there will be a great many who has
claims there that will be much disappointed next
season, who think they have struck it just as big as
those others, but they or no person else can tell what
is under the ground. They have not been working
on any other Creeks this winter except one claim on
Antler.

There is great excitement about peace River this
winter & I think there will be quite a rush there this
season coming. Provisions is just as high this winter
as last, and it is supposed that they will be just as
high next summer as they were last. Flour is selling
in the mines now for $1 per lb. Bacon 1.50 Beans
c90 & other things in proportion.

Well Thomson, I have put in a very lonesome time
of it this winter, here all alone from morning till
noon & from noon untill night in this great big
house & I have not been more than fifty rods away
from it for over two months. Whilst here alone I
often get thinking about the Boys and wish some
of them would come along and I often go to the
window at the lower end of the house to see if some
of them are coming, but I have looked & looked
again in vain. I can see nothing but mountains on
every side but still winter will soon be gone and
summer will come again. And though I am here all

alone through the day, I can enjoy myself much better than in the evenings when the other Boys are here for it is very unpleasant to sit & talk or listen to them talking when every other word is an oath. You know what the people in this country are for swareing. There is only two stopping here besides Bill & myself & they were both strangers to me. They are clever enough men only very wicked & sware. I think I could enjoy myself if I could have the priviledge of sitting and chatting with my old friends, for an hour or two once in a while or the chance of hearing a good sermon. Well I would be satisfied if I could hear one once a month, but that is played out up in this part of this country & will be as long as I stay here likely.

This has been the most pleasant winter ever known in this part of the Country. It has been the most pleasant weather that I ever seen in the winter season. There has been only two snow storms this winter here, the first one was about the 1st Dec. the second right after New Years & the snow has not been over one foot in depth all winter. We had one week of very cold weather & the rest of the winter has been like one of the most pleasant days in April at home. There has not been any rain this winter at all & scarcely any wind. It has been lovely & only for that I do not know how I ever could have stood it through the winter in this lonesome place.

I have not heard anything from any of the Boys only what you wrote me, excepting Pickens. Frank knew all about him but nothing about any of the rest. I should like very much to hear from them.

I do not know whether I shall stay here this season

or not. I am waiting for Mr. Davidson to come up &
if he will give me enough wages I will stay. I commenced writing to Lora the 27th Jan & have not
had any chance to send my letter, so I thought I
would [write] a few lines to you and let you know
that I am still well.

I have not yet taken the small pox & I think there
is no danger now. The Indians have got over it now
all around. There was 12 of them died here. They
were camped right over at the Creek where you used
to get the water sometimes, when the stream would
be dry. There was 15 of them & only 3 of them
lived & at Beaver Lake out of fifty-one only three
survived. There were 4 white men died at the Forks,
3 sick at deep Creek but got better. One died at Lake
La Hache but we have all escaped clear of it here.
I hope you had a pleasant passage home, found Mary
& your littl pets all well and all the rest of the folks
at home & may you long live to enjoy the Comforts
of home friends & society which I am deprived of.
May God bless us all & if we are never permitted to
meet again at home, May we all meet in a home in
Glory. Ever pray for me,

From your Affect. Brother

Anson

Write me a long letter. Direct to Williams Lake
P.O., B.C.

To James Thomson 25 April 1864
From William Scott, Mimico

Mimico, 25th April, 1864

My Dear Cousin,

I am ashamed on looking at your kind letter to
see that it has already lain by me a month un-
answered and lest old procrastination should again
step in to break up our correspondence I sit down to
write you a few lines as this wet morning keeps me
indoors at any rate. Accept dear friend our sincere
sympathy in the loss you have sustained by the
arrival of your beloved father[1] to another and I hope
a better sphere. . . . It must have been trying for you
to part with him although you must have been in a
great measure prepared for the event, seeing that
only by reason of more strength he had outlived
nearly all his generation. You have reason to bless
God that you have been permitted to watch over him
to the last and to see him depart in peace. The sudden
death of your sister-in-law[2]—cut off in the midst of
life in the bloom of youth amid all its hopes and
aspirations—must have been a severe trial for your
dear partner. . . .

I have give up all my public business and must
now try to make up my own leeway. I am sorry to
hear that you have had your own difficulties in
worldly matters but it is no wonder to me when
I see the most cautious and prudent men of business
have failed on every hand during the last 5 or 6

1. Alexander Thomson.
2. Lora Ann (Sissy) Armstrong.

years. The fever of excitement begun with our railway speculations drove many against their better
judgment as they must either go with the tide or get
out of the way. . . . The failure of our wheat crops
following immediately upon the heels of the land
fever, though no way connected therewith has tended very materially to augment the trouble at least
in this part of the country which was one of the best
wheat growing districts in Canada. We have not had
a good crop of wheat since 1856 and many of our
farmers are quitting it altogether in despair. . . .

Give our love to Mary and all the other branches
of the family. Write us soon and why should not
Mrs Th or Aunt Helen write a few lines if you are
too busy or too lazy to do so.

P.S. When you write again tell us all about your late
sisters family as well as your own—Also whether
Helen has no sense of her responsibility now that
she has adopted this new country for a home. . . .

APPENDIX A

Testimonial on the death of James Thomson

Moved by J. R. O'Reilly, Esq. and seconded by John Carruthers, Esq. and resolved;

That the Liberals of South Grenville in convention assembled desire to place on record their profound feelings of sorry for the death of their highly esteemed fellow Liberal, Mr James Thompson of Cardinal.

They desire to testify to his solid worth, his value as a citizen and to the long and honorable career that closed with his death.

They desire further to convey to the family of deceased their profound sympathy.

Be it further resolved that a copy of this resolution be published in the public press and engrossed by the Secretary of the Liberal Association and forwarded to Mrs Thompson.

John Carruthers
President

Prescott, Feby 16th, 1895

APPENDIX B

Gravestone Inscriptions

Cardinal, Ontario

Face One

James Thomson died
Feb 10, 1895
aged 72 years
Wife: Mary Armstrong
died March 14, 1916
aged 80 years

Face Two

James Melville Thompson
1855–1938
Colin Havelock Thompson,
B. May 25, 1858
died Nov 14, 1944
Edwin Scott Thompson
Born May 21, 1870
died Jan 3, 1962

Face Three

Henry A. Thompson
died June 1856
aged 1 year
Lora M. Thompson
died May 7, 1877
aged 17 years
Children of James
and Mary Thomson

Face Four

Alexander Thomson
died March 2, 1864
aged 82 years
and his daughter Helen
died Jan 4, 1877
aged 58 years

SECOND MONUMENT

STUART A LYTELL, 1887–1931
Ella M. Thompson (Lytell) 1863–1930
James Edwin Lytel, 1898–1929

336

APPENDIX C

A Temperance Song; The Landlords Pet

I was once a Landlords pet when I had money to spend
I spent it in drink and did verily think
That it never would come to an end.

Chorus)   So now Ive got nothing but rags to my back
             My boots wont hide my toe O oes
             And the brim of my hat goes flap flip flap
             Against my rum blossomed nose.

But every thing has got an end
And some Landlords chalks have got two
But the money that bought me such respect
To the Landlords pocket soon flew

The Landlords coat is good broadcloth
And his pants are no worse of the wair
But the Landlords coat was bought by the sot
And so ware his cane bottomed chairs.

The Landlord he called me a deacent fellow
And O but I was vain
For he got my cash and I got his trash
To soake my poor silly brain.

The Landlord who Keeps at the sign of the fox
Soon kicked me out of his door
For the Landlord can tell by instinct full well
When a bodys confoundedly poor.

So now I have got a sprinkling of sense
I'll sign the pledge to abstain
And old harry may cook me up for a mess
If I ever tuch their trash again.

For I fain would have something but rags to my back
And boots that would hide my toe O oes

337

And the brim of my hat shall no longer flip flap
Nor rum discolour my nose.

Written by George Armstrong at Matilda, 14th Feb. 1851
[see fn. 1, p. 215]